AT CHRISTMAS AND ON RAINY DAYS: TRANSPORT, TRAVEL AND THE FEMALE TRADERS OF ACCRA

Duafe
(dee AH fih)
Symbol of the wooden comb which stands for the positive qualities of women: patience, fondness, care.

At Christmas and on Rainy Days

Transport, Travel and the Female Traders of Accra

MARGARET GRIECO
Africa Region
World Bank
Washington DC

NANA APT
Social Administration Unit
University of Ghana
Legon

JEFF TURNER
School of Architecture
University of Manchester

Avebury

Aldershot • Brookfield USA • Hong Kong • Singapore • Sydney

Published by
Avebury
Ashgate Publishing Limited
Gower House
Croft Road
Aldershot
Hants GU11 3HR
England

Ashgate Publishing Company
Old Post Road
Brookfield
Vermont 05036
USA

British Library Cataloguing in Publication Data

At Christmas and on rainy days: Transport, travel and the
    female traders of Accra. – (Perspectives on Europe)
    1. Retail trade – Ghana – Accra   2. Women merchants – Ghana –
    Accra   3. Women – Ghana – Accra – Economic aspects
    I. Grieco, Margaret   II. Apt, Nana   III. Turner, Jeff
    381'.09667

    ISBN 1 85972 172 9

Library of Congress Catalog Card Number: 96-83228

This book reflects the views of its authors: it does not represent the views of
any official institution or agency.

Printed and bound in Great Britain by
Ipswich Book Co. Ltd., Ipswich, Suffolk

Contents

vi

Figure, plates and tables

Acknowledgements

To the one thousand and more Ghanaian respondents who gave of their time, a hearty thank you for your trouble. Thanks to Phil Fouracre, TRL for setting up the initial research project; thanks also to E.A. Kwakye, Ministry of Transport and Communications, Ghana, for providing support and guidance in undertanding the local transport context. ODA's contribution was critical: its mainstreaming of gender provided the impetus for the research. The research was supported and developed by a large and excellent team of local interviewers, some of whom helped shape our text and whose names appear against the chapters they contributed to. Our thanks also to the University of Ghana, Legon which provided administrative back-up for the project and to those colleagues and students who bore with us as we strived to conduct and complete our research. Saija Katila made the journey from Finland to Ghana, a journey which gave us an excellent research administrator as well as an interesting and lively research colleague. Mandy Fouracre read many of our early drafts and gave an abundance of encouragement when it was much needed. To Ken Williams, the Resident Representative for UNICEF in Ghana, our thanks for his belief in our ability to portray Ghanaian reality. To Ishrat Z. Husain, Division Chief, AFTHR, World Bank, our thanks for her interest and encouragement as this task reached its end stage. To Andy Norton, ODA/World Bank, our thanks for keeping an open office on the social anthropology of Ghana: his support and interest were much appreciated. Thanks also to Prosper Agika for his photographic skill. Finally, our thanks to Ravi Kanbur who made his home our research station whilst we struggled to shape a text on Ghanaian traders and travel which did justice to the complexity and vitality of the interaction. To all we say, Medwiase.

In celebration of the resilience of the Ghanaian female trader and to Katherine Kpemasor and her daughter Matilda who traded, toiled and travelled the social distance necessary to make us aware of their story.

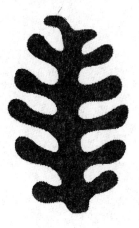

Aya
(ay YAH)
The fern, a symbol of
defiance, independence and
fearlessness.

1 Expected to earn, constrained to trade: Trading a customary role for Ghanaian women

Memunatu Attah, Nana Apt and Margaret Grieco

1.1 Introduction: beyond the orthodoxy: the economic role of Ghanaian women

At Christmas and on rainy days, the female traders of Accra, Ghana often make use of the more comfortable and superior forms of informal public transport. These are the terms in which they themselves describe their transport choice. In order to understand the character and scale of the demand for informal public transport (Fouracre et al., 1994) in Ghana, it is necessary to understand the specific gender features of economic involvement in this region (Turner and Fouracre, 1995). Women dominate the trading sector (Katila, 1995; Cutrufelli, 1983; Twumasi, 1976; Garlick, 1971; Little, 1973; Apt and Katila, 1994): the absence of strong retail distributional systems means that these female traders carry the organisational and social responsibilities for ensuring the local availability of goods. They are major actors in the area of transport organisation: they both adapt their transport behaviour to the poor quality and low reliability of existing informal public transport systems (Fouracre et al., 1994; Mbara and Maunder, 1994) and creatively adapt the local informal public transport system to their business needs (Clark, 1991). In respect of the former, we shall find that girl children provide the labour which compensates for the absence of their elders imposed upon businesses by transport delays: variability in public transport journey times have real consequences for girls' access to education (Odaga and Henneveld, 1995). In respect of the latter, we shall find that traders come to arrangements with drivers for the overloading of public transport vehicles in order to accommodate their restocking needs: the absence of strong retail distributional systems has consequences for the safety and efficiency of public transport (Grieco et al.,1994; Turner, 1994).

3

This chapter collects together both Ghanaian and international literatures which indicate the substantial scale of female trading in Ghana and establishes the customary character of this female occupational niche. It sets the context for subsequent chapters by providing the reader with the necessary information about the social organisation of trading in West Africa, information which is largely absent in the conventional literature on women's employment status and occupational lives (Cleaver and Schreiber, 1994).

1.2 Household organisation and customary obligations: spousal separation and independent domestic economies

Recent reviews of gender issues in Ghana have highlighted the complexities of Ghanaian household organisation (NCWD, 1995; ODA, 1994): male and female 'household' members frequently operate under separate domestic economies (Woodford-Berger, 1981; Lloyd and Brandon, 1993). Indeed, there are problems of applying Western concepts of the household to Ghanaian structures (Clark, 1989; Woodford-Berger, 1981). The classic work of the anthropologist Meyer Fortes (1974) on Ghana, commenting on the Akan, provides us with guidance on the issue:

> Matrilineal marriage in Ghana tends to be associated with an open domestic system with split residence – split in space, split over time, both in the individual's life time and in the sequence of generations, split for the spouses, split for the children and so on.

Similarly, the work of Jette Bukh (1979, p.50) discovers practices of physical spousal separation within working marriages and the separation of domestic economies even where spouses inhabit the same accommodation within the Ewe community:

> Husband and wife usually have separate economies and there are relatively clear expectations as to who should pay what. But there seem to be quite wide limits to the question of how much of the responsibility for the daily necessities can be pushed onto the woman, if the man, for some reason or another, is indisposed to take on his share. Because it is the woman's work to see that there is food in the cooking pot every day,and because the women feel themselves more closely related to the children and also more directly responsible, it is they who ultimately carry the burdens which many of them think ought to have been equally shared with their husbands.

Recent economic reviews of household structure across Africa have achieved similar understandings: for example, the recent work of Cleaver

4

and Schreiber (1994, p.74) focuses upon the 'female headed household syndrome' which is widespread across Africa:

The female headed household is a widespread and increasing phenomenon in many parts of sub-Saharan Africa. It has always been common in societies that practice polygamy and spousal separation of residences, or in which divorce has been easy and frequent. In some regions, where long term or seasonal male out migration is particularly prevalent, female headed households account for fifty per cent or more of total rural households ...

The concept of the female headed household is often misunderstood or misinterpreted. It is not a static concept, but a life cycle issue. African women may move in and out of being household head several times in the course of their lives (due to marriage, divorce, husband's death, remarriage, husband's outmigration, husband's return). Female headed households are not simply a marginal group – remnants of nuclear families that have lost their male heads due to death, divorce, or migration. They are a common and economically and socially important reality with far reaching applications for development policy. The great majority of women in sub-Saharan Africa who reach adulthood are likely at one or more time throughout their adult lives to head a household that is without a resident adult male.

Of course, a key element in the prevalence of female headed households is the ethnic dimension. Spousal separation is a cultural practice which attaches to some but not all ethnic groups in Africa. Ghana, like much of sub-Saharan Africa, has a complex ethnic structure: contemporary estimates identify the presence of 90 distinct ethnic groupings. Boateng (1993) divides Ghana's population of 15 million (UN estimate for 1990) into 44 per cent Akan, 16 per cent Mole-Dagbani, 13 per cent Ewe and 8 per cent Ga-Adangbe. In Ghana, our own and other evidence shows (Apt, 1995; Fortes, 1994; Kilson, 1974; Abu, 1983; Apt et al., 1996; Woodford-Berger, 1981), spousal separation as a strong cultural practice for the Ga, Ewe, Ashanti (Akan) and Fanti (Akan) ethnic groups. The predominance of the Akan ethnicity in the population as a whole, given its cultural practice of spousal separation, results in the now widely recognised outcome (ODA, 1994, p.3):

pooling of resources and joint decision making between men and women in households is generally not the norm, with men and women tending to have separate income and expenditure streams.

Recent evidence indicates that around 60 per cent of Ghanaian urban households depend solely upon the income of women in meeting their household survival needs (Ardayfio-Schandorf, 1994). One argument that

5

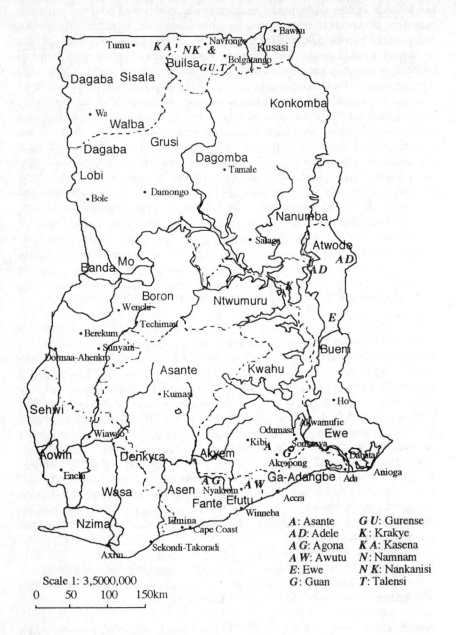

Figure 1 Ghana: ethnic groups

has been put forward to explain these dramatic figures on female-headed households is the widespread existence of polygamy, coupled with the practice of spousal separation, in the Ghanaian context (Ardayfio-Schandorf, 1994). Generally, polygamy is taken as evidence of the economic weakness and low status of women, however, in the Ghanaian context, it is easily seen that whilst the heavy economic responsibilities of women add to their labour and toil, their roles as earners and heads of household expand and extend their decision-making and decision-taking powers beyond those enjoyed generally by women. One element of this bitter-sweet female role of head of household is the responsibility for the organisation of the activity pattern and time budget of the household unit: trading is an occupation which harnesses the household's human resources, most particularly its children (Joekes, 1994; Johnson et al., 1995), and permits the female head of household the flexibility to schedule and reschedule her tasks according to the household's routine and crisis needs (Whipp and Grieco, 1989; Grieco, 1996). The next section investigates this occupational fit between women's domestic need for finance and their family need for time.

1.3   Trading for time: a fitting occupation for a woman

As a consequence of their domestic financial responsibilities, women are highly economically active in Ghana. Their opportunities for economic activity are, however, primarily concentrated in the informal sector and within this sector they are primarily to be found as traders (Little, 1973). Indeed, the majority of traders are women. Over 25,000 traders turn up daily at the various markets in Accra, 85 per cent of whom are women (Cutrufelli, 1983). In addition to women's dominance in central market trading, they are also prevalent in the area of petty trading. In fact, petty trading is the predominant form of commercial activity. Women are extensively involved in petty trading at the local level. Petty trading activity varies from very small doorstep trading activities to more conventional commercial arrangements based in kiosks or converted cargo containers: petty trading takes place on the doorstep, by the kerb side, on small local markets where a low capital base is required, in small kiosks in local neighbourhoods or through the hawking of goods on local byways and highways. There is thus a panoply of trading forms and women move between these different forms of trading according to life cycle needs.

Research in urban Ghana indicates women's possession of sophisticated and refined customary strategies for managing the timing and movement across these various trading forms (Apt and Katila, 1994; Clark, 1991; Katila, 1995, 1996; Apt et al, 1996). The trading experience of a woman typically starts with her involvement in supporting the business of her mother or other elder female relatives whilst she is still at school; she uses

Plate 1   **Kerbside commerce: the world of petty trading**

this experience to build up skills and financial capital; sometimes she creates her trading capital on her own but more usually, after a period of assisting her elder relatives, she receives premises and capital as an occupational gift. The expectation is that she will carry on the business and give support to her elder female relatives as well as using the income to support her own offspring. In the period where she assists her senior female relatives in business and in which she begins to bear children, she will operate a 'branch' of the family business from the doorstep of the family home. When she takes over the family business in the central market area, mother and daughter switch trading locations with mothers moving from the main 'branch' of the family business in the central market areas to the doorstep location and daughters moving out of the domestic environment into the larger commercial world. As women grow older and physically weaker, the volume of trading they undertake diminishes but, nevertheless, their trading continues on the doorstep into the advanced stages of old age (Apt et al., 1996).

The practices of occupational socialisation and inheritance amongst female traders in Ghana, and in West Africa, are beginning to receive considerable attention as it is increasingly recognised that the economic and social models of the West do not readily encompass the history and social organisation of the African informal sector. The occupational gifting system of Ghana's female traders exists in a context where the social welfare system is weak, women's responsibilities are great and customary organisation supports kin networking amongst women (Kilson, 1974; Gabianu, 1990; Apt and Katila, 1994). Among the customary forms which support women's intergenerational economic exchanges within the kin structure is the existence of the ancestral or family home (Woodford-Berger, 1981) which provides a physical anchor for the enforcement of social and financial responsibilities: the entitlement of a woman to be in the ancestral home is inalienable. This places her within the context of her female kin. As we have already seen, female headed households are a feature of Africa: our research in Ghana suggests that part of the explanation lies in the resource base afforded by the ancestral home.

Given the range of trading experience of the urban Ghanaian women, it is appropriate to talk of the career structure of female trading. Inside this structure, there is little promotion from the informal sector to the formal sector (ODA, 1994) but this should not be allowed to mask the many important differences within the informal structure as perceived by the women themselves. However, these perceptions are not simply a matter of cultural identity, for these various gradations in the trading structure have their own considerable activity pattern, travel and transport implications.

Looking at the career of the Ghanaian female trader, we see that she is to be found trading on the doorstep at a number of stages of her life: whilst a young girl; when heavily involved in child bearing; and when she begins to age and experience infirmity. Doorstep trading permits the combination of domestic presence with economic activity. In periods where social protection is needed, employment can be managed without her being exposed to external dangers. Linking the economic with the domestic is a possibility offered in developing societies, with their lower levels of business regulation, which is no longer readily available in the Western context.

Security is not the only benefit of these arrangements, for the scheduling flexibilities provided by doorstep trading are a major consideration. The ability of young mothers to offer both child care and economic productivity simultaneously is critical in a context where financial responsibilities for children are deemed to be a female responsibility. Similarly, trading in the informal sector even where this is at market venues offers women enhanced time flexibility. When family circumstances demand, women field proxies to perform their business duties in the market area. Other family members take over the task of protecting the goods and conducting sales when the market stall owner has other responsibilities to take care of. Employment in the formal sector would offer no such flexibility. Of course, this family flexibility also benefits female traders in conducting their economic business; while the female trader is travelling to the wholesaler to restock her enterprise, her daughter is busy ensuring that the outside world meets with 'business as usual'. As we have already indicated, it is primarily daughters who are allocated this task, the view being that it represents part of their occupational training rather than constituting a loss of educational opportunity.

Women's time needs and time responsibilities clearly contribute to their presence in the trading profession but it is also the case that their restricted incomes serve to direct them en masse into the lower capital base forms of this sector (ODA, 1994). Women have poor access to credit and capital for investment in enterprises (Cleaver and Schreiber, 1994). The merging of women's two roles, domestic and economic, is easily seen in female traders' management of finance. The household and the business budgets are merged: 'chop' money, e.g. the food budget, is married with that of the business. Typically no separation of the business and household accounts occur. Whilst many observers have focused on the need to teach book-keeping skills in order to preserve the business budget and enable the graduation of the petty entrepreneur into the formal sector, the flexibility that such transfers between household and business accounts provide in terms of changing family circumstances has largely gone unnoticed. In fact, many female traders are able to continue with their trading activities as a consequence of remittances and transfers which come to them from children who are based elsewhere. The use of the female traders' business budget for the upkeep of children in their youthful years appears to receive an intergenerational return in later life.

Female trading is a fundamental element in the survival strategies of many low income households. It is an extension of the customary rural responsibility of women to provide the food for the cooking pot (Bukh,

1979, p.50) and an outcome of customary practices of spousal separation. Financing the upbringing and education of children is the woman's lot. Correspondingly, our research has shown that matriarchs, e.g. female heads of household, often carry the responsibility not just for financing the upbringing and education of their own offspring but also that of their offspring's offspring and of the offspring of their siblings (Goody, 1978). Indeed, the pressure to feed and educate grandchildren explains the continued economic activity of many of Ghana's elderly females. One consequence of this household survival pattern and strategy is the prevalence of fostering rural children in urban households: foster children are both responsibilities in terms of feeding and clothing requirements, and often education, and resources in terms of additional sources of labour for plying the family trade. Children hawking goods and serving at the counter is an everyday feature of Ghanaian life.

1.4 The transport demands of petty trading: the commercial use of informal public transport

As we have seen, women form the majority of the Ghanaian trading sector (Apt and Katila, 1994). Purchasing, transporting and selling goods is primarily a female responsibility: women's involvement in the economic activity of trading results in high levels of regular urban travel. The restricted capital base but regular turnover of goods inherent in petty trading necessitates frequent travel between wholesale markets and their local neighbourhood selling places on the part of female traders: petty trading is generative of a larger number of journeys than occur where the availability of sufficient capital permits bulk buying. Petty trading not only takes place in a context where the capital base of the majority of traders is highly restricted but also in a context where the organised delivery and distribution of goods to small retail outlets is not commonplace. Thus the majority of traders have to replenish their stock through regular small load journeys to central markets. Given the scale of personnel involved in the petty trading sector, and the number of journeys each trader must make, the total number of restocking journeys made by traders is substantial (Clark, 1991). Although each trader is moving small loads at any point, the number of traders involved in the activity and the prominence of petty trading in the Ghanaian economy guarantees that the volume of travel generated in this way is significant, although no comprehensive survey has yet been undertaken. Indeed, the small load characteristics of these journeys have served to disguise the extent to which the informal public transport system represents part of the commercial retail distribution system.

Female traders make use of the public transport system, in combination with supplementary services found in the developing world such as

11

portering, to meet their travel needs. Thus women are disproportionately involved in the making of load carrying journeys on the public transport system. Such commercial and travel responsibilities are coupled with substantial domestic responsibilities. This combination of economic and social roles, and the constraints associated with these roles, means that in a context where there is considerable variability in travel times, female traders generate a set of travel and transport strategies.

Viewed from an activity approach (Jones, 1989; Grieco, 1995), the making of these regular restocking journeys, in an environment where journey times can be unreliable, is reported as requiring considerable coordination at the household level (Clark, 1991). Most particularly, co-ordination occurs between school age girls and adult female traders of the same household. The research shows a strong pattern of using girl child labour in operating petty trading outlets whilst their elders engage in the purchasing of the goods for sale, a finding which fits with other materials collected on the early occupational socialisation of girls (Sowa, 1994). The use of family labour is important in providing traders with flexibility in making travel arrangements and organising transport. Furthermore, such flexibility is of great importance in a context where the stocking or restocking of businesses involves the trader him- or herself in making the journey to the wholesalers and other points of purchase several times a week or every day. It was found that members of large households also appear to travel less per household member, as their greater numbers give them a better ability to organise the provisioning of the household using fewer trips. Households operated a system of 'domestic anchors' where a junior adult female of the household stayed around the home and sold things from the front of the house: in a number of households, this role was, in fact, performed by the second wife. A similar pattern has been found for Yoruba households in Nigeria. This allowed other household members, particularly women, to travel greater distances and more frequently for work and trading as a result of the greater flexibility achieved.

Attention must also focus upon the relationship between this trader demand for the commercial use of the informal public transport system and its influence in creating a differentiated transport supply within Accra. The weak capital base of the bulk of female traders prevents them from being able to purchase dedicated transport facilities. Even large traders rarely have their own vehicles. In this context, informal public transport vehicles become temporarily customised and coopted to traders' needs. Women traders not only make conventional use of the famous tro-tros (Fouracre et al., 1994) or urvans as individual fare paying passengers but also hire and divert these vehicles off their normal routes by making 'customised' arrangements with their drivers. In undertaking petty commercial journeys, women traders also make extensive use of taxis and of non-motorised transport, i.e. hand pulled trucks or trolleys. The evidence is that there is considerable differentiation in the urban transport market.

Differentiation is partly the consequence of the variations in traders' load carrying requirement. However, an equally important factor is the dependence of transport supply on the importation of second hand vehicles. There is often great variation in the reliability and roadworthiness of these imported vehicles (Clark, 1991). These variations generate the circumstances necessary for the existence of different charges and fares for the same journey length. New and old vehicle operators have different charging capabilities and consequently serve different market sectors. Young and old female traders frequently have different financial horizons: advanced age often accompanies access to the poorest qualities of transport.

The informal public transport sector of Accra is characterised by considerable negotiation between customers and transport operators as to the fares which should apply on any journey; similarly passengers frequently make on-the-spot side payments to brokers in order to gain access to seats and storage space on public transport vehicles. The interaction between Ghana's female petty trader and the informal public transport system is, like much of Ghanaian life, one of bargaining, negotiation, preferencing and patronage: brokerage is at the heart of the Ghanaian public transport system.

1.5 Conclusion

This chapter has shown that household organisation in Ghana is fundamentally different to that of the Western societies on which most models of economic, development and transport planning are based (Okpala, 1977). It has been shown that female trading has developed as a local response to the survival needs of the regional situation. The time budget consequences of female trading have been outlined and the ways in which the time flexibilities of trading fit with women's domestic requirements have been described. The role of girls in compensating for constrained financial and transport resources has been shown to have educational consequences. The predominance of women in the trading sector, and the magnitude of journeys created by the interaction of their time and capital restrictions, results in a level of commercial use of the informal public transport system which has gone unrecognised in the literature. The consequence of the arguments presented in this chapter is that development planning which assumes women are not economically integrated but seeks simply to incorporate women's labour in economic growth is misplaced. It is the enhancement of women's economic role that is important and not the construction of a first access to employment.

The next chapter, Chapter 2, provides a description of transport organisation in Accra and explores the cultural attitudes and travel behaviours which explain and accompany that transport organisation. It focuses on the informal public transport system of Accra and the role which this plays in meeting traders' working needs. Analysing the public transport system, as opposed to retail distribution systems in this way, represents a departure from the existing literature.

Chapter 3, building on the insights of Chapter 2, advances the key argument that the scale and prevalence of petty trading has consequences for the organisation of the transport sector. It focuses on the frequency of trips which have to be made as a consequence of the constrained capital base of female traders. It also describes the improvements in the transport sector which have occurred with the revival of the economy as recounted by the traders themselves. In this respect, the chapter contributes to the present debate on the impact of Economic Recovery Programmes and Structural Adjustment.

Chapter 4 describes the extensiveness of the female porterage of goods within the petty trading economy of Accra. It analyses the interaction between the customary transportation role of women in Africa, e.g. head load carrying (Cleaver and Schreiber, 1994, p.6; Turner and Fouracre, 1995; Howe and Barwell, 1987), and the extensiveness of petty trading as an employment form. The chapter describes the social organisation of Ghana's female head load carriers, locally termed as 'kayayoos'. Particular attention is paid to the role of rural migrant girl children in this urban occupation.

Chapter 5 describes the organisation of wheel based porterage, e.g. trolleys and wheelbarrows, which are locally termed as 'trucks'. Trucks are operated by males only and the chapter explores the social organisation of this occupation. Overall, the argument is made that these non-motorised forms of transport play a key role in a low income economy and are unlikely to disappear in the foreseeable future. The small load character of much petty trading provides great opportunity for the commercial use of the bicycle but cultural attitudes work against women's access to the bicycle and the majority of petty traders are women. These cultural barriers to cycling by women are described and discussed, within the chapter, in terms of developing a sustainable transport policy for sub-Saharan Africa.

Chapter 6 examines the activity patterns of households in the low income areas of Accra and describes the relationship between activity bundles and household organisation of time in the complex and varied range of household structures which were found to exist. It prepares the ground for the discussion in Chapter 7 of the ways in which traders make use of family labour, most particularly school age girls, in order to compensate for the long journey times and considerable variability in journey time. In particular, Chapter 7 focuses on the consequences of family labour and income requirements for girls' education. It examines the contribution that transport organisation makes to this educational loss. This argument is of consequence for educational policy in a context where the low enrolment of girls is a major policy issue.

Chapter 8 produces a shift of focus away from the trading activity of the young towards the conventionally neglected trading activity of the elderly. Doorstep trading in Ghana is shown to provide elderly women with both social and economic opportunities for integration in the life of their communities. The chapter makes a contribution to the literature on the role of the extended family in providing social welfare, through the social organisation of its trading 'career' structure, in the absence of formal social insurance systems.

Chapter 9 provides a description of female traders' occupational histories and life circumstances in their own voices. The tales of the young, of the old and of those in their middle years, have been collected together to demonstrate the resilience of Ghana's female traders against a set of national and gender circumstances which has frequently appropriated from them the benefits of their earnings.

Chapter 10 concludes the book by considering the case for a more sensitive policy approach to informal public transport in developing countries. It argues that transport planning must take account of the persistence of non-motorised transport and make appropriate infra-structural provision for these low income transport needs. In particular, it is shown that the interaction between petty trading and the informal public transport sector requires more considered policy attention.

The intention in putting this volume together is to indicate how complex the interaction between the trading system, the transport system, the travel system and the gender system is in urban Accra. Although simple text can never convey the feel of the richness of Ghanaian excitement and endurance in travel, we invite the reader to attempt this journey through the tool of travel research.

Mmra Krado
(mm RAH KRAH doh)
The lock, or seal of law and order – a symbol of the authority and power of the court.

2 Trading and the tro-tro: A description of the informal public transport sector of Accra

Jeff Turner

2.1 Developing countries, informal sectors and informal public transport

The 'tro-tro' is the key component of Accra's informal public transport system. 'Tro-tro,' a local term, conveys the meaning 'pick up and drop off': its very description on the local scene is one of informality and casualness. Contemporary tro-tros are minibuses in varying states of roadworthiness that ply the journey between local neighbourhoods and the central areas carrying fare paying passengers and their loads. Historically, tro-tros were small lorries with slatted wooden covered backs in to which passengers would climb and remain for the duration of a journey. These vehicles combined the functions of carrying goods and fare paying passengers. The traditional tro-tros were of a uniform design and are now referred to as mammy wagons. Modern tro-tros exhibit no such standardisation. Accra has a large fleet of tro-tros or minibuses imported from a variety of locations. These vehicles are mostly second hand.

There is an extensive literature on the importance of the informal sector in developing countries. Indeed, there is a sizable literature on the significance of the informal sector in Ghana. There is a small but growing literature on the existence of informal public transport systems in developing economies (Fouracre et al., 1994; Gardner et al., 1989; Fouracre and Maunder, 1979; Silcock, 1981). What precisely constitutes an informal public transport system is yet to receive a definitive treatment within the literature: the variations existing within the developing world have worked against a simple definition of the terrain. Practically, definitions of informal public transport convert into the absence of municipal fare-stage buses, a low level of fixed routes and the provision of fare paying transport services by small scale operators. Despite the recognition of the importance of understanding the operations of the

Plate 2   Bulk buying, little comfort: the mammy wagon

informal economy for development and despite the recognition of the importance of the informal public transport system for the mobility of the urban poor in developing countries, there has been no corresponding attempt to link the operation of the informal public transport system to the workings of the informal economy.

In Ghana, the informal sector is the primary location of employment for women. Their mass employment as traders makes clear demands upon the informal public transport system for the accommodation of their load carrying needs. The informal economy is a petty economy with specific transport needs: flexibility in the carriage of load size is crucial. The low level of regulation of informal public transport better serves this commercial requirement than would be possible within a more formal fare-stage, fixed route system. The opportunity to negotiate variations in routes, fares and size of load carried, e.g. on the roof space or interior of vehicles, is more readily available inside the informal structure of a large number of small scale operators. There are more chances of striking an appropriate travel and transport bargain. Indeed, our research shows that negotiation on fares, routes and size of load carried is at the core of Accra's informal public transport operation. This chapter provides a description of transport organisation in Accra and explores the cultural attitudes and travel behaviours which explain and accompany that transport organisation. It focuses on the informal public transport system of Accra and the role which this plays in meeting traders' working needs. Analysing the public transport system, as opposed to retail distribution systems in this way, represents a departure from the existing literature.

2.2 Getting at the core of the informal public transport system: surveys and sources of evidence

The research on which this book is based was conducted over two years (1993–5) in Accra, Ghana. It was conducted by the Overseas Centre, Transport Research Laboratory, UK, in conjunction with the Ministry of Transport and Communications, Ghana and the Social Administration Unit, University of Ghana as part of an ODA-funded research programme. The research explored the characteristics of low income urban travel in the developing context. Within this general area of low income travel, specific attention was paid to gender in designing the research. The recognition that women were highly active in the economy of Ghana and that the nature of their activity, e.g. trading, was likely to have a strong travel and transport dimension resulted in a specific focus on female traders as a research object.

The research was organised into a number of sub-studies. These were designed so as to highlight the travel behaviour and the activity patterns of female traders and of low income households. As part of its focus on the

21

transport and travel strategies of low income women, the research also explored economic decision-making around the use of non-motorised transport and of human transport, e.g. head load porters.

The key objective of the research was to demonstrate that the transport choices of low income households are influenced by the form of household organisation, e.g. spousal separation, separate male and female domestic economies, etc., and that the range of travel and transport choices available to households in the developing world is greater and more diverse than has previously been understood. Non-motorised options – e.g. trucks, trolleys and porters, the availability of domestic servants, the use of children's labour to increase time and travel flexibility, the diversity of vehicle types and transport arrangements – all of these factors indicate that there is a need for a more detailed approach to the travel transport choices of the urban poor in developing countries. The next section describes the range of vehicles available within the informal public transport system of Accra as described by the female traders themselves.

Interviews were conducted in local languages by experienced researchers and ethnic data was recorded. In this respect, the research differs from the large scale surveys conducted in recent years in Ghana where the ethnic dimension has not been incorporated (World Bank, 1995): this, despite the fact that Ghana contains over 90 well defined different ethnic groups (ODA, 1994). In the course of the research, 1,013 people were interviewed, either individually or as part of a household or an occupational group (Table 2.1).

2.3 A vehicle for every purpose: the range of vehicles and transport services in the informal public transport system

The traditional tro-tro, now called the mammy wagon, and the modern tro-tro, a fleet of fare paying minibuses or urvans which are owned by a large number of small private operators, have already made their entrance as part of the furniture of Accra's informal public transport system. But within the category of tro-tro itself there is a range of vehicle types. And the tro-tro and mammy wagon do not constitute the outside boundary of the informal public transport system, for there are many more vehicle types and transport services in play. Within the informal public transport system taxis, operating under a number of different charging regimes, play a key role in the commercial carriage of traders' loads. There are also various forms of non-motorised transport such as trolleys, trucks and human porters which should be considered under the description of informal public transport. This is an area which is typically neglected in transport and travel analyses of the developing world despite its vitality, persistence and centrality to the travel arrangements of the petty traders in the developing city. We argue that non-motorised transport should be viewed as part of or an extension of the informal public transport system; however, for reasons of ease of presentation, the non-motorised aspect of the informal public transport system is presented in Chapters 4 and 5. In this chapter, we will deal only with the range of motorised vehicles and motorised transport services.

Table 2.1
Data sources: a listing of surveys conducted

	Topic	Date	No. of interviews	Household/ Individual
1a	Household organisation	April '93	14	Household
1b	Household organisation	March '94	40	Household
1c	Quantitative household organisation	November '93	242	Household
2a	Cycling	April '93	16	Individual
2b	Cycling	November '93	30	Individual
3a	Traders	April '93	8	Individual
3b	Traders	March '94	60	Individual
3c	Traders	April '94	102	Individual
3d	Traders	March '94	5	Group
3e	Traders	November '94	50	Individual
3f	Traders	December '94	50	Individual
4a	Porters	April '93	4	Individual
4b	Porters	November '93	12	Individual
4d	Porters	March '94	60	Individual
4e	Porters	March '94	5	Group
5	Working children	August '94	10	Individual
	Total		708	

The Accra informal public transport system is comprised of a large fleet of small private operator vehicles which largely move along the city's arteries between the central termini, e.g. lorry parks or tro-tro stations, and the local neighbourhoods. The lorry parks or tro-tro stations operate under the rules set by the GPRTU (Ghana Private Road Transport Union), the informal public transport association, and vehicles are meant to operate according to a fixed, fare charging schedule as set by the GPRTU.

Women, in their role as traders are significant consumers of transport, thus play a major role in shaping the demand for informal public transport services. The evidence collected suggests that there is considerable differentiation in the urban transport market and that it is the predominance of petty trading in the Ghanaian trading structure which

Plate 3   Getting the most out of the motor: informal public transport

gives rise to the existence of such a differentiated market. Within the petty trading structure, traders experience considerable variations in capital, trade and stock and this results in considerable variation in the transport requirements of individual traders.

Transport supply in Accra provides regular facilities for traders to transport each and every sized load. The petty trading structure, with its abundance of small load journeys[1] and variability in load size, provides important business for the varied supply of transport vehicles. Petty trading provides considerable business for taxis and urvans: traders are an important source of taxi and urvan custom. The traders themselves identify a hierarchy of vehicle types and services (Table 2.2), with the same traders frequently making use of more than one level of this hierarchy in the regular transportation of their goods.

For taxis alone, three different operating practices were identified, all of which appear to be used at some time by respondent traders. They are: *Chartering*, where the passenger arranges with the taxi driver to wait while s/he undertakes activities at different locations and then delivers her/him to a particular destination; *Dropping*, where the passenger is taken from point of pick up to a particular destination – under this arrangement the driver has no right to pick up other passenger in the course of the journey; *Joining*, where passengers pay set fares for a point-to-point journey and other fares will be picked up en route.

The considerable variability in the size of loads which traders have to transport results in considerable variability in the modes used by the individual trader. Traders who at one point in their trading cycle are carrying loads which are so small that no transport charge is made for them, at another point in their trading cycle are required to charter a vehicle because the load is so large. Traders report themselves as using a variety of modes, the choice of mode being determined by their position in business capital/income cycle. The traders who make use of taxis are the very same traders who at other points in the week or month or year are forced to make use of the less comfortable modes such as the old fashioned mammy wagon or the battered and poorly ventilated tro-tro.

> *Female trader in provisions at Madina.* Sometimes she uses a small lorry (minivan), sometimes a taxi. She uses a taxi when she has too many goods – which is not often. She usually uses kayayoos and tro-tros to transport her goods.

> *Female trader in oil, onions, paste, ginger, spice at Madina.* She normally uses a tro-tro – it does not matter which type. Sometimes when her load is too large she takes a taxi. Normally she will take whatever tro-tro is available to her; she always uses the kayayoos to transport her goods when she uses a tro-tro.

25

Table 2.2

The Accra Urban Transport Market as described by Accra market traders

Type	Quantity	Quality
Taxis	Plentiful compared with three years ago. Large number of second hand taxi vehicles came on the market three years ago.	Great variation in the condition of vehicles. Variations in roadworthiness of taxis produce variations in charging capabilities. Variations in charging capabilities result in considerable negotiation over price.
Urvans	Number of urvans in operation has dramatically increased through influx of second hand vehicles from Europe.	Considerable variation in roadworthiness.
Cargo trucks/ Benz trucks	Substantial imports of second hand vehicles.	Considerable variations in roadworthiness. Ability to carry larger loads than taxis and urvans.
Mammy wagons		Varying conditions of roadworthiness. Ability to carry larger loads than taxis and urvans.
Hand pushed trucks	Increased provision of service.	Ability to carry greater loads than head porters.
Porters	Increased provision of service.	Can provide a head loading service where other vehicles can not pass. Provide service for petty traders who require small loads to be carried short distances.

Type	Formal service	Informal
Taxis	Taxis can be hired under several different regimes: 'Chartering', 'Dropping' and 'Jobbing'. Three years ago dropping and chartering services were difficult to obtain. Charge for goods not set; at taxi driver's discretion.	Help in loading. Dropping at a joining fare. Old taxis more prepared to carry bulky, unwieldy goods.
Urvans	Urvans operate under a number of different regimes. Charter or hire of an urvan for sole use by customer. Fixed person fares with fixed charges for carriage of goods on fixed routes. Fixed person fares with discretionary charges for goods on fixed routes.	Dropping: where urvan drops at personal destination after other passengers have got off at fare stage. Preferencing of traders for seats in busy periods especially end of day services. Bookmen: brokering seats to traders on earliest departing tro-tros.
Cargo trucks/ Benz trucks	Chartered independently: purchaser accompanying goods. Chartered at the warehouse to deliver goods without purchaser having to accompany vehicle.	Collective chartering of vehicles.
Mammy wagons	Charter. Fare paying passenger and goods	Collective charter. Assistance in loading goods. services.
Hand pushed trucks	Not regulated.	Carriage of goods within markets. Carriage of goods between markets and lorry stations or to pick-up points. Carriage of goods across the city as a cheap but slow alternative to motorised transport.
Porters	Not regulated.	Head load carrying between markets and lorry stations. Export goods in taxis for traders as part of regular arrangement between kayayo and customer.

Female trader in cloths, shoes, jewellery, hair goods at Madina. She takes a taxi twice a week. If her load is small she takes a tro-tro which is not often.

Female trader in rice, provisions and soap at Madina. When she buys in bulk she takes a taxi, when they have a small load they can take a tro-tro, but it is rare.

The variability in load size results not only in the selection of different modes but also of different transport options within the same mode. Traders may use the same mode for both inward and outward journeys, using a 'dropping' option for the return half of the journey but a routine fixed route option for the outward trip. There is a strong preference for the 'dropping' option when goods are being transported in any volume. This preference for the dropping option frequently results in taxis being the chosen mode of goods transport, as well as for passenger transport (Abane, 1993). Whereas 'dropping' by urvan or other vehicle forms typically involves a prior arrangement or some waiting, dropping by taxi is a service which is almost immediately available.

Variability in load size also has consequences for the cost of the journey, with many traders routinely operating both 'high cost' and 'low cost' arrangements for transporting goods (See Appendix). There is evidence that traders are willing to pay higher charges when there is rain (with the possibility that goods may be spoiled if the normal arrangements are used), on holidays or when they are in a hurry. At Christmas and on rainy days, the more expensive transport forms are used. Christmas, like the other festivals, creates increased demand for goods and the combination of the traders need to transport her own goods and to be present at the selling point to capture the seasonal custom gives rise to the use of higher priced transport forms. In discussing low cost options, it is important to note that very small loads are not charged for on the urvans. Therefore it seems likely that traders purchase smaller than optimal volumes in terms of their sales potential in order to hold their transport costs down, at least in the early days of trading.

The bulkiness, unwieldiness and character of goods transported is also a factor in mode choice. Where goods are both bulky and unwieldy, they are likely to be transported on the top of an urvan or in a chartered urvan or in a well-worn taxi. Newer taxis are reluctant to provide transport services to traders with goods which are likely to spoil the fabric of their vehicle. Where goods are relatively compact and relatively fragile and have been purchased in wholesale quantities, they are likely to be transported in a taxi and to be attractive as a source of custom to newer taxis. Taxis do not simply accept any custom which presents itself but take an active hand in determining the character of their customer base.

Apart from the variability in informal public transport vehicle design and size, there is variability in the roadworthiness of vehicles which results in substantial variations in the reliability of vehicles. Variability in roadworthiness and in design result from the dependence of Accra's informal public transport system on the mass importation of second hand vehicles for the provision of its fleet.

Female trader in provisions at Nima. The transport system has been improved with more second hand taxis coming into the system.

Female trader in cloth, sponges, bags, sewing materials at Teshie. The vehicles are not in good condition: many are second hand, and clothes can be torn.

Vehicle unreliability, as a consequence of poor roadworthiness, creates a pressure upon traders to escort their goods rather than simply to arrange for their transport (Clark, 1991). Consequently, although there was some mention of the commercial delivery of goods, i.e unescorted trips, to traders, the majority of goods transportation took place within the arrangement where the trader accompanied her/his goods on public transport: the unreliability of Ghana's vehicle stock may very well be making its own contribution to the failure of a fully developed commercial distribution system to emerge. In the absence of such a distribution system, traders in the Accra transport market continue to be heavily dependent upon public transport in conducting their trading activity.

Women traders have use for a variety of vehicles of different sizes and qualities depending on their load carrying, time and cost needs. Money and time have to be traded off in this choice. As we have seen, the public transport market in Accra appears far less homogeneous than the literature implies (Fouracre et al., 1994). This lack of standardisation in the transport supply results in greater variability in public transport conditions than is conventionally assumed in the discussions of low income transport in developing countries.

Women are also suppliers of transport: women are involved in the ownership of both motorised and non-motorised transport. Though no official or comprehensive data exists on this issue, informants repeatedly indicated that women's financial role in owning urvans and taxis is significant. Women did not, however, combine the careers of transport owner and trader: amongst the female traders interviewed for this research, access to or ownership of a private vehicle for the transporting of goods was highly restricted. Amongst all the traders interviewed, only three respondents had any access to a private motor vehicle, of which two had restricted use: traders in the Accra area are clearly dependent upon public transport in conducting their trading activities. In measuring the importance of the informal public transport structure in the conduct of

29

traders' economic activity, it is important to appreciate that access to private transport in this context is negligible.

From our evidence, it thus appears that there are two key factors which are contributing to the differentiation in the informal public transport market, the petty trading structure which results in substantial variations in traders' load carrying requirement and equally importantly the dependence of this market on the importation of second hand vehicles. The great variation in the condition and roadworthiness of the vehicles creates a policy dilemma as to whether safety or economic considerations should predominate in respect of the importation of vehicles. Although, there is an official mechanism for ensuring the roadworthiness of vehicles – a six monthly testing of vehicles roadworthiness (Fouracre et al., 1994) – in practice, this mechanism is not effectively enforced, a fact which is obvious from even the most casual inspection of vehicles trafficking the streets. Such variations in the condition of vehicles generate the circumstances necessary for the existence of different charges for the same journey length. New and old vehicles have different charging capabilities and consequently different trading markets.

2.4 Order of departure: the ground rules of Accra's lorry parks

In order to understand the willingness of traders to pay higher fares in the busy trading seasons, during bad weather or when in a hurry, it is important to appreciate that there is a considerable difference between waiting times for different types of vehicles and the time taken for the journey once it has begun. Where traders are using more than one mode, there is often a substantial difference in waiting times for these respective modes. Taxis are not only more frequent than urvans but they also commence their journey immediately the passenger enters them or shortly afterwards, even if the driver insists on obtaining a full load before setting off. In the case of tro-tros or urvans departing from the termini, however, the vehicle does not depart until it is full. In the case of other older, larger vehicles, this can take up to two hours.

> *Female trader in provisions at Medina.* On new urvans, etc., the trader can get a space immediately upon arrival at the lorry station; however, it takes one hour for the vehicle to fill and commence upon its journey. On old vehicles, the trader can get a space immediately upon arrival at the lorry station; however, it takes two hours for the vehicle to fill and commence upon its journey. In the morning and in the afternoon the urvans will be there but won't fill quickly. It takes two hours for old vehicles to fill up during the mornings and afternoon, but they fill quickly in the evening. In the evening the cars fill quicker.

Some traders report that they have no flexibility as to which vehicle they join, for the regulations of the lorry station require vehicles to leave the lorry station in the sequence they entered it (Fouracre et al., 1994). Thus the first vehicle to arrive must be filled and depart before the next tro-tro in the queue can depart. Under these circumstances, some traders simply join the first vehicle due to depart, some traders change to a different mode of transport and some wait until a vehicle which meets their requirements reaches the top of the queue for departure. Under this system, the reluctance to join old vehicles with their problems of reliability slows up the stream of new vehicles departing the lorry station, depending on the position of the different categories of vehicles in the queue. Likewise the size of vehicle is not taken into account when determining the order in which vehicles should leave the lorry station, thus those with large loads may have to wait through the departure of a number of vehicles before a vehicle sufficiently large enough to accommodate their load reaches the top of the queue.

> *Female trader in oil, onions, paste, ginger spice at Medina.* She prefers big cars because they can carry the goods well; her goods get spoiled easily in small cars.

There is a noticeable variability in waiting times according to time of day. Afternoons are marked by the length of time vehicles stand waiting to depart for lack of customers, early evenings are marked by the time passengers stand waiting for even the superior forms of transport to become available. Spare capacity in the afternoon contrasts with a shortage of capacity in the evening. However, for the individual trader these two situations have a similar appearance as in the event of spare capacity in a vehicle, the vehicle does not leave the terminus until the vehicle is full. In the words of one respondent, 'vehicles operate according to the flow of market women'.

2.5 Negotiating a fast track back: respect payments and brokerage fees

Cultural norms around the respect payments due to those who enable any activity or provide any form of patronage, together with the recent history of transport shortage in Ghana, have combined to produce a situation where travellers and traders are paying out side payments – 'dash' – in order to go about their business. For example, traders wishing to gain timely access to departing public transport vehicles pay unofficial fees to the locally termed 'bookmen', i.e. transport brokers, in order to obtain a seat and place for their goods above on departing vehicles. Knowing which urvan will be the first to depart and gaining a seat in it can, therefore, save valuable time. Respondents routinely negotiate with a 'bookman', who for a fee can provide this information and influence. The trader faces the choice of either paying a higher unofficial fee or losing the opportunity of time saving.

The extent of the informal services provided and the frequency of the contacts reported between specific traders and specific transport providers raises the issue of whether transport supply in such a context should be understood as a market or a network form. We return to this issue more fully in Chapter 3; however, what is clear is that the negotiation which takes place between transport operators and traders around the seating availability, position in the sequence for departure and fares is outside of the routine description of a public transport service.

> *Female trader in oil, onions, paste, ginger, spice at Madina.* There are no special arrangements, I take whichever car is available. When the cars are hard to come by I make arrangements with the bookmen; I dash them about 200 cedis for the arrangement. The bookmen arrange with the driver to reserve space for me and my goods.

Old vehicles are perceived to have a reliability problem and are, therefore, obliged to charge less for journeys compared with new vehicles and old vehicles are prepared to carry larger and more damaging loads than their newer counterparts. Reliability is an important factor in a context where traders are obliged to wait until a vehicle is full before it leaves the terminus, a process which often takes over one hour and frequently two hours in the case of older vehicles. A breakdown on the route home can be very costly indeed when such lengthy periods of time are involved in gaining access to another. Traders with tight time requirements pay higher charges for reliable vehicles or wait until a sufficiently roadworthy vehicle presents itself at the lower charge.

> *Female trader in cloth, shoes, jewellery, hair goods at Medina.* She waits until a new vehicle comes, she will not take an old vehicle ... Sometimes the cars will kneel down (break down) during the trips or a taxi driver may run out of petrol.

Variations in charging capabilities as compared between older and newer vehicles, together with the variations in load size, result in substantial negotiation around fares between traders and transport operators. Even where fares appear to be fixed, negotiation regularly occurs. There is substantial discretion on part of drivers/conductors as to what charges should be made for goods. Such discretion is largely the outcome of the difficulties involved in determining and enforcing standardised charges combined with prevalent cultural practices of 'dashing' the service provider for any 'favours' given.

2.6 Conclusion

Traders frequently experience lengthy waiting times for access to the lower cost forms of public transport. On the evidence, a key element of the delay to journey experienced by traders is accounted for by the considerable variations in the size and condition of vehicles which form the one queue for departure at the lorry stations. One solution to the substantial delays presently experienced by traders at the termini (lorry parks) would be to classify vehicles according to their capacity and form separate queues for departure accordingly.

The research found that despite the existence of regulated fares for tro-tro journeys, there was considerable evidence of negotiation and bargaining within the Accra transport market. Even where a tro-tro is used by a trader, the set fare often only represents one component of the cost. Traders talked of variability in the fares charged for the carriage of their loads by tro-tro even when load size remained the same; similarly, traders indicated that side payments were frequently made to 'bookmen', i.e. brokers, to obtain a seat on the earliest departing vehicle. That paying such a fee in order to get access to public transport where the fares are officially 'fixed' or 'set' is both routine and necessary raises the question of what the real transport costs are and how they are determined. Informal charging practices appear to interact and dovetail with formal charging ones. As a result, traders transport costs and public transport operators profitability may be higher than suggested by the artificially low level of regulated fare. Policies of increasing fares, therefore, in an attempt to improve the quality or quantity of investment in vehicles may merely increase the cost to users and the return to small private investors, without changing the nature of supply.

The informal public transport market of Accra is characterised by a substantial degree of spontaneous bargaining and negotiating around transport charges. Female traders, by virtue of their business needs and load requirements, are well woven into this web of transport and travel negotiation.

Note

1   See Boampong (1981) for information on the difficulties experienced by Ghanaian women traders in gaining access to capital through the formal institutions. Note that, given the predominance of women in the trading sector, this lack of access to capital has consequences for the size of load routinely transported. See also Gabianu (1990) for information on self-organisation, i.e rotating box credits, by market traders aimed at ameliorating this situation.

Afuntun mmireku
Denkyem mmireku
(ah FOON toon mir eh KOO
den CHEM mir eh KOO)
Two crocodiles that share the
same stomach – a symbol of
unity between different
groups of people. It recalls
the proverb, 'Bellies mixed
up, crocodiles mixed up'.

3 Petty trading in a reviving economy: The implications for motorised transport organisation

Nana Apt, Margaret Grieco and Yaw Dankwa

3.1 Economic revival: its impact on traders' transport needs

Hopping on the local bus, having your goods delivered or arranging for transport is no simple business in present day Ghana. Travelling with or without load frequently involves negotiating both the costs and timing of a journey with transport operators or their brokers. But travelling is now a lot better than it was in the past: services are more frequent, more varied and more plentiful. This chapter describes the improvements in the transport sector which have occurred with the revival of the economy as recounted by the traders themselves. In this respect, it contributes to the present debate on the impact of Economic Recovery Programmes and Structural Adjustment. This chapter, building on the insights of Chapter 2, advances the key argument that the scale and prevalence of petty trading have consequences for the organisation of the transport sector. It focuses on the frequency of trips which have to be made as a consequence of the constrained capital base of female traders and explores the role that this plays in the scale of negotiations within the informal public transport sector. Traders strike contracts with transport operators in order to meet their own specific routing needs, diverting vehicles temporarily out of the public transport system and thus become route makers. Economic revival provides both the vehicles and the custom to ensure the vitality of 'contracts' in the Accra informal public transport system.

3.2 Tracking traders' travel: the sources and scale of data

Data was collected in three survey waves. The pilot research took place in April 1993. Interviews with eight traders revealed the centrality of travel to the conduct of trade in Ghana: traders do not simply sell goods but must

37

Plate 4   Fitting it in, a fine art: taxis as a distribution system

also go to fetch them. The second wave took place in March/April, 1994. 196 interviews were conducted where traders were asked about their motorised transport choices and preferences. In November/December, 1994, 50 traders were interviewed about the use of non-motorised versus motorised options and 50 elderly doorstep traders were interviewed about their trading and travel circumstances. Traders' views on non-motorised transport are presented in Chapters 4 and 5: elderly traders' experiences of doorstep trading are reported in Chapter 8. This section focuses on the demand for 'informal'[1] public transport as described by traders and petty traders in urban Accra. Four types of interviews were conducted:

* 50 interviews were conducted with traders in different local neighbourhoods who buy their wares wholesale from the central markets. These interviews focused on the overall pattern of commercial transport arrangements of the traders. The sample was drawn both by interviewing people both in the central Accra motorised transport terminals who were going back to the different local areas of Accra and in their local areas, even their homes.

* 10 interviews were conducted with traders who trade in different products in the Accra central market area itself.

* 102 supplementary interviews were conducted explicitly on the transport costs of traders.

* 5 group interviews with market traders were also conducted as the group interview frequently brings to the forefront issues which remain buried in individual discussions.

The distribution of traders interviewed on the operation of the motorised transport market by trading district is given in Table 3.1.

Traders were asked to identify the range of transport they used, the range of costs they faced and paid in undertaking the carriage of their goods, the difficulties they experienced in making use of the transport system and the arrangements they made to overcome these difficulties. A common perception amongst the traders was of a radical improvement in transport provision and in ease of access to transport for load carrying purposes in the recent past. The next section investigates the reasons for this improvement.

Table 3.1
Number of traders interviewed by trading district

District	Number of traders interviewed			Total
	Individual	*Group*	*Supplementary*	
Abeka Lapaz	3		4	7
Agbo Boloshie		7		7
Accra Central	10			10
Achimota			10	10
Adenta			1	1
Alajo	1			1
Bubuashie	1			1
Burma Camp	3		6	9
James Town		21		21
Kaneshie	3		21	24
Kwashieman	1		2	3
Lartebiokorshe			2	2
Madina	21		12	33
Mallam-Atta	7			7
New Town	2			2
Nima	4	6		10
North Kaneshie	1			1
Tema			25	25
Teshie	3		11	14
Total	60	34	102	196

3.3 Restriction, regularisation and revival: traders' access to motorised vehicles in Ghana

According to respondents, there has been a marked improvement in the supply of urban transport in Accra over the past three to five years, in line with the recovery of the Ghanaian economy. Respondents indicate that there are now many more vehicles in the system than was previously the case.

Female trader in cooked foods at Alajo. These different forms of transportation are always around; there are so many cars in the system these days that any time you go you can get a car. Right now the transport has improved greatly than previously when one had to queue for an hour before getting a vehicle.

40

In addition, new types of service are also offered. Previously, according to respondents, traders could only obtain transport along a restricted number of routes and make use of a restricted number of vehicle types. Now traders are able to take services between termini which are proximate both to their buying and selling locations. The number of routes now offered by urvans has also considerably expanded. Traders talk of the increased penetration of local areas by transport operators over the past three years and draw attention to the increased convenience they experience in transporting their goods as a consequence of this improved penetration: traders now have goods 'dropped' by urvans and taxis at their doorsteps, a service which was not available in earlier periods of economic hardship due to government restrictions. Furthermore, it is now possible for traders to arrange with transport operators to be picked up from their point of purchase and deposited at their point of sale. Individuals are now free to 'charter' vehicles: once again this option has not always been available, with both scarcity and restrictions playing their part in killing supply. Taxis and urvans have been very important in providing these new services.

> *Male trader in rice and eggs at Bubuashie.* The transportation system in the city has improved unlike some three years back; immediately after shopping you are assured of getting a taxi or an urvan to cart your goods straight to your doorsteps.

Whilst market traders perceptions are of an increase in the types and numbers of vehicles available for the transport of goods in the Accra region (Fouracre et al., 1994), their view is that this increase in numbers has not been associated with a decrease in fares, although other evidence suggests that it has been associated with an increase in trade (World Bank, 1994b; ODA, 1994). There does, however, seem to have been a decrease in waiting times. In traders' statements, this is associated with an increase in the range and not just the number of vehicles available.

> *Female trader in yam and plantain at Medina.* At this present moment unlike some years back you have all sorts of transport services ranging from taxi to tro-tros available for one to transport her goods from the market; this makes us cart our products easily and faster unlike previously when you have to wait for a longer time ... waiting for the tro-tro.

Similarly, whereas previously traders had to escort their goods back from the wholesalers themselves, new services have been developed whereby goods can be delivered to their destination without the trader having to accompany them. There is general agreement amongst respondents that there has been an improvement in both the quantity and quality of the services as compared with the recent past. This improvement has been a consequence of an increase in the number of vehicles in the system due to the mass importation of second hand vehicles: this mass importation was itself enabled by relaxation of the restrictions on vehicle imports.

Improvements in the informal public transport system have clearly assisted traders in plying their business. As we have already seen, the trading sector is primarily composed of women. The statistical evidence is that during the period of economic adjustment in Ghana, female headed households have been coming out of poverty faster than male headed households (World Bank, 1995). It may very well be that it is the role of females in the trading sector which explains this economic revival of female headed households. The recovery of the Ghanaian transport system registered here may, given the role of women as traders, be one dynamic which has fed into the improvements in the fortunes of female headed households.

3.4   Preferred customers: restocking, routemaking and the regularity of trips

Gracia Clark (1991), talking of traders' occupational language in Ghana, recognises the extent to which traders in the Ghanaian context are aware of the embeddedness of social exchange (Grieco, 1996). Buying and selling, or renting and hiring, are not seen as one-off events, something that happens on a market once, but rather as part of a pattern of continuing exchange between the dyad involved.

> Ghanaians use the English word, customer, reciprocally for dyadic personalised commercial relations without directly implying or ruling on the superiority or dependence (of either party).
> Kumasi traders recognise and value binding dyadic relations, which have a long history in Ghana and West Africa generally. They refer to both regular buyers and suppliers as their customers ... The landlord/ broker system of clientship common in the savannah trading networks provides another locally familiar dyadic model.

These patterns are precisely reflected in traders' transport arrangements. As we saw in Chapter 2, the payment of brokerage fees and respect taxes was a common feature of the informal public transport system: traders entered into repeated sequences of bargaining with the same individuals to 'tame' the transport system to their individual needs. In our interviews with traders, the prevalence of special arrangements between a taxi operator, a tro-tro driver and a trader emerged. When chartering tro-tros, traders are frequently diverting them out of the public transport system to meet their own specific route requirements. Thus even where vehicles are meant to be operating along fixed routes, the bargaining between traders and operators results in the traders' ability to design routes to their own requirements. Traders are route makers. In order to understand how such 'contracts' occur, it is useful to think about the transaction space which petty trading interacting with the informal public transport sector affords.

Some of this ability to design routes is given by the large number of traders and the large number of transport operators in the system. The very informality of the transport sector creates the space for route making. When the number of restocking journeys is added to the number of traders and operators in the system then the space for diversion of vehicles and the corresponding payment of 'dash' becomes clear. As we have already indicated, petty trading generates a larger number of journeys than would occur under a developed retail distribution system or where the capital base of trading permits bulk buying, either in a collective or individual form. This is well demonstrated by Table 3.2.

Table 3.2
Frequency of restocking journeys to/from Central markets

Frequency of restocking journeys	Number of traders	Percentage
More than 3 times a week	11	5.6
3 times a week	23	11.7
2–3 times a week	4	2.0
2 times a week	50	25.5
1–2 times a week	12	6.1
once a week	45	23.0
once in 2 weeks	25	12.8
once a month	11	5.6
not known	15	7.7
Total	196	100.0

These three features (the large number of traders, the large number of transport operators and the large number of journeys in a petty trading economy) increase the scale of the transaction space in the Accra transport environment. More transactions are taking place, there is a greater volume of 'contracts' between operators and passengers, with correspondingly more opportunities for the striking of bargaining strategies and arrangement of side payments or 'dash' (Grieco, 1996). That this interaction between a highly populated, small operator economy and a cultural practice of respect payments and informal service provision generates a greater volume of contracts and portfolios of transport and travel solutions than exists under Western conditions is clear from respondents' accounts.

Female trader in provisions at Madina. I have a particular driver who picks me when I go shopping; I only inform him in advance and he comes over to pick me at a particular spot after shopping. When the product I buy is in small quantities I take a taxi; however when they are in large quantities I hire a Datsun pick-up or Peugeot caravan.

Female trader in rice, soap, provisions at Madina. I have a particular taxi driver who picks me up from town whenever I (go) off to buy goods; I arrange with the driver at a particular place and time; at that time he comes and pick me home of the buying my goods. When I go to buy rice in a larger quantity I hire an urvan; however when the goods are in a small quantity I take a taxi.

Female trader in provisions and textiles at Madina. After shopping I move to the street side and arrange for any available taxi; however; when the goods are many I arrange with the urvan driver to pick me up at a specific time at a particular place.

Female trader in oil and rice at Madina. Because of the drums of oil a prior arrangement has to be made with the driver. When the oil exceeds a drum and there is more than five bags of rice then a cargo is preferred considering cost. By nature of the load it's better to use cargo because the cost is lower comparatively. The services operate when the services of a driver is needed

Special arrangements are made, according to traders, as one way of overcoming the deficiencies in the routine informal public transport market. As we have seen, the scope of special arrangements extends to the unofficial chartering of tro-tros which are diverted out of the public transport system for the duration of the charter and are thus diverted from general public transport use. Traders' comments show that, despite a degree of progress, there is still room for considerable improvement in the delivery services offered by cargo trucks, e.g. mammy wagons, as well as other forms of public transport vehicles: in the absence of appropriate commercial or public transport arrangements, the unofficial chartering of vehicles provides an ad hoc solution to traders' needs.

Female trader in stationery at Accra Central. If a more organised cargo transport could be in place so that when you need it you can go there for such service to be rendered for you.

Traders have their preferences but transport operators also have theirs. As we saw in Chapter 2, taxi drivers take an active hand in determining who is acceptable to them as a customer. Similarly, urvan drivers and conductors prefer traders to other passengers and permit them to jump the

44

queues for urvan places in the evening rush hour. Whether such preferencing is related to the transport operators' ability to obtain higher fares from the traders on account of their loads is not discussed, however, such preferencing of one category of customers over another is far removed from the world of first come, first served and fixed prices of a formally regulated market.

Female trader in tomatoes, onions at Madina. In the mornings and afternoon I wait for about 15 minutes (for an urvan); however in the evenings, even though there are long queues drivers give preference to traders with goods so I wait for about 30 minutes.

Female trader in smoked fish at Kaneshie. In the morning and evening because I have load it is easy to get a car (urvan).

Female trader in yams at North Kaneshie. Drivers are very particular and want to take load as soon as they see it.

Female trader in vegetable oil at Abeka. These forms of transport are always available especially for us, who have loads.

In Chapter 2 we noted the problems around order of departure at the lorry parks and indicated the space this created for negotiation around charges in the informal public transport situation. In terms of preferred customers, drivers wishing to fill their vehicles in order to meet the requirements necessary for departure from the termini also actively broker their own services.

Female trader in cassava, plantain, groundnut oils at Madina. In view of the many vans around the drivers rather makes connections with the traders.

Transport brokers are not simply a feature of the minibus transport market but are also active in respect of taxi business. In this case, however, it is the taxis who pay the broker's fee. Traders making use of these brokers as a way of gaining access to taxis have the security advantage that they can remain alongside their goods at a kerbside spot close to where they have purchased those goods whilst the 'agent' fetches a taxi, as well as the convenience with which the arrangement provides them.

Female trader in rice, provisions, soap at Madina. If there isn't a taxi, they make arrangements with other people to hire taxis for them; these people find the taxis, pack the goods and take commission from the taxi driver; the taxi drivers hire these people to find jobs for them thus the market women do not pay.

45

Female trader in plantain, fish, tomatoes, spices, oil at Burma Camp.
After I buy my goods I takes them to a particular place. There are
boys there who get cars for us; we do not pay the boys, they are paid
by the taxi drivers. The boys are always there to find me a car; I rely
on them.

Female trader in rice, gari and yam at Teshie. There is no special car,
she always takes a taxi from the same place – from the place where she
buys her goods. There are people who serve as agents to get taxis for
her.

The brokering function is also present in the mammy wagon sector of
the transport market. The evidence is that wholesalers take an active part
in organising transport for those customers who purchase from them.

Female trader in rice, groundnuts, beans, oil at Teshie. When the
mammy trucks aren't there she takes a taxi – but that's rare. The
people who sell goods to her make sure she has a vehicle to join – they
organise the mammy wagons; the market does it for them to get more
customers.

These services are not confined simply to ensuring that the trader gains
access to transport for the carriage of her goods home but also stretched to
the provision of unescorted delivery of goods. Whether the wholesalers
pay a fee to the drivers for their services is not mentioned, but given their
role in the organisation of the transport it is not unlikely.

Female trader in rice, groundnuts, beans, oil at Teshie. It can take two
hours from the point of loading before the mammy wagon is full and
finally sets off. The drivers know the traders so they usually just load
their goods and the traders take some other earlier departing form of
transport back to Teshie. They will get their goods later in Teshie;
they do not dash the drivers anything; they got to know the drivers
from the people they buy from.

The extent of the informal services provided and the frequency of the
contacts reported between specific traders and specific transport providers
raises the issue of whether such transport provision should be understood
as a market or a network form. At the very least, it is clear that patron-
client relations are a feature of urban transport organisation in Ghana.

Female trader in second hand clothes at New Town. Depending on the
weight of her goods she may make a prior arrangement with a taxi
driver friend to come for her.

Female trader in smoked fish at Kaneshie. She uses same vehicle anytime she goes for her fish.

Female trader in provisions at Madina. The driver which brings the load is often given a prior information to carry the load home.

Female trader in stationery and text books at Accra-Central. Sometimes we make a special arrangement with a known driver to convey the goods to the sales point for the purposes of convenience.

Female trader in yams at North Kaneshie. Normally arranges with tro-tro drivers in her locality to convey goods to her residence. She complained of the way some drivers behave and of the problem of off-loading wares at her house.

Female trader in rice, maize, sugar, oil, milo and flour at Okaishie. We get to the transport yard and arrange with them to convey the goods from the various wholesalers at a charged cost irrespective of time involved.

As we shall see in Chapters 4 and 5, one area of transport provision in which these special contacts are very evident is in the use of human transport, i.e. porters. The distances from the wholesalers to the transport stations mean that traders frequently make use of female porters (kayayoo), male porters (kayanoo) or truck boys (hand pushed or pulled carts) when transferring their goods between these points. Similarly traders frequently make use of more than one wholesaler when restocking; in such circumstances, they have to walk around the market areas in order to obtain their stock and thus make use of porters when putting their stock together before finally heading for the lorry station. Traders who use taxis also make use of kayayoos when assembling their stock. Traders report making repeated use of the same porter. Gaining the services of a 'good' kayayoo appears to be an important consideration, a consideration the importance of which is reflected in the ratio between the kayayoos' payment and the payment made for the use of the urvan on the return journey. We shall return to these issues in Chapter 4.

3.5 Finding a full load, sharing a ride: spontaneous cooperation amongst female traders

Ghanaian traders do not routinely combine to share in economies of scale, either in respect of the purchase of goods or of their transport. Such cooperation as exists is primarily of a spontaneous quality; one-off arrangements, made on the spot, which hold only for the trip from the

47

central markets back to the home neighbourhood. Collective organisation by traders in respect of transport arrangements is limited. This limited quality of collective organisation in the trading sector is compatible with Garlick's finding (1971) that sole proprietorship is the main form of business organisation within the predominantly female Ghanaian trading sector. However, higher levels of cooperation between female traders might reasonably have been expected given the widespread presence of self-organised savings schemes within this group (Gabianu, 1990). It seems probable that the variability in stock requirements, variability in capital availability and the range of goods each trader offers within a petty trading structure works against cooperative transport organisation. For any group of traders to synchronise repeatedly along these dimensions, and this is what would be necessary for cooperative transport organisation, is problematic. Petty trading may be inimical to collective transport organisation.

Of the collective arrangements which existed, the greatest number, both around buying and transport and for transport only, were found in the Madina area, a relatively distant low income suburb of Accra. A handful of collective transport arrangements were found amongst traders in the inner low income districts. The greater part of the female trading community makes minimal use of collective transport arrangements.

Female trader in rice, provisions and soap at Madina. No, she does not cooperate with anyone to buy goods. She pays about 2000–3000 cedis; if she shares a taxi it is a lot lower (1500 cedis). The tro-tro charge 200 cedis per sack and 100 cedis per carton, if they have two sacks and two cartons (or below this amount) they will take a tro-tro; otherwise they will take a taxi.

Female trader in oil and rice at Madina. This trader cooperates with two other persons who deal in same goods and sell in same market; the cost is shared according to load.

Female trader in provisions and silver pans at Madina. I cooperate with another trader who lives in Madina. When the driver charges 5000 cedis or 4000 cedis, we only divide the money into two and pay him his fare.

Female trader in provisions at Madina. Another trader who trades in the same locality; two persons are involved; the transport is organised on the quantity of goods a trader buys, e.g. when a driver charges 4000 cedis for the trip, the trader with more goods will pay more than the one with less goods. The collective arrangement is only for transport.

Female trader in yam at North Kaneshie. She arranges transport with her friend who is also a trader in Yam; 'we divide it equally among ourselves to pay. When it comes to purchase of goods I do it alone.'

Female trader in secondhand clothes at New Town. She organises transport with one other trader; 'I normally ask her to pay one quarter while I take the rest'.

Female trader in spices and oils at Kaneshie. She was first cooperating with three other traders for transporting their wares, the cost was shared according to the load of the person or otherwise equally.

Female trader in provisions at Malata. About 2000 cedis when I charter a taxi but about 1000 cedis when we are about two or more, 1500 cedis per trip when the goods are many.

Collective organisation around purchasing was of a very limited character and even less common than collective arrangements in respect of transportation.

Female trader in secondhand clothes at New Town. Sometimes cooperates with her sister when purchasing goods.

Female trader in yam and plantain at Kwashieman. She sometimes buys things for a friend in her area but she does not charge her any transport since sometimes she does it on her behalf.

Female trader in oil, onions, paste, ginger, spice at Madina. She usually buys her goods herself but sometimes she does not have the money to buy in bulk so she and another woman at the market will share the cost.

Collective arrangements within our sample often have a spontaneous rather than a planned quality, involving minimal levels of cooperation and collective organisation. Typically, each journey involves only a small number of people cooperating.

Female trader in vegetable oil at Abeka. She does not necessarily make collective arrangements around transport but 'we may happen to meet at the station and then we take the same fare'.

Female trader in rice, provisions and soap at Madina. If their load does not fill the whole taxi then they ask someone to fill the taxi and they share the cost; she does not share with anyone in particular. She cooperates with anyone she meets in Accra going to the same area; just with one other person. They share the costs according the distance each person goes.

Female trader in plantain, fish, tomatoes, spices, oil at Burma Camp. She will share a taxi with others to come to Burma; if there is no one coming to Burma she will join to Labadi or Osu and pay the rest to come to Burma. They recognise each other from the market, thus they can cooperate in town; she cooperates with about four others. If they are all going to Burma Camp they will each pay 600 cedis. She does not cooperate with anyone to buy the goods.

Female trader in provisions at Malata. Occasionally, when she meets traders from the same district in the market, she cooperates with them in organising transport for the return journey. There are usually just two traders involved. 'We share the cost depending on each person's quantity of goods.'

Female trader in provisions at Madina. If by chance she meets a co-trader at the market she may transport the goods together. She will do this with any trader dealing in similar goods. Each trader pays according to her load.

However, this spontaneous cooperation is based in the large numbers of market traders moving between the same urban origins and destinations. It can be argued that the prevalence of petty trading in Accra, combined with the recent availability of more plentiful transport as compared with a past history of extreme shortage, has reduced the need for planned cooperation in undertaking these commercial journeys. It should also be noted that the transporting of small loads associated with petty trading easily lends itself to spontaneous combining in respect of return journey transportation.

Even where there is a degree of collective organisation and cooperation, this is frequently concerned with the generation of time rather than cost benefits. Traders organise with others going in the same direction to fill a vehicle with passengers and their goods so that the waiting time between the trader entering the vehicle and the vehicle departing from the terminus is reduced. Traders organising in this way pay the same fare but have the benefit of a greatly shortened waiting time.

Female trader in rice, groundnuts, beans, oil at Teshie. With the mammy wagon they try to cooperate with other buyers to fill the vehicle quickly; they sometimes share a taxi.

Female trader in oil, onions, paste, ginger, spice at Madina. She cooperates with a friend in Medina who sells her goods here – they are two together. They pay according to the quantity they buy. When she

50

shares a taxi they pay 2000–2500 cedis together.

Female trader in yam at Burma Camp. Sometimes when her load is not much she cooperates with women going to Labadi, they are two or three. For every 100 yams she had she must pay 2000 cedis. Thus sharing the costs doesn't matter. She doesn't buy her goods with anyone.

There are certain barriers to collective organisation and cooperation operating in respect of transport costs: in particular, drivers are able to charge each passenger independently of the fare paid by the other passengers. Drivers, on occasion, also deter customers from combining in organising their journey.

Female trader in cloth, shoes, jewellery, hair goods at Madina. Yes, sometimes I combine with some other trader if the driver is willing; but I do not cooperate with anyone in particular. When I cooperate with another, the costs are allocated according to the size of the load; we meet at the lorry station (before approaching the vehicle) but are charged as individuals.

Female trader in vegetable oil at Abeka. In such a case (where traders have combined at the station to take a taxi) the driver is the one who will decide on how much he is charging each one of us.

Female trader in rice, maize, groundnut, beans at Abeka. She cooperates with other traders in the same market for a car but what happens is that in such a case the driver determines how much to charge each of them.

Female trader in rice, gari, yams at Teshie. She does not cooperate with anyone in particular in getting a taxi – she combines with anyone who happens to be coming to Teshie (it doesn't have to be a market woman). They are charged separately. She doesn't cooperate with anyone to get her goods.

Female trader in rice, groundnuts, oil at Teshie. She cooperates with someone from the market, one other person, when arranging transport; they are charged separately. They don't purchase goods with anyone else.

Female trader in cassava, plantain, groundnut oil at Madina. She organises transport with three other traders; they are charged individually.

Female trader in yam at Madina. She organises transport with a neighbour selling Akpeteshie (local fire-water), the driver charges them separately. The arrangement doesn't extend to wholesale purchase of goods.

Male trader in soft drinks at Accra Central. He cooperates with a co-mineral seller in organising transport. 'I bear the whole transport cost', i.e. they are charged a 'dropping fee' and a per item fee independently of one another.

When negotiating cooperation, no matter how transitory, traders have to consider such barriers to collective organisation. However, there are clear time advantages to traders in involving themselves in organising full loads for the transport operators and thus reducing waiting times. There is some evidence from our sample to suggest that collective arrangements around transport by traders were more important in the past when the transport market was less active.

Female trader in yam and plantain at Madina. Some five years ago, we had a bus that conveyed yam sellers to our selling districts but with the construction of the bus station, all these buses have moved there

Equally evidence from other sources[2] indicates that a high degree of collective organisation and cooperation amongst women traders is a feature of the long distance rural-urban, urban-rural transport market. Robertson (1975/6) argues that Accra market women were traditionally long distance traders but with the advent of motorised transport and the arrival of dealers in imported goods, these traders have over time become sedentary merchants operating in local as opposed to long distance trade. It may very well be that the movement from journeying to sedentary trader diminishes the logistical imperatives for collective organisation. In support of this understanding, our trader group interviews revealed collective organisation of urban/rural journeys by charcoal traders. Charcoal trading is largely an illicit activity as a consequence of environmental protection regulations. This illicit status requires a correspondingly higher level of collective organisation on the part of the charcoal traders in order to meet 'dash' payments, fines, etc.

However, in the present and on the evidence of our sample, collective arrangements around intraurban transport are largely confined to the spontaneous combining of traders at the lorry stations in order to gain time advantages on the return journey. There is little evidence of collective arrangements around the purchasing of goods. Similarly, outside of the family context, there is little evidence of cooperation between traders in operating their businesses so as to minimise the impact of such time expensive journeys on trade.

Female trader in smoked fish at Kaneshie. There is no one to take charge of the place while I am away; anytime I go for fish I don't come to the market that day. I have no choice than to use the whole day so I don't bother myself about coming early.

Female trader in provisions at Malata. No arrangements, nobody staffs her stall.

Female trader in provisions at Malata. She closes the store.

Female trader in rice, onions, beans, pepper at Madina. No arrangement, nobody takes charge of the stall in her absence.

Female trader in soft drinks at Accra Central. No arrangement made with any member of the family or other people; 'I lock the stall whilst away'.

In any future study, it may be useful to focus upon the barriers to cooperation which exist in the Ghanaian transport and trading context. This research has indicated that taxi drivers often 'subvert' the cooperative intentions of female market traders and it may be useful to consider what public transport charging regimes are most compatible with the goal of economic development. Finally, our interviews revealed little awareness of any ethnic differences in the organisation of trading and related transport activities on the part of our respondents.

Female general merchant at Accra Central. Basically, the migrant traders like the Ashantes, Fantis, Ewes etc. like to take taxis whilst the indigenous, e.g. the Gas, like to take urvans in the conveyance of their goods.

Female trader in stationery and text books at Accra Central. The Ewes and Fantis like to take taxi while the Gas like taking tro-tro to convey their goods.

Female trader in shoes and uppers at Accra Central. The Gas like the urvans, while the Ashante like pick-ups and the Ewes use the different forms: but this depends on the type of goods traded in.

Female trader in rice, cooking oil, minerals, toilet soap at Madina. With the exception of some people from the same ethnic background who prefer using drivers who are their tribesmen in transporting their goods; I don't think there is any difference in transporting their goods.

Female trader in bread, gari, beans, beverages at Madina. People who sell similar goods around the same area who belong to the same ethnic group (e.g. Hausas) make the same arrangements to buy goods and transport them home.

Male trader in rice and eggs at Bubuashie. I know some Ewe and Hausa traders team up to buy goods from wholesale and transport the goods as a team home.

Group of female traders in plantain and cassava from Nima. Nima is a traditional Muslim community, respondents with similar ethnic background cooperate with each other as far as buying and transporting of goods are concerned.

The majority of respondents were not aware of any ethnic differences; amongst the respondents who perceived differences, few viewed these as being of any consequence.

3.6 Conclusion

The chapter reported that traders perceive a major improvement in the Accra intraurban transport supply over the last half decade. This improvement has been based upon a large supply of small vehicles. Currently, there is a municipal and transport planning interest in promoting the introduction of larger vehicles into the system. Promoting the introduction of larger vehicles into the transport supply of Accra (Fouracre et al., 1994), whilst increasing the quality of service and number of en route seats, may produce longer waiting times; careful consideration should therefore be given to who this might impact upon.

Female economic activity creates an important user group, female traders, within the Accra intraurban transport market. It appears women engaged in this activity have some influence over adapting supply to meet their needs. Petty trading generally lacks reserves of working capital, thus making travel to restock a regular occurrence. It also means that there are significant fluctuations in how much extra stock is needed or can be afforded depending on demand, seasons and stage of traders 'career'. Around these fluctuations, a complicated bargaining structure has developed within the informal public transport sector: traders and transport operators develop 'contracts' for customised routes.

Understanding the influence that women petty traders currently have on transport supply and understanding the impact that the existing form of supply has on petty traders' time and transport costs are critical activities in shaping appropriate transport and travel arrangements for urban Ghana. To shape policy by merely mirroring the arrangements of the developed world has been an all too frequent mistake in transport history of the developing world. In this chapter, we have attempted to indicate that the transport culture and transport supply are complex phenomena which are likely to vary as between different geographical locations. Any attempt to implement technology or policy which fails to pay appropriate attention to such institutional barriers or resources is likely to create problems, particularly for women meeting their economic and transport needs. Success lies in understanding the details and harnessing them in transport policies appropriate for the area or region seeking development (Okpala, 1977).

Notes

1 As defined by Fouracre and Maunder (1979), Silcock (1981) and Rimmer (1986).

2 Interviews with small farmers in the Afran Plains, Ghana, July 1992.

Gyawn Atiko
(JOW en ah TEEK koh)
Symbol of great courage
and determination.

4 Bearing the weight: The centrality of head loading in a petty trading structure

Vida Asomaning, Fred Amponsah, Memunatu Attah, Nana Apt and Margaret Grieco

4.1 The transport gap: traditional streets, restricted accessibility and the functional need for porterage

In Accra, 'the load that women carry' is not simply an expression, a figure of speech for the tedium and toil that is women's lot, but a virtual description of their task as porters. This chapter describes the extensiveness of portering as part of the goods transportation system within the trading economy of Accra. It analyses the interaction between the customary transportation role of women in Africa, e.g. head load carrying (Cleaver and Schreiber, 1994, p.6; Turner and Fouracre, 1995), and the extensiveness of petty trading as an employment form. The transport contribution of rural women in Africa has recently received substantial attention (Howe and Barwell, 1987). An important finding of this body of research is that women and girls are used and use themselves as a means of transport. The historical custom of human carriage of produce as opposed to carriage by beast or machine in Africa contributes to and normalises the contemporary use of human labour as a primary means for the transportation of goods. In particular, the urban head loading of goods by women as a transport service is a 'natural' extension of the role played by rural African women and girls in the transportation of firewood and water for domestic use. This chapter describes the social organisation of Ghana's female head load carriers, locally termed as 'kayayoos'.[1] Particular attention is paid to the role of rural migrant girl children in this urban occupation: girl children and women temporarily migrate from the North to Accra in order to earn the income which will enable them to begin trading in their home areas. Portering is viewed as providing a path towards trading.

Plate 5   No space to manoeuvre: petty trading and portering
needs

60

Urban design also makes its contribution to the persistence of female portering in this developing economy: the design and human traffic density of market and trading areas favour the easy passage of pedestrian load carrying as compared with motorised or even hand pulled or pushed technologies. The following sections explore this interaction between customary roles, urban layout and developing economy.

4.2 The female porter, a human link in the transport chain: enhancing accessibility in the central market area

Portering plays a critical role in the informal public transport system of Accra. The petty trading nature of the economy not only generates a complex array of motorised transport services but also a demand for the porterage function (Agarwal et al., 1994; Apt et al., 1994). The extensive petty trading environment ensures the plentiful supply of smaller transport loads, sufficiently large to be arduous in terms of human carriage but not impossible to carry. Very often the kayayoo moves around the central market area carrying the goods the trader accumulates as she purchases the range of items she stocks from the various wholesale outlets.[2] The small scale but wide range of each individual trader's purchasing activity and the design of the central trading areas preclude this portering service being offered by motorised transport. The trader surrendering her goods for carriage can easily accompany, escort and police the movement of her goods when on the head of a single kayayoo; head loading largely protects against the theft of small volume goods. A kayayoo escort permits a trader to circulate around the market area without constantly having to keep her eye on the goods she has purchased at each point. However, there are concerns about the possible theft of goods by head load porters and these give rise to a preference for females as head load porters on the part of female traders. Women are substantially involved in the supplying of porterage where, apart from the physical transport of goods around the central market areas and to the various central transport termini ('lorry parks'), they also perform the function of escorting goods in taxis to the traders' place of business thus freeing traders' time. Whilst each transaction between a head load porter and a trader is itself a minor economic transaction, the practice is extensive and the number of such transactions make the practice a major feature of the transport organisation of the Ghanaian trading structure. The requirements of petty trading – the dominant form of trading in the Ghanaian economy - give rise to the demand for head load porters. These factors are likely to ensure the continued existence of an urban market in Ghana for female human transport for the foreseeable future.

Women are not involved in performing either of the other two portering roles which have been identified: loading and offloading vehicles and

Plate 6   Heading to market: the normalisation of human transport

transporting goods by means of hand pushed or pulled truck or trolley. There is some head load portering by men and boys but this appears to be primarily in connection with the loading and off loading of vehicles carrying goods. Where men and boys are involved in this form of head loading, they also often form part of the truck boy teams which ferry goods between the trading districts. However, the two services appear to be distinct and different operations provided to different types of customers. Some males operate purely as head loaders but this appears to be a phase at the beginning of male portering careers where the porter has neither the capital to purchase or hire trucks and trolleys nor the social connections which could afford him membership of a truck boy team. Head load portering is used as a way of earning the income for purchasing or hiring a trolley by new entrants to the occupation: it is the beginning not the end of a male porter's career.

Three waves of research were undertaken into the workings of female porterage in Accra. Pilot research on the topic was undertaken in March/April 1993. Four female porters were interviewed to gain insight into the porterage function. This was followed by a more detailed set of interviews with 12 female porters in November 1993. A third set of interviews with 45 kayayoos was undertaken in March/April 1994. The first round of research indicated that female migrants were a strong feature of porterage in Accra. The second wave of research gave further confirmation: it focused on the experiences of 12 kayayoos and their contacts in the kayayoo trade.

Table 4.1
Number of kayayoo contacts by ethnicity of the respondent

Code number	Kayayoo contacts	Ethnicity	Region	District
01	0	Northern	Upper West	Nandom
02	0	Gonja	Northern	–
03	2	Kotokoli	North Volta	Jasikan
04	10	Kotokoli	North Volta	Jasikan
05	41	Dagomba	Northern	Tamale
06	11	Dagomba	Northern	Savelegu
07	52	Dagomba	Northern	Savelegu
08	28	Dagomba	Northern	Kombungu
09	12	Dagomba	Northern	Zabzugu
10	15	Dagomba	Northern	Savelegu
11	5	Dagomba	Northern	Zabzugu
12	21	Mumprusi	Northern	Walewale

The third wave of research contained 117 interviews with porters, 45 of whom were with a female head load porter. Tables 4.2, 4.3 and 4.4 provide basic information about the age profile, the ethnicity and the duration of kayayoo employment. Evidence from the third wave confirmed the findings of the first and second. Northerners from rural areas are strongly represented in this occupation; duration of the occupation is short and motivation for undertaking the task is linked with the need to raise capital for trading, for marriage and for investment in occupational goods, e.g sewing machines, etc., for the future. The inability to earn a cash income in the rural areas brings a constant flow of female girl child labour into the urban area.

There are clear gender divisions in the organisation of the Accra portering market. In Ghana, head load portering is culturally defined as women's work; portering by men almost invariably involves the use of a technology, such as a hand pulled cart or wheelbarrow. Both male and female porters were asked about when and why customers chose the services of the different types of porters. The predominant explanation of this pattern of choice was in terms of the difference in the distances and in loads which each of the three categories of porters traded in. Kayayoos dealt in short distances and lighter loads whilst truck boys offered the transport of longer distance, heavier loads to the various districts of Accra and male head load porters provided an on-the-spot offloading service.

Table 4.2
Age profile of sample

Age	Male porters/ truck boys	Female porters	Total
8–15	1	1	2
16–20	7	4	11
21–25	12	7	19
26–30	11	3	14
31–40	5	4	9
40+	4	1	5
Not known*	32	25	57
Total	72	45	117

* The exact ages of some respondents were not obtained. Of the 25 female respondents whose precise ages are not given, nine kayayoos were aged between 12–15; nine kayayoos were aged between 16–25; and seven kayayoos were aged between 26–30 plus.

Table 4.3
Occupational duration: kayayoos

Starting age	Present age							Total
	8–15	16–20	21–25	26–30	31–40	40+	n.k.	
8–15	1							1
16–20		4						4
21–25			7					7
26–30				3	1			4
31–40					3	1		4
40+								
n.k.							25	25
Total	1	4	7	3	4	1	25	45

Table 4.4
Ethnic composition of Accra porters by gender: female

Ethnic group	No. of female porters
Baasare	1
Dagomba	36
Dandama	1
Ewe	1
Hausa	1
Kotokoli	1
Kusasi	1
Moshie	1
Wala	2
Total	45

Both male and female porters indicated that there was also a clear spatial division between the genders in the portering occupation. There are districts and markets in which kayayoos do not operate. The main location for female portering is the central trading district of Accra, with kayayoos' services being scant or non-existent in other locations. The centrality of the Accra central markets area in respect of female portering is perhaps best explained by the role played by the kayayoos as both transporters of and escorts to the goods of the petty traders as they move around the central trading district accumulating their stock. The traders' stock purchasing activities in the market area are, given the structure and style of purchasing (lengthy queues, slow service, selection of goods/cash desk/receipt/pick up of goods system), time consuming and kayayoos accompanying traders on their stock purchasing tasks are engaged for correspondingly lengthy periods. The traders require no such service at the other end of their journey, for whereas accumulating the stock involves attendance at many venues, disbursing the stock will take place at a single point.

36 year old Grushie truck boy working at Kaneshie. We truck boys carry heavy loads. There are a few boys who carry head loads of goods anyway. Kayayoos are most found in central Accra.

32 year old Nzema truck boy working at Agbogbloshie. We carry drums of palm oil or palm kernel oil and second hand clothes. There's no competition; kayayoos are mainly in Accra at Okaishie.

42 year old Fante truck boy working at Achimota Station. You can see yourself there are no kayayoos here. You see them in Accra.

30 year old Fante truck boy working at Mamprobi Tuesday Market. No competition. They are in Accra where they carry goods from store to store or to stations.

26 year old Ga truck boy working at London Market. There is no competition between the truck boys and the kayayoos because it is only the truck boys who work here. The kayayoos are virtually absent in this particular market, so all types of customers either carry their luggages or employ the services of the truck boys where the load is heavy.

Group of eight Ga truck boys working at London Market, Jamestown. Mobility between different markets is not flexible due to competition among the truck boys for loads and the type of organisations existing in the various marketing centres do not permit any easy shift in operations in any one of the markets. There are no kayayoos operating in the London Market except for those petty traders who solicit their services and they render it and return to their work.

Part of this pattern of segregation of female and male porters in terms of function and district can be explained in terms of the different conditions of mobility pertaining in different areas of the city. Many respondents drew attention to the advantages head load carriers possessed within the market area and its immediate environs as compared with trucks (or, indeed, motorised transport) whereas on the main road network trucks possess an advantage over head load carriers. The density of human traffic in the central trading areas makes it easier for kayayoos to move faster

66

than trucks and this, taken together with the prevalence of petty trading in the economy, provides an explanation for the persistence of a substantial volume of human transport in an economy where the availability of motorised transport is widespread.

19 year old Ga male head load porter working at Okaishie. No the four wheel truck is not suited for use in a high density area. I only operate in a small area.

22 year old Ewe truck boy working at Makola Market. Customers who buy small items and walk short distances to car parks use head load porters. Kayayoos and head load porters can walk freely in the market. Boys can't push trucks freely in the market whereas petty traders with their kayayoos can move freely in the market.

15 year old Ewe truck boy working at Madina. Because the petty trade can move fast with the kayayoos in the markets.

20 year old Dagomba truck boy working at Madina. I think traders who buy small small items use kayayoos and head load porters. Because they want to go fast since the market is crowded.

29 year old Sandama truck boy working at Tema Station. Petty traders with smaller loads are often in a hurry so they prefer kayayoos. They can also police the kayayoos.

28 year old Akan truck boy working at Tema Station. Customers who buy few items use kayayoos. Maybe they are in a hurry so to avoid traffic which may delay truck pushing.

22 year old Baasare working at Makola. We are plenty. Yes, when there is plenty of load it does happen that sometimes they are even faster than we are.

In the same way that the use of trucks and trolleys offers a transport service at a substantially lower cost than motorised transport, so female porters offer their transport services at lower rates than their male counterparts. Customers choosing to use the services of more than one kayayoo simultaneously in order to transport a bulk load are trading off the convenience of supervising one vehicle on its journey against the higher cost of such a services as compared with head load carrying. The different costs of female and male porter labour with their resultant difference in transport costs are part of the equation which maintains the presence of female porters in the Accra transport market.

23 year old Northerner truck boy working at Makola. Also the truck will charge higher than kayayoos even for the same load.

Group of 12 Dagomba truck boys working at the Timber Market. Mostly the well established traders who deal in heavier goods use we the truck boys, while those with light and manageable weight use the kayayoos who are able to carry for long distances at reduced costs.

15 year old Dagomba kayayoo working at Makola Market. Because of the weight and quantity of load involved and the cost in transporting it.

30 year old Dandama kayayoo working at Kantomanto. Customers who have a heavy load which cannot be carried on a single trip use the truck boys and those with less load use the kayayoos. Those who don't want to pay more use we kayayoos. Because of the size of our equipments used in carrying the goods and also the cost involved in paying for the services offered.

28 year old Dagomba kayayoo working at the Timber Market. Petty traders, cooked food sellers and passengers use kayayoos whilst big time traders who trade in large goods use the male truck boys and porters. Because of the quantity of goods involved in transporting and the cost of transporting such goods.

Group of ten Dagomba kayayoos working at the Timber Market/Tudu/ Makola/Kantomanto. Because of the cost in transporting the items and easy and fast mobility associated with each type.

Group of 15 Dagomba kayayoos working at Agbogbloshie/ Kantomanto/Makola/Tudu. Because of the differential access to technology use and the quantity of goods needed to be carried and also cost-effective wise.

For women, there is no career progression through the portering occupation; they begin and end as head load porters (kayayoos). Their career progression is to be found in saving sufficient income to commence trading back in their home areas. The principle difference between new entrants to the occupation and the longer term members of the trade lies in ownership of the technology used for head loading: new entrants typically rent their head pans, longer term members of the trade own their head pans. Occasionally, these independent kayayoos form spontaneous teams for the transportation of an exceptionally large load; however, the normal arrangement is that each girl and woman typically works on her own and for herself. For the majority of kayayoos interviewed, portering is a short term form of employment and is used as a mechanism for generating income for household and occupational needs on the part of female migrants from areas where sources of paid employment are scarce. It is the social organisation of the kayayoos – often very young, migrant females from Northern Ghana, who work as porters for only short periods and are accommodated within families of relatives in Accra – that enables them to offer their services at very low costs. The widespread availability of low cost portering labour enables traders to connect with the other informal public transport modes operating in the Accra urban system: traders routinely make use of female head porters. As women traders use kayayoos to move their goods between markets or purchasing points and transport facilities, i.e. lorry parks, tro-tro stations, this travel arrangement must be viewed as part of the informal public transport structure of this Third World country. Transport functions which are performed by technology in the First World are performed by human energy in the Third World; human transport is an integral part of the transport structure. Head load carrying is itself a petty form of trading; head load carriers are self-employed, informal sector workers. Girls and women frequently enter the 'kaya business' as a way of saving the necessary capital to invest in technology and equipment to enter other less arduous and more profitable occupations. Entering the 'kaya business' requires less investment than other informal sector trading activities, though as we shall see, there are some investment requirements even with head loading, and entry to the occupation is neither regulated formally or informally.

4.3 An occupational journey south: exiled from home to prepare for marriage and trade

Girl children are sent from their home towns and villages in rural areas to Accra in order to undertake the kaya business. Kayayoos are disproportionately drawn from the north.[3] All 12 of the head loading porters that were interviewed in the second wave came from rural Ghana and were not indigenous Accra people. All were from northern areas of Ghana (Upper West, Upper Volta, Northern Regions). The respondents all suggested that they had moved to Accra from a rural area and that they returned there at regular intervals and some said that they intended ultimately go back to their home areas to stay. Within these 12 interviews with kayayoos, each was asked to talk about both their own and the experience of other kayayoos they know. In all, our pilot interviews contain information on the fortunes of approximately 200 kayayoos. A subsequent wave of interviews with female porters reinforced the finding that they are predominantly from the north: of the 45 kayayoos interviewed in the third wave, 36 were Dagomba, a northern tribe. This pattern has been confirmed by yet another wave of research into the social conditions of Ghana's street girls commissioned by UNICEF and conducted by Apt and Grieco (1995).

The kayayoo trade seems to represent something of an ethnic occupational niche for northern females. Previous research by Apt et al. (1992), however, indicates there is a pattern of short term migration by teenage Krobo girls who are transported in small groups by their adult relations to Accra from the Eastern region for approximately three months employment prior to the initiation rites which prepare the girl for marriage. There also appears to be some involvement of local Ga girls and women in the kayayoo trade (Apt van Ham, 1992, p.35). However, our own sample has not generated any respondents from these areas and precise information on the scale of their involvement in the kaya business is nowhere presently available. In the case of Northern female porters, the mechanism by which they came to be working as kayayoos was reported mostly to be through family connections. Typically they exist within an occupational chaperoning context; either an older sister, cousin, home town acquaintance or distant relative is involved in arranging accommodation, ensuring that the girl child works and in enforcing savings activities on the part of the child in the interest of the larger family unit. In this arrangement, these young girl children are separated from their parents and their original social context.

15 years old, kayayoo (Kotokoli). She came down with her sister to Accra who is also a kayayoo.

Respondent is a kayayoo with age eleven years. According to her she was invited by her sister who herself is a kayayoo. She is a Kotokoli girl from Northern Togo (Apt et al., 1992).

Typically, they talk of their return home when sufficient income has been earned. From the evidence collected so far, it seems that kayayoos from the north spend roughly six months to one year in Accra. It is inappropriate to consider kayayoos under the category of 'street children', if 'street children' is taken to mean children who have either abandoned or been abandoned by their families. Myers (1991) indicates the problems involved in applying the description 'street children'. As UNICEF recognised in 1986, many children work on the street without having weakened or severed ties with their families. Appreciating the difference between children 'on the street' and children 'of the street' is important in identifying the appropriate policy moves to benefit such children. In the case of Accra's girl kayayoos, these are children who are deeply embedded in a family structure. They are responsive to their families requirements for cash income, obedient in remitting their earnings back to their parents in the north and expect to return permanently to their family contexts. Many of these children do, however, sleep on the street or in very low grade accommodation. Through our interviews, we have established that girls as young as eight years old are financed by their parents to travel from the north to Accra to undertake employment as kayayoos. On present evidence, it seems that many of these young girls see employment as a kayayoo as a way of getting together the goods which are necessary for their marriage and future earning. For these girls from the north, being a kayayoo is one step in their career towards marriage: a marriage which is likely to entail plentiful financial domestic responsibilities. The kaya business is not confined to young girls, however, for adult kaya women come from the north to Accra shortly after the birth of a child and remain with the kaya business in Accra until such time as the infant is toddling, when they return to the north. The financial pressures of motherhood on rural women have their register in the urban labour market.

Having established the general features of the kaya business in Accra, the rest of this chapter will investigate: technology constraints which adversely affect the quality of life of kayayoos; the social organisation and savings behaviour of kayayoos; business education; and savings facilities which could improve the social life of kayayoos and will outline the case for sensitive policy intervention in this complex social process. At present, there are no statistics which would allow us to estimate the total number of kayayoos active in Accra. It is, therefore, impossible to assess at this moment the total number of girl children who fall within this category.

4.4 Carriers of culture: women as a means of transport

Human transport is a routine African reality. When men perform the transport function, they typically do so with the aid of technology. Whereas women are substitutes for transport technologies, male transport activities incorporate transport technologies. What explains this difference? Why are women used as a means of transport and men not? How do men acquire technology? and why do women not make use of the same technologies? The experience, satisfactions and problems of kayayoos have to be explored within this context, a context in which there are established cultural differences between the transport functions of women and men.

Load bearing by female children has to be understood as part of the female occupational career structure. In line with the general cultural relationship of gender to transport technology, female porters, unlike male porters, make little use of technology. As adult women do not make use of technology in their load bearing, girl children following this occupation are consequently restricted to the same transport practices, which rely solely on human energy. The girl children are performing the same tasks in the same manner as adult women, with the qualification that younger girls are typically bearing lighter loads. In order to improve the working situation of girl kayayoos, it is necessary to identify what the barriers are to the use of technology by females.

From the evidence we have collected so far, the barriers to technology use appear to be more socio-cultural than financial in character. Kayayoos, when starting in the business, typically have to rent the head pan in which they carry the goods, the cost of which is 70 cedis a day (Apt et al., 1992).

Interview with 15 year old kayayoo, November 1993. But I was hiring/renting the head pan/basin used in carrying the luggage/items. This ranged from 50 cedis to 100 cedis. Until such time that I gathered enough money and bought my own which costed 1,500 cedis for an old/already used head pan/basin (i.e. a bigger and wider enamel bowl).

Male porters hiring trolleys rent at 200 cedis a day. Trolley rental charges are distributed between teams of three to six boys and men who work the load together. The renting of a trolley greatly increases the weight and volume of goods that can be carried and thus the earning potential of the work group. Yet whereas men combine to rent and subsequently to own trolleys, women's portering operates on a more individualistic basis with each woman renting or purchasing her own head pan even though combining into portering teams would permit the financing and use of superior portering technologies.

Whether the use of technology is a consequence of operating in a different carrying market or whether cultural restrictions on the market in which women can operate negate the use of technology, the outcome is that female and male porters operate in different carrying markets. Female porters carry the smaller loads of petty traders and travellers, male porters transport the more remunerative, heavier loads of larger traders and over greater distances. The exception to this relationship between distance travelled and the gender of the porter is to be found in the special arrangements between particular customers and particular porters where the 'kayayoo' plays the role of commercial escort to the customer's goods. The customer hires a taxi to transport goods across the city from the point of purchase to the point of sale and, instead of travelling with these goods herself, hires the kayayoo to travel in the taxi with the goods. This arrangement frees the customer to attend to other business and ensures that neither taxi nor kayayoo absconds with the goods. However, this arrangement depends upon the high level transport technology available to the customer and not upon the kayayoo's independent access to transport technology. The kayayoo's contribution to this longer distance travel arrangement lies in her reputation and the customer's knowledge of her previous escort performance.

In looking at the organisation of kayayoos' activities, it becomes very clear that there are customary carrying routes and distances. The expectation of both kayayoos and their trader customers is that these women porters will carry their loads from the specific local markets to their corresponding local transport termini. However, despite the

72

customary character of these carrying markets there are surprisingly, perhaps, no set fees either in terms of load or distance carried. The price for each individual load is a bargaining game between trader customer and carrier. In this bargaining game, there is a trader preference for teenage girls as load carriers because they are unencumbered with children; adult women involved in this trade tend to have infants strapped to their back and this is regarded as a disadvantage by customers, presumably because it makes the load carrier less flexible. In this bargaining game, girl kayayoos frequently experience verbal abuse from their trader customers who are trying to push the rate down.

> *Kotokoli girl kayayoo, aged 15 years.* Respondent said it was not always that the people she carries their load for treat her nicely. They sometimes try to cheat her and in the process scream on her if she does not agree to their payment. She thinks they at times feel she will abscond with their goods.
>
> Respondent said she carries load to anywhere that the person requests at a fee ranging between 100 to 300 cedis. She carries them either to Novotel, CMB, Agboloshie etc.; however, the distance and the weight determines the price that she charges. Most often the people she carries the load for do not pay her what is due; as such she does not force herself to carry loads which are too heavy.

In discussing why women make no use of technology as local porters and men do, it may be useful to think about the social dynamics of the migration/gender relationship involved here. On present evidence, the boys and men involved in local portering are either indigenous to the area, or are long time residents of the area, or have the expectation of becoming long term residents. Furthermore, there appears to be an internal career structure within the local male portering occupation. Young boys are apprenticed to elder men who either rent or own the technologies which they help to work. Males of different ages play different roles on these work teams. On the other hand, females enter the occupation of porter for a short term, with adult women and girl porters occupying the same role. Girls and women are not entering the occupation on terms which favour investment in the purchase of higher levels of technology; the short term migrant experience does not favour grouping together with others in order to invest in longer term projects. Whilst migrant status may explain why girls and women do not group together in order to purchase technology, it does not, however, completely explain why girls and women do not group together to rent technology. This is particularly the case where these same women and girls join together in a range of other pooling behaviours such as savings, the organisation of accommodation and the provision of cover for illness.

In concluding this section, we wish to draw attention to the high costs of petty purchase and hiring structures. The hiring cost of the head pan faced by the kayayoo at the start of her carrying career imposes a substantial burden on the girl child: similarly, purchasing the head pan is likely to happen under a credit arrangement which is equally burdensome. In designing measures likely to benefit the kayayoo and especially the girl kayayoo, easing the financial path to technologies, whether these be as simple as head pans or more complicated like hand pulled or pushed trucks and trolleys, requires consideration.

4.5 Suffering to save: social organisation and savings behaviour amongst the kayayoos

Earnings in the kayayoo trade on a good day are approximately 2,000–2,500 cedis. Earnings per load carried vary, but younger girls appear to earn less per load carried than adult women: whereas an 11 year old girl reports earning roughly between 50–100 cedis per load carried, adult women are reporting between 200–500 cedis per load carried. Yet both adult women and young girls are reporting the same daily earnings. If these preliminary findings are true across the head load carrying market it implies that younger girls are making more carrying trips per day than their adult counterparts. Despite, and perhaps because of, these low levels of earning, there is evidence of a high degree of social organisation within the kayayoo occupation. Both our current research and previous research by Apt et al. (1992) reveals a high degree of cooperation amongst groups of individuals engaged in this occupation in respect of meeting accommodation costs, providing support when illness strikes and forming savings units. Whilst not all of the kayayoos interviewed were involved in such pooling of resources and informal insurance arrangements, the majority were.

> A Kotokoli girl I interviewed disclosed to me that they have something like an association made up of all Kotokoli girls in Accra working as common-carriers and sleeping in the streets. They all contribute some money and give it to any of their members who may not be able to work due to illness.

The majority of kayayoos interviewed were involved in regular savings arrangements. These arrangements lay outside of the formal banking structure and took two major forms: susu and adashie. Susu describes the arrangement whereby individual women pay a daily contribution to an 'informal banker' who holds their savings for them for 30 days and at the end of that 30 days pays them back the lump sum they have saved with him minus a charge for the security service provided (Gabianu, 1990).[4] The kayayoo has a card and the susu man has a corresponding card upon which the value of the savings deposited are tallied. From the evidence collected, savings with the susu man are used for investment purposes, e.g. the purchase of the items necessary to make a good marriage, to change to a more profitable occupation, etc.

Table 4.5
Basic kayayoo income, savings and remittance data

Age	Rate per load	Daily income earned	Daily savings		Monthly remittance to home area
			Susu	Adashie	
15	100–300 c	1,200 c	300 c	500 c	
Adult	200–500 c				
Adult	200 c	2,500 c			
11	50–100 c	2,000–2,500 c	1,500–2,000 per day saved with sister		Not known by respondent
16			500 c	300 c	4,000 c
13			400 c	400 c	4,000 c
8/9	She knows she saves with adashie and susu but does not know how much as her sister manages her money.				
32				700 c	
11			400 c Sister manages this money		
15			400 c	400 c	
35			500 c		
14			400 c	400 c	10,000–12,000 c

The adashie system of savings is arranged within the kayayoo community itself – it is a form of rotating box credit (Ardener, 1964; Besley et al., 1993). Groups of 10–20 women save together, contributing a set amount daily. At the end of the month, the adashie will pay out to a particular set of individuals in accordance with the turn-taking rules of the group. In this way, each woman has a relatively large sum available to her at some point in the year from which she can purchase the goods needed for normal use. On present evidence, savings from adashie appear to be used for relatively short term survival needs. The adashie system also appears to be used as a mechanism for protecting the kayayoo against the immediate consequences of income loss through sickness. Under the adashie system, the advent of sickness can lift the individual kayayoo up higher in the queue for her turn of the adashie. The adashie thus performs the function of a medical insurance scheme, and, noteworthily, a self-organised medical insurance scheme. Most of the respondents appear to be trying to save as much money from their meagre earnings as possible, with children and adolescents saving more than their adult counterparts.

15 years old, kayayoo (Kotokoli). According to her she is saving so that she can get enough money to buy a sewing machine and go back to Jasikan to her mother to learn how to sew.

14 year old kayayoo, Mumprisi from Walewale. I buy some household utensils but I have also bought a sewing machine home (Singer model).

35 year old kayayoo, Dagomba from Zabzuga. (On the basis of the savings from kayayoo activities.) I hope to start doing some petty trading activities particularly in cereals such as groundnut, beans, etc.

Respondents' reports of their savings arrangements typically involve the mention of other kayayoos and the information received on the size of these savings associations indicates that such savings behaviour is not merely a function of our sample but is indeed a widespread practice within the kayayoo occupational community. In order to save on such low incomes, their daily expenditure has to be minimised. Sharing accommodation and forming savings clubs are two of the important survival strategies adopted by kayayoos. Some respondents gave quite detailed break-down of their routine living expenses.

Kayayoo at CMB lorry park. The respondent lives with a sister who is also a kayayoo. They, together with eight other kayayoos, live in a small room. According to the respondent, she pays 50 cedis a day for rent and this amounts to 1,500 cedis per month. This means that the ten of them who live in this small room pay about 15,000 cedis a month. Besides this the respondent makes other expenses like bathing – 30 cedis a day, toilet 20 cedis a day. Therefore toilet and bathing runs into 600 and 900 cedis respectively. Respondent therefore pays double this amount since by the nature of her work she has to use these facilities twice each day.
    Eating takes 300 cedis of respondent's daily income. Her total income for the day is between 2,000–2,500 cedis. This means that the respondent saves an amount between 1,500 to 2,000 cedis a day and this money is kept by her sister.

It appears that they coordinate such things as accommodation and food between themselves, with a view to reducing the cost to the minimum possible and so are prepared to put up with overcrowding. In order to reduce transport costs, they seek to live as near work as possible. The 'rooms' referred to by the kayayoos typically refer to the wooden sheds around the markets which are used for trading purposes by day and as night shelter for the kayayoos when the trading day is finished. They pay a fee for the use of this shelter and typically sleep either on cardboard, sacking or upon the piece of cloth which forms a part of Ghanaian female dress. That this shelter is available to them only by night means that they have no secure place to store possessions. Insecurity of accommodation may provide one of the explanations for the well-developed savings behaviour found amongst this group. Being a kayayoo, on the basis of the information received, involves the separation of the community of women and the community of men. The information we have collected on accommodation arrangements indicates that these women are present in the city without any accompanying men folk. The only males sharing space in these overcrowded wooden shed are infants who are strapped to their mothers' backs. The insecurity of kayayoos' accommodation is given by the fact that they either rent by the day or by the week. The fact that they enjoy night shelter only means that infants have to be taken with their mothers to the place of work. Frequently such infants are tended by young girls of about six to eight years of age who operate as kayayoo nannies before moving upon the occupational ladder into the conduct of kayayoo work itself.

Kayayoo accommodation is clearly of a poor quality, but it should not be forgotten in this discussion that 'economising' on accommodation costs is part of a kayayoo savings strategy. The less spent on survival needs in the urban context, the quicker can be the return to the rural context. Even where kayayoos are sleeping outside, their accommodation practices are organised. They sleep together as a group to provide both for safety and identification purposes. Visitors from rural areas can locate their relative in Accra even when she is living on the street by virtue of the outdoor sleeping territories which groups of kayayoos deriving from a particular district or area outside of Accra occupy. Living in the street does not mean in local terms that kayayoos are without an address at which they can be found. Friends and families can find them by way of their night time 'residential' arrangements and even come to visit at these haunts. Sleeping in the open does not of course imply that the kayayoo has no accommodation costs, as night watchmen require a payment to turn a blind eye to these night time residents.

> This (Kotokoli) woman has come to visit with a daughter who sleeps in the street. She hopes to stay with her for one week (Apt et al. 1992, p.51).

Whilst it is clearly the case that kayayoo girls and women are involved in arduous labour and it is clearly the case that they do not rank amongst the high earners of Ghanaian society, it is also the case that being a kayayoo is seen as an honourable trade amongst the migrant groups who provide its personnel. Coming to Accra requires an initial investment on the part of

Table 4.6
Accommodation arrangements of kayayoos

Age	Quality of accommodation	No. sharing room	Daily cost per person
15	She lives in Nima where about 10 people sleep in one room.	10	50 cedis
Adult	No information	NI	NI
Adult	No information	NI	NI
11	Stays with a sister in one of the sheds behind CMB lorry park: ten kayayoos in one room.	10	50 cedis
16	She lives at Kantomanto market: with over 40 females some of whom have children in one room. She sleeps on her piece of cloth.	approx. 50	50 cedis
13	Ten women plus their children living in one room in Tudu (commercial area).	approx. 16	NI
8/9	Lives with her sister among a group of kayayoos with 50 people sleeping in the room. 'We sleep on any material that we lay hands on – from mats to empty packing cases and empty cocoa jute sacks'.	50	NI
32	Sleeps at Agbogbloshie inside one of the wooden structures. Currently we are just a few (i.e. 10 adults) but initially we were 25+ in the room.	10–25	50 cedis
11	I sleep at Nima 441 (prostitution area). We are 8 of us who sleep on a narrow verandah. We sleep on mats.	8 sleeping outside on a verandah in a group	NI
15	Sleeps at Tudu with 10 other female adults plus their children: appears to be sleeping in the open.	approx. 15 in the open	NI
35	Sleeps on verandah with 4 other women.	5 on a verandah	NI
14	Sleeps in front of the State Insurance Corporation building at night with over 20 others.	over 20 sleeping together in the open	NI

NI = no information

the kayayoo and her family, as the cost of travel has to be met. Being in Accra is seen as a short term activity which provides an opportunity for putting together a level of capital that would not be possible in the rural area. Being a kayayoo is seen as the short term cost to be paid for a long term gain – change to a better occupation, a better marriage or the purchase of capital goods necessary for training for a better occupation. From the urban Accra perspective, the occupation is not regarded as honourable and urban legends abound of kayayoos who have absconded with the goods, tales of which the kayayoos themselves are aware. Not surprisingly, this perspective has served to disguise the extent to which a high level of social organisation is a feature of the kayayoos' social existence. Kayayoo girls are certainly exposed to arduous labour but they are in no sense abandoned children.

4.6 Improving the kayayoos' lot: some appropriate policy measures

It seems unlikely that girl children will disappear from the economic scene in Ghana. As with much of the rest of Africa, the survival requirements of low income families dictate the inevitability of children continuing to work for a living (OAU, 1992). Legislation already exists which prohibits children under 15 years of age from working in Ghana. However, where children find themselves forced to work as part of the survival requirements of their families, such legislation can operate as an extra burden upon children, leaving them open to extortionate practices on the part of minor officials (Adenike Oloko, 1991). Added to the arduous character of the task, the stress of escaping official detection does little to better a child's welfare. If child employment cannot be legislated away, what policy improvements could be made which would benefit these child workers in the present and contribute towards their future development?

Taking this line of approach, there are a number of measures which warrant our attention. Firstly, it seems on the basis of existing evidence that the combination of insecure place of residence and poor access to the formal banking sector results in kayayoos placing their savings with informal bankers on disadvantageous terms. Improved access to the formal banking sector where interest is paid could do much to benefit both girl and women kayayoos. The present susu system operates on primitive tally system, a system which, given the low numeracy levels of the kayayoos, is well suited to the present environment. However, educating kayayoos so as to enable them to check the accuracy of the susu account would be a valuable service. Secondly, women might be encouraged to adopt less arduous forms of technology in the conduct of their portering duties. Discussions of the costs and benefits of technology could usefully be coupled with discussions about the injurious consequences of head load carrying. The kayayoos have many health problems which they meet by self-medication with drugs which serve to numb their occupational pain. The health education of kayayoos is important, for there is evidence of extensive self-medication using drugs which dull present pain and permit continued working but which are pernicious to the body in the long run. Indeed, the occupational use of drugs is so endemic that a drug used to deaden feeling in the nerve endings is referred to as 'even the old lady can play ball'. Business education which incorporated health education could usefully be harnessed to challenging the gender assumptions which provide men with a technology and make use of women as a technology.

A third policy measure which might reasonably be considered is that of providing accommodation shelters for female porters at the market locations, most particularly for those groups of female porters whose company includes young children and working girls. In order to attract kayayoos, such accommodation would need to be low cost. Related to this issue of improving upon present accommodation arrangements is the matter of providing secure facilities in which such girls and women can store their valuables. Where the provision of sleeping quarters proves too costly to contemplate, a safe deposit facility for female porters could still do much to improve the quality of their life. It would enable the storing of small sums of money until sufficient cash was in hand to make a deposit at a conventional bank.

Fourthly, the organisation of a low cost credit scheme which would enable kayayoos to purchase their equipment and perhaps even enable them to move towards the use of better technology would be a useful policy development. The human transport market has not received any explicit academic or policy recognition, yet human transport is an active feature of the African transport situation. As a consequence of this failure to identify the human transport market and its importance for the African economy, ways of improving the lot of this sector have also been neglected. At present, hiring charges and credit terms for equipment are very unfavourable. Children seeking to acquire this equipment to ply their trade are subject to commercial exploitation; yet, setting up a pooling system whereby new entrants rent at reasonable rates coupled with a financing scheme for own acquisition of equipment would be a relatively easy move to make. Such schemes are perhaps the only way in which those workers whose incomes are so low as to place them outside of the formal banking sector can get financial assistance on terms which are not exceedingly exploitative. The evidence on kayayoo savings behaviour suggests that such schemes would not run aground due to high levels of non-payment.

4.7 Conclusion: the case for sensitive intervention

To summarise, there is a set of key features of the human transport sector which can be identified. Firstly, there is a market for very short distance transportation of goods around the central market area and between the market area and motorised transport termini which is primarily served by the kayayoos. Secondly, involvement in the kaya business is viewed by the kayayoos as short term, the purpose of involvement being to achieve sufficient savings to convert to a more lucrative and less arduous occupation. Thirdly, head load portering is primarily a female activity. Fourthly, girl children are heavily involved in the kaya business; many such girl children are part of a pattern of labour circulation between the north of Ghana and Accra. A large number of the kayayoos have become involved in the business because they have either dropped out of school or have never enrolled and they see self-employment as the only way to acquire minimum assets for better marriage prospects and greater economic stability. Fifthly, although the kayayoos are clearly within the low income earning categories, they exhibit a high degree of social organisation.

Child labour is common within this community but such children appear to be self-determining in terms of the acceptance or rejection of loads carried and in terms of setting their own rates. Pre-pubescent girls appear, however, to have little control over their earnings although they are very aware that they are involved in savings and investment activities. These girls do not expect to be involved in this arduous work in the long term but expect to be free from the burden and to return home within six months to one year. Adolescent girls appear to have more control over their monies earned, although they save at the same rate and allocate their monies amongst the same uses. Despite the fact that earnings in this occupation are low, those pursuing this occupation arrange their living arrangements so as to maximise their savings – overcrowding, proximity to place of employment, etc. The rigours of the occupation, the low income and the degree of overcrowding associated with being a kayayoo should not blind us to the degree of organisation already present. The object of policy must be to supplement the existing degree of organisation and to take care that in the cause of improvement, existing arrangements are not destroyed to be replaced by even worse ones.

With this in mind, we would suggest that the regulation of the kayayoo trade would be unlikely to be successful and would most probably introduce the space for the illegal taxing of children's work by minor officials. A child working illegally will have to pay bribes to continue, the volume of work will thus have to be increased to achieve the same level of income. Enabling children to obtain better terms for what work they do may be the appropriate path to improvement. Redesigning education for working children so that it is compatible with their occupational hours may be one of the most fruitful methods of approaching the problem of non-enrolled children or drop-outs ending up in the little education/low pay trap.

Whatever policy interventions are considered, policy intervention in terms of the girl kayayoos should take the form of making the income-generating activities more efficient and thus the task less burdensome. Stamping out the practice seems an unlikely prospect in an African country where women are economically active in the informal sector and girl child labour forms part of the occupational socialisation process. Hiring the transport services of the girl child will continue as a petty trading practice.

Notes

1   Kayayoo is a term used by the Ga people, an ethnic group in the Greater Accra region, to describe women who engage in carrying wares for a fee. Etymologically, this term is derived from two words, one from Hausa and one from Ga: 'kaya' from Hausa meaning wares or goods, whilst 'yoo' is from Ga meaning woman (Coffie, 1992, p.6).
2   Research into the transport organisation of petty traders indicated that such traders frequently trade in a range of items which are purchased from different wholesale sources (Grieco, Apt, Dankwa and Turner, 1994).
3   Attah (1993) interviewing 122 rural women involved in income generating activities in the Western region of Ghana found no evidence of this community operating as kayayoos in the urban context.
4   See Gabianu (1990) for more detailed information on the development of the susu (informal savings and credit) system in Ghana.

Kuntinkantan
(koon tin KAHN TAHN)
Associated with the saying,
'Do not boast, do not be
arrogant'.

5 Putting the cart before the car: Traders' use of wheeled non-motorised transport options

Fred Amponsah, Felix Donkor-Badu, Nana Apt and Margaret Grieco

5.1 Wheeled non-motorised transport: a vital cog in the transport system

Accra's traders continue to make use of the hand pushed or hand pulled cart for moving their stock across the city. This chapter describes the organisation of wheel based porterage, e.g. trolleys and wheelbarrows, which are locally termed as 'trucks'. Trucks are operated by males only; the chapter explores the social organisation of this occupation. As we will show, these non-motorised forms of transport play a key role in a low income economy. As with female head load portering, in Accra the congestion of market areas and the distance between trading areas and transport termini create a context where wheeled portering flourishes. The low costs of labour as compared with the comparatively high costs of motorised transport technologies have generated a set of conditions where hand pushed or hand pulled trolleys or trucks are a routine mode of transport for goods. These manual vehicles mingle with motorised traffic creating considerable delay and experiencing high accident levels in this interaction with motorised traffic. On the existing evidence, it seems unlikely that the importance of wheeled portering in this transport structure will diminish in the near future. Given the consequences of non-motorised transport arrangements for the operation of motorised transport and vice versa, the operation of wheeled portering in Accra requires some investigation. This chapter provides a first approach to understanding the role of wheeled portering in the transport organisation of an urban area in a developing African country.

The chapter then moves on to consider the fit between the small load characteristics of a petty trading economy and the development of a sustainable transport policy based upon the bicycle. It explores the ways in which existing cultural and infrastructural barriers work against the

Plate 7   Pushing the package: truck boys in traffic

utilisation of the bicycle by female petty traders. Currently, cycle paths are being developed for Accra with little explicit consideration of the cultural barriers which operate to prevent women cycling. If female petty traders are to avail themselves of these new transport and travel opportunities, cultural changes must accompany this infrastructural investment. Strong cultural rules against women's entitlement to ride have to be combated in order to permit the neat fit between petty trading and a sustainable transport policy to become effective.

5.2 Teaming up on the job: providing traders with collective muscle power

In the case of males, their involvement in the portering occupation displays a different set of characteristics to those of females recorded in Chapter 4. Males frequently work in teams. This is particularly the case where four tyre hand pushed trucks are used to transport heavy loads such as bulk goods extending to provision kiosks. Large, bulky loads which are conveyed by motorised transport in Western countries are transported by hand pushed, wheeled transport in Ghana. The weight and bulk of such loads requires team strength and coordination to move it safely to its destination. This section explores the migration, gender and work task factors which result in the greater prevalence of team working amongst male porters as compared with female porters. Interestingly, this greater prevalence of team working amongst male porters contrasts with the higher degree of social organisation exhibited amongst female porters.

Interviews were conducted with 72 male porters to gain insight into the workings of the wheeled non-motorised transport sector. Their age distribution and length of time in this form of employment are given below. It should be noted that truck boys are offering a low cost, manual option to the higher cost, motorised modes of tro-tro and taxi. The extent to which traders make use of the truck/trolley option is under-represented in our own main study of petty traders in Accra and their transport organisation (Apt, Grieco, Donkor-Badu and Turner, 1994). This was partly due to the fact that many traders were either sampled at the motorised transport termini or in the outlying trading districts of Accra and partly due to the fact that we had not initially understood the importance of non-motorised wheeled transport in the transport economy of Accra. This deficiency was corrected by conducting a supplementary set of interviews with traders who made use of non-motorised transport in order to gain an understanding of the attributes of this form transport from the traders' perspectives. 50 interviews with traders using non- motorised transport were conducted, ten interviews in each of five districts of Accra. The districts researched were: Adabraka, Jamestown, New Town, Osu, Tudu. 33 females and 17 males were interviewed in the course of the research.

Table 5.1
Age profile of sample

Age	Male porters/ truck boys	Female porters	Total
8–15	1	1	2
16–20	7	4	11
21–25	12	7	19
26–30	11	3	14
31–40	5	4	9
40+	4	1	5
Not known	32	25	57
Total	72	45	117

Table 5.2
Occupational duration: male head load porters and truck boys

Starting age	Present age							Total
	8–15	16–20	21–25	26–30	31–40	40+	n.k.	
8–15	1	2	3					6
16–20		5	4	4				13
21–25			5	6				11
26–30				1	3	3		7
31–40					2	1		3
40+								
n.k.							32	32
Total	1	7	12	11	5	4	32	72

Table 5.3
Gender of traders interviewed by district

Trading district	Male	Female	Total
Adabraka	5	5	10
Jamestown	3	7	10
New Town	2	8	10
Osu	3	7	10
Tudu	4	6	10
Total	17	33	50

These two surveys, combined with the study of female porters, uncovered clear gender divisions in the social and work organisation of portering: i) indigenous males or long term settlers versus short term migrant females; ii) team organisation as normal for males versus independent operation as normal for females; iii) use of wheeled technology by males versus no use of wheeled technologies by females. There are also major differences in the type and scale of goods carried, the distance over which such goods are transported and the costs per trip at which such goods are transported. Both genders report that there are customary divisions between the genders as to who should carry what type of goods where and by what method. Although a few individuals perceived the situation between male and female porters as a competitive one, most viewed the divisions which exist as 'natural' and had little interest in changing them. More concern was expressed about competition within the categories, i.e. within the ranks of male porters and within the ranks of female porters, than about competition between the categories.

There is well recognised division of labour which serves to regulate the competition between the genders: there are three occupational roles – kayayoos, kayanoos and truck boys. These correspond with:

a) short distance head load portering;

b) loading and offloading of vehicles;

c) and medium distance transportation of goods on the urban road network by hand pushed or hand pulled trolleys.

The first of these roles is typically performed by females: the latter two by males. There are several factors which explain this apparent lack of competition. Firstly, there appear to be different protocols for collecting customers as between the genders: kayayoos move about looking for customers, male head load porters and truck boys wait for customers to come and select them. Male porters and truck boys talk of being tied or linked to particular sections of the markets. Similarly, there is discussion of the same porters routinely being chosen by the same customers. This is the case for both male and female porters.

17 year old Akan head load porter working at Kaneshie Lorry Station. It depends on the type of portering. In Accra male head porters have to arrange to hang around the front of business premises or stores to carry things. Women head porters roam the streets to be called. In Kaneshie market here there are no kayayoos at all.

25 year old Ga truck boy working at Makola. No competition since we are stationed at the Law School and the kayayoos move about looking for loads to convey.

26 year old Bisa truck boy working at Knutfort Avenue. There is no competition, we the truck boys give some of the load to the kayayoos to help convey to the destination of customers while we wait for the heavier ones because they cannot do the work the truck will do.

36 year old Grushie truck boy working at Kaneshie. I usually carry sugar cane from the Kaneshie market to Zongo and sometimes Chorkor. On my return if perchance I get a load I carry it. I always return to the sugar cane section of the market. There are no kayayoos.

25 year old Kusasi female porter working at Kantomanto. There is no competition between us since we all have defined loads to carry.

According to our respondents, female and male head load porters provide different services to their customers and thus have different customer bases. Particular attention fell upon the ability of male porters to load and offload goods. In the absence of locally available technologies which reduce the physical effort necessary, such a service is considered to be beyond the physical capabilities of women. The goods escort service (e.g. carrying the traders' goods around the market as she purchases additional stock) provided by female kayayoos, with all of the attendant waiting time involved as the trader stocks up on goods at the various purchase points, does not appear to have a widespread counterpart within the male portering role.

Group of 12 Dagomba truck boys working at the Timber Market. Because of the nature of technology we use in operating and again our ability to climb into long vehicles and offload loads which the kayayoos can not do.

21 year old Dagomba kayayoo working at Accra Central markets. Petty traders use we the kayayoos while those who deal in more heavy items/goods use the male truck boys in unloading and transporting their goods, e.g. cereal, onion and cassava sellers.

38 year old Moshie[1] kayayoo working at Tudu and Kantomanto. Those who have small/light items use we kayayoos and those with the heavy load use the male porters/truck boys. They are able to take more and they also carry out of vehicles.

Yet another consideration which affects the customer's choice between the different human transport options is the different security characteristics of these various options. Traders discuss their motorised transport choices in terms of the security characteristics, i.e. protection against theft of goods. Not surprisingly perhaps, their portering counterparts revealed considerable awareness of these concerns on the part of traders in the non-motorised sphere of human transport. Traders' concern to reduce the opportunities for and the possibility of theft was seen as the principal explanation of the individual trader preference for a particular porter. Likewise, male porters typically saw the choice of a truck for transporting large loads of goods as being more secure from the traders' perspective than splitting the same load amongst a number of kayayoos for its conveyance, as one truck is more readily policed than are many kayayoos. This contrasts with the female porters' view that traders view the use of female porter labour as a form of protection against theft.

24 year old Kwaku truck boy working at Okaishie. Every customer has his or her porter or kayayoo customer but the most cases for the purpose of theft the customers like to take the truck where supervision is more effective than the kayayoo who may disappear with the goods.

35 year old Blusa truck boy working at Okaishie. It depends on the amount/quantity of goods being bought and the ability of the kayayoos or porter to convey the goods. For fear of theft that the kayayoos will run with the goods, they take trucks and follow them.

24 year old Hausa truck boy working at Knutfort Avenue. The difference is due to the quantity of goods involved but ideally some customers like the truck since with that supervision and escort to the destination is more effective.

There was little indication of any change in this customary division of labour, though how long it has been customary has not yet been established. Only one male respondent indicated that any form of substantial change in this respect was in process.

49 year old Frafra truck boy working at Kantomanto. We carry any kind of load. WC pots, wheelbarrows, mesh, iron rods, iron sheets and so on and so forth. Kayayoos have come in our midst. They are supposed to be in the market to carry foodstuffs. They have taken our work.

There have been some local changes in the types of loads carried by truck boys as a consequence of the movement of markets or certain functions of markets to other areas. Such a case is to be found at the London Market in the Jamestown area.

Group of eight Ga truck boys working at London Market, Jamestown.
Because of the shift in market we carry seating forms/chairs
(furniture) for funeral gatherings, cooked kenkey, fish and any other
goods that come our way.

Neither our respondents' accounts nor our researcher/interviewer
observations generated any instances of female porters using trucks or
trolleys in the transportation of goods. The gender segregation in the use
of wheeled non-motorised transport appears to be complete and
comprehensive. The majority of both male and female accounts of why
such gender segregation exists were in agreement: women are not strong
enough to make use of wheeled non-motorised transport; traffic conditions
make the use of such wheeled technology dangerous for women; and
gender roles in respect of this segregation are too strongly established to
be easily broken. Untangling the practical difficulties which women would
face with the technology in its present form from the gender stereotype
which custom has constructed is no easy business. The traffic conditions
facing truck boys are indeed treacherous and are made even more so by
the absence of brake pedals on such vehicles. Brute strength is essential to
the control of the vehicles on slopes: indeed, a number of truck boys
within the sample reported having had an experience of such an accident.
The redesign of these vehicles to make them more suitable for women had
received little consideration by either male or female in our sample.
However, when the possibility of such redesign and its implication for
female use of the technology was put to them, the majority of the male
respondents and a substantial number of female respondents rejected the
notion on the grounds that it would interfere with customary roles and
divisions of labour.

The men's view:

25 year old Frafra working at Kantomanto. God wants me to push a
truck and a woman to carry loads on the head.

42 year old Akan truck boy working at Kantomanto. Men can carry
heavy loads whereas women can only carry light loads. Women
naturally will be careless in using these things.

29 year old Sandama truck boy working at Tema Station. Because men
and boys are stronger than the women and also women don't have the
sense for truck pushing.

43 year old Akan truck boy working at Kantomanto. A woman cannot
push a truck, she may run into a vehicle.

15 year old Ewe truck boy working at Madina. Owners may feel reluctant to rent the trucks since they know that the women can't push them. Because of the physical strength. Women are not strong to push trucks. Also they fear crossing gutters and cars.

24 year old Kwaku truck boy working at Okaishie. For women, access to capital to buy it will be a problem in the first place. Descending a hill, there will be the problem of steer control. In facing an oncoming vehicle, fear may grip them and they will lose control. They will not be able to control the steering when the load is heavy.

35 year old Blusa truck boy working at Okaishie. It may be rented to them but the difficulties are that they may not be in position to control the steering and this may cause damages to people's goods or properties.

25 year old Ga truck boy working at Makola. Women are unable to control it in the midst of a heavy traffic. They may cause damage to life and property. They do not also have the skills.

The women's view:

38 year old Moshie kayayoo working at Tudu and Kantomanto. We are experts in carrying on the head just as we do when carrying water and fuel wood.

21 year old Dagomba kayayoo working at Accra Central. No, it's men's work and our roads are not too safe for women to push the trucks around.

28 year old Dagomba kayayoo working at the Timber Market/ Agbogbloshie. It depends on the type of trucks to be introduced but I feel we shall not be very keen on using trucks/trolleys.

45 year old Ewe kayayoo working at the Timber Market/CMB. Because they are physically more enduring (strength) than we women do. They are also more skilful in operating the trolleys.

32 year old Dagomba kayayoo working at the Railways area. It is not good for females considering the risks involved in pushing these especially on the streets. Men are stronger and we have babies which will be very difficult to push trucks with.

20 year old Dagomba kayayoo working at Agbogbloshie. They are stronger than us.

Whilst gender stereotyping clearly plays an important part in determining who undertakes what portering tasks, the requirement of physical strength in ensuring the ready manoeuvrability of the current design of vehicles in hazardous traffic conditions is an important factor militating against female use of wheeled technology. Any attempt to move the load from female heads onto trucks or trolleys will require the substantial redesign of locally available technology. Apart from their physical strength being viewed as inadequate for the operation of the current generation of trucks and trolleys, the extent to which women are encumbered by the children strapped to their back is also a consideration. Many of the female head load porters carry their loads with an infant strapped to their backs. Female respondents draw attention to the difficulties of truck operation with a child strapped on the back. With a head load, the child's position remains upright and constant; when pushing a trolley the child would be moved constantly between horizontal, vertical and upside down positions.

24 year old Hausa truck boy working at Kaneshie. I think the main reason is that portering work is such that only men can use trucks and trolleys whereas women can head loads. Some of these women carry babies on their backs.

32 year old Wala kayayoo working at Kokomba Market. It will be very cumbersome and also dangerous for us and most of the time we have babies on our back and thus would be dangerous for us. Women do not use those things because as I have already stated trucks are heavy in themselves and to put loads on them will make them more heavier and as such pushing will be difficult.

21 year old Dagomba kayayoo working at CMB. Because of the body build up it makes the male stronger than the female. No, I think it will be difficult for them to use. We do not like the pushing, it is dangerous for us nursing mothers. Men are daring and as such can conveniently push the trucks into the streets but women will not even attempt it.

22 year old Baasare kayayoo working at Makola. I think because we are female we will find it difficult to push these trucks. Pushing is difficult for some of us women especially for some of us with children at our back.

24 year old Dagomba kayayoo working at CMB. I think female porters will find it difficult to push it because of its cumbersome nature. Boys don't have children at their back and we do and they are stronger than we.

Our porters, both male and female, provided cultural and physical rationales in abundance for the comprehensiveness of gender segregation in portering. However, the resistance to the idea of female 'truck boys' is not simply a matter of practicalities: it also has to do with respect and honour. Concerns about women being exposed to traffic are partially concerns about women being placed in situations where they will be dishonoured. Whilst being shouted at by motorised users or hooted at by motorised traffic is acceptable for a male, it places a female in a situation of shame. Male porters repeatedly made reference to women's 'fear' of interactions with traffic: whether such fear is learnt as part of a cultural role or a simple reaction to physical danger, it operates to shape a form of seclusion or exclusion. Women do not belong on the technology highway, no matter how simple that technology may be.

26 year old Hausa kayayoo working at Kantomanto. Because of the many vehicles around, even I see the men sometimes being shouted or hooted at when they are on the street with their trucks. The men will be stronger and will be able to push these things despite the vehicles but we are also afraid.

As can be readily seen from these respondents' comments, the negative attitude towards women's use of non-motorised wheeled technology is very widespread. It is a combination of safety concerns and conservative customary role restrictions. No such restrictions exist, however, on women's ownership, as opposed to use, of the technology. Indeed, there was evidence to indicate that women do indeed own trucks and trolleys.

24 year old Hausa truck boy working at Kaneshie. They cannot push trucks but they can own them and then hire boys/men to push the trucks for them.

32 year old Nzema truck boy working at Agbogbloshie. They can't push trucks/trolleys. If however they own these they can give these to boys to use them.

30 year old Fante truck boy working at Mamprobi Tuesday Market. I rent it for 500 cedis a day. It is a woman who owns it.

35 year old Ga truck boy working at Mamprobi Tuesday Market. It's for my mother so I'll say it's my own. I do give my mother some of the money I realise from portering.

In Chapters 2 and 3, we saw that it was rare for female traders to have access to or ownership of motorised transport. Female traders' ownership of trucks or trolleys, however, appears to be more common. Female traders do not operate these trucks or trolleys themselves but arrange for truck boys to move their goods between storage and selling facilities at the beginning and end of the trading day. During the day, traders frequently hire out their trucks and trolleys to truck boys for use by other parties.

20 year old Ga truck boy working at Kaneshie Market. But I know that some women especially market traders own trucks and trolleys for the purpose of conveying only their wares.

Within the truck boy teams, there is a form of apprenticeship structure through which young boys progress to the full male role, with commensurate differences in the share of the earnings enjoyed by the young as compared with their older brothers. There is some evidence that in the case of males there is an occupational hierarchy in portering which is related to age. The language used by our respondents to describe this hierarchy and the information collected on the age of entry to the occupation confirms the existence of an old apprenticeship structure. Ghana inherited the apprenticeship system from the British. Whilst the form has disappeared in Britain, it persisted into the present in Ghana, most particularly in the informal sector. Apprenticeships have flourished in Ghana's informal sector as part of the structure of underemployment, with present day apprentices frequently being beyond their teenage years and often in their late twenties (Peil, 1995, p.7).

Group of eight Ga truck boys working at London Market, Jamestown. Six of us started in 1979 (14 years ago) as truck mates and boys to older ones. We all rent it. It was rented to us by those retired Ga truck men whom we worked with as apprentice/mate boys 14 years ago. Our predecessors (retired masters) give it to us and we make weekly payments of 1,000–2,000 cedis plus depending on how much we earn per week.

Group of 12 Dagomba truck boys working at the Timber Market. When this particular group of respondents get their monies at the end of the day's work, they put everything together and share amongst themselves. The eldest amongst the group takes the higher proportion of the income and the younger ones take equal amounts but with the very youngest taking the smallest amount.

As the existence of the apprenticeship structure demonstrates, truck boys are working as teams, as contrasted with the kayayoos who typically work as individuals. The collective work organisation of male porters and truck boys is stronger than that of kayayoos, whilst the collective social organisation and support provided by these female porters to one another is stronger than that found amongst their male counterparts. Whereas kayayoos provide more social support for one another, e.g belong to informal savings associations, than do their male colleagues, male porters and truck boys are more likely to work in occupational teams and thus provide more work-based support for one another.

26 year old Blusa truck boy working at Knutfort. I use a four tyre truck for portering. It was bought on a group basis. The equipment was financed through the savings of all the members of the group. I have about 15 friends, relatives and home town acquaintances who also work in the portering trade.

30 year old Akan truck boy working at Mamprobi Tuesday Market. There are around 10 or 15 of us (truck boys) here. We don't have a union but we have a nominal head. We don't have a lot to operate on. We were moved from the church. But we don't have any land. We pay money to the landlord, in addition to the rates, dues, taxes we pay to AMA (Accra Metropolitan Assembly).

25 year old Frafra truck boy working at Kantomanto. We are at least ten (truck boys), there are also people from my home town.

49 year old Frafra truck boy working at Kantomanto. We are 14 truck boys, they're all my boys or my brothers. They are all from my place.

42 year old Fanti truck boy working at Achimota Station. We are eight truck pushers including me. I'm the head here.

The team dimension of truck boy work comes out more strongly and directly in the group interviews than it does in the individual interviews with truck boys and male head load porters.

Group of eight Ga truck boys working at London Market, Jamestown. (On the equipment used) We all rent it. It was rented to us by those retired Ga truck men whom we worked with as apprentice/mate boys 14 years ago. (On why customers use truck boys.) Because our trucks make it possible for us to carry heavy and more loads at a time using many boys to push. But kayayoos don't have this opportunity.

Group of 12 Dagomba truck boys working the Timber Market. We prefer to stay (sleep) at the market and keep the company of our colleagues and friends who have no homes and also to have the opportunity to start work early as a team and close late.

Whilst male respondents made little direct comment about the widespread and readily visible existence of truck boy teams, female porters were more vocal on the issue. Female porters appeared to be aware of the advantages that group working conferred on their male colleagues.

28 year old Dagomba kayayoo working at the Timber Market. Because boys and men grow up learning how to operate trucks and trolleys while we women learn how to carry on our heads. Also men do it in groups while we do it individually and have different durations of stay here.

22 year old Dagomba kayayoo working at Kantomanto. Because the men and boys are stronger. They also operate in groups and assist in pushing but women do so individually.

21 year old Dagomba kayayoo working at Accra Central. Because they operate in smaller groups but we operate individually. They stay longer in Accra and we don't. They are stronger than we are.

Group of 15 Dagomba kayayoos working at Agbogbloshie/ Kantomanto/Makola/Tudu. (On why men use wheeled technology for portering and women do not.) Because they have been socialised into doing it. They team up to rent and use, share profits but we do so more on an individual basis.

They also reported that whilst female portering work was mainly conducted on an individual basis, on occasions work teams were formed to carry particularly large loads. Such team efforts may be foiled by the trader's preference to harness the convenience of the male operated truck.

Group of 15 Dagomba kayayoos working at Agbogbloshie/ Kantomanto/Makola/Tudu. All types of customers use kayayoos but those with more heavy loads use the truck boys (e.g. onion sellers) but we kayayoos often organise ourselves and share the heavy loads and carry for customers.

19 year old Dagomba kayayoo working at Agbogbloshie. I carry all types of load except filled maximum jute sacks of onions and cereals. No competition between us; but once in a while yes. when it involves transporting 100 tubers of yam and we mobilise to share it and carry they refuse and wish to convey it once in the truck which they normally succeed in doing so.

In addition to the teams which are formed for pushing the heavy loads carried upon the four tyre flat bodied trucks, at least two other forms of male portering teams are in evidence. The first of these is owner/user teams and alternating user teams which lie outside of the simple commercial relationship of renting/hiring.

30 year old Akan truck boy working at Mamprobi Tuesday Market. It is my elder brother's but I give him a portion of whatever I realise from the operations at the end of the day.

25 year old Ga truck boy working at Makola. We rent it in shifts. While I am using the truck, the hirer remains idle; and when I am tired I rest for my co-worker/hirer to use it.

17 year old Akan male head load porter and occasional truck boy working at Kaneshie lorry station. (On access to portering equipment.) I don't have any I carry the load on my head. But if I get too many things to carry at a time, I rent a truck from one of those boys who have rented at truck to carry the heavy load, after which I give him the 100 cedis or an amount agreed upon.

The second form of team exists to circumvent the physical and infra-structural barriers which present porters with difficulties.

17 year old Akan head load porter and occasional truck boy working at Kaneshie lorry station. It is difficult to carry heavy loads on the overhead bridge. Normally I arrange with a friend to collect the load from the other side of the wall divide in the road. There is competition among we kaya boys here.

Why do male porters form work teams and female porters not? Part of the answer lies in the demands of the technology, part of the answer lies in the different migration profiles of male and female porters. As we have seen, female porters are predominantly short term migrants from the northern regions of Ghana. In the case of male porters and truck boys, there is a higher percentage of southern ethnic groups involved in the occupation. Even where male porters and truck boys derive from ethnic groups which are northern, such male labour is more likely to have been born or been long term resident in Accra than is its female counterpart. Whereas female porters have only been resident in Accra for a short term and express the intention of spending specified short terms in Accra, male labour has often been present for longer in Accra and expresses the intention of remaining for longer periods. Female involvement in the portering occupation is typically connected with the short term generation of income for investment in occupational and domestic goods whereas male involvement in the portering occupation is typically connected with meeting the requirements of daily survival. The migration profiles of male and female porters are thus very different, a difference which is reflected in the different ethnic composition of the of these two categories of porters (see Tables 4.4 and 5.4). Ethnic differentiation is also present at the local level. According to our respondents, particular ethnic groups have the monopoly of certain markets. However, in other markets respondents remark on the multi-ethnic origins of porters. According to our respondents this multi-ethnic mix is a new development, with this mix now encompassing members of ethnic groups which previously would have been above entering such a lowly occupation.

Table 5.4
Ethnic composition of Accra porters by gender: male

Ethnic group	Male porters/truck boys
Akan	10
Blusa	2
Dagomba	13
Ewe	4
Fante	3
Frafra	3
Ga	16
Grushie	1
Hausa	2
Krobo	1
Kwako	1
Northener*	2
Nzema	1
Sandama	1
Upper regions*	12
Total	72

* Specific tribe not recorded on interview sheets.

Group of 12 Dagomba truck boys working at the Timber Market. In this particular market, it is only Dagombas who work here and we are more than 40 truck boys here (but a varying number of relatives and friends).

43 year old Akan working at Kantomanto. No because of the multi-ethnic origins of porters, they are not interested in common activities. Portering is not a dignified job, in the past Akans were not doing portering work, but what do you do these days? We have dominated the business.

There are differing levels of awareness amongst respondents of both genders about the ethnic composition of the portering occupation. However, the social organisation of female porters along ethnic lines appears to be more developed than amongst male porters. An explanation of this difference may be found in the short term character of female migration to the portering occupation, such short periods being insufficient for building an independent domestic base and thus rendering kayayoos more dependent on their relatives, friends and acquaintances for support. Male porters have typically been present in Accra for some time before entering the portering occupation and thus have better access to independent domestic resources.

On the existing evidence, it appears that there are two explanations as to why male porters are more commonly to be found working in teams than are female porters. Firstly, the nature of the technology and the weight of loads carried required more strength than one individual can muster. Secondly, the social circumstances of male porters and truck boys, most particularly their long term residence in Accra, favour the formation of working teams. However, even where female porters attempt to form teams to capture some of the benefits enjoyed by their male colleagues, they are often thwarted in this attempt by the traders' preference for a transport form which, in the case of bulk loads, is more convenient and offers more security from theft.

Both male and female porters were largely of the opinion that there was surplus labour in the market. There is some evidence of self-regulation and of semi-official regulation around the portering trade. The porters express concern about the harassment by the city authorities which frequently takes the form of the confiscation of their trucks. Confiscation generates major problems for a truck boy or truck boy team; a truck is necessary for participation in the more remunerative trade and its acquisition requires substantial savings. Not surprisingly, in a context where such equipment can be confiscated at will, hiring another vehicle is no easy business. Reputational guarantees are required (and often have to be paid for) and the hiring cost reflects not only the owner's risks in terms of potential damage to the vehicle in the interaction with traffic but the potential danger of confiscation in the interaction with authority. These 'economic' hazards results in truck boys pooling their resources to manage their environment.

Attention can usefully be given to the development of low cost technologies which could contribute towards making the bearing of goods and other burdens by human beings less arduous. Respondents made specific suggestions for improvements that could be made: two key suggestions were the fitting of a brake pedal to these hand pushed vehicles and the fitting of a motor to make the operation of the truck faster and less physically exhausting: this is not a fanciful idea, for in the 1960s milk carts operating on such a system were to be found in London, UK. The present muscle power requirements of wheeled non-motorised transport accentuate the need for teams and a collective dimension in male portering work arrangements which is rarely present in that of the female porters.

5.3 Trolleys, trucks and traffic congestion: cost and time in traders' non-motorised transport choices

Female and male porters alike viewed the interaction between wheeled non-motorised transport and motorised traffic as hazardous, most particularly for women. Similar perceptions were found amongst traders. The study of 50 traders (Amponsah et al., 1994) using non-motorised transport i.e. hand pulled trucks and trolleys, was conducted in order to gain insight into the factors determining the choice between non-motorised and motorised modes found that the majority of users of non-motorised transport are also users of motorised transport (Table 5.3 above). The choice of mode depends upon weather conditions, traffic conditions, accessibility conditions, load size and cost. During rainy weather, traders shift mode from non-motorised to motorised transport in order to avoid spoilage of goods, particularly foodstuffs. Similarly, seasonal considerations produce a change in mode; at Christmas and on rainy days, traders switch from non-motorised to motorised modes: the increase in the demand for goods in festival seasons results in traders transporting larger loads than under normal business conditions. Larger loads mean a change in mode.

> *Trader in plastic goods, New Town.* I use motorised transport when I am taking larger quantity of plastic goods especially getting to the Christmas and the New Year or Easter. Aside the occasion days when I usually use motorised transport the only way by which I transport my goods is through the use of truck.

> *Trader in beans, rice, groundnuts, New Town.* I use motorised transport when the goods are plenty and not belonging to me only. Also when the weather is bad i.e. cloudy, I use motorised transport. On the other hand I use non motorised transport (kayayoo or truck) when all the goods belong to me and the weather is good, i.e. when there is no fear of rains.

Interestingly, it was found that in congested conditions non-motorised transport is faster over shorter journeys. Two specific accessibility conditions are relevant to the choice of non-motorised transport here. Firstly, congestion reduces the available parking space for loading at wholesale points. Secondly, many stores are located in such a way that motorised access to the doorstep is not available. In these conditions, non-motorised transport has an advantage. Non-motorised transport is also significantly lower in cost compared to motorised transport. It was also discovered that 60 per cent of the traders interviewed had experienced an accident when using non-motorised transport. The majority of these accidents occurred in the interaction with motorised traffic: however, a number of accidents involved other non-motorised road users. The use of non-motorised transport, in a transport culture which views non-motorised modes negatively, also carries the risk of the traders goods (along with the 'truck') being confiscated by the Metropolitan authorities (Grieco, Turner and Kwakye, 1995). Traders confirm truck boys' accounts of harassment by municipal authorities and of the unwarranted seizure of both trucks and goods.

It was also found that, despite the cordial relationship existing within the trading community, the majority of traders operating near to Central Accra do not have any cooperative arrangements with other traders in transporting their goods to their stalls, stores and kiosks. Only ten out of the 50 traders interviewed cooperate with other traders in transporting their goods from central Accra to their respective trading districts. Similarly, traders selling in roadside stores and kiosks do not have associations which assist them in organising the transportation of their goods. Yet other occupations have indeed developed such associations in Ghana, i.e. tailors and dressmakers and private commercial drivers, and those traders selling in market places are well organised with leaders, locally termed the Market Queen Mothers (Katila, 1995). 26 out of the 50 traders expressed their desire to see a formal Traders Association developed.

Table 5.5 below summarises traders experiences of using non-motorised transport in respect of accidents and coordination of transport. Two key features of traders' experience are immediately apparent: traders using non-motorised transport are highly exposed to the risk of loss of load through accidents and traders making use of non-motorised transport are typically doing so on a solitary rather than a cooperative basis.

Table 5.5
Traders' experience of non-motorised transport

Trading district	No. with cooperative arrangement for transport	No. experiencing accidents	No. experiencing theft	No. with arrangement with particular truck team	Total interviewed in each district
Adabraka	0	7	1	9	10
Jamestown	2	6	1	5	10
New Town	3	4	2	6	10
Osu	5	5	0	6	10
Tudu	0	8	1	9	10
Total	10	30	5	35	50

There were a number of factors used to explain their patterns of mode shifting between motorised and non-motorised transport forms by traders. The bulkiness of goods frequently determined which mode was to be used: however, where the bulkiness of goods led some traders to select motorised transport it led others to select non-motorised transport. Distance also entered the equation. Where goods could be obtained locally then non-motorised transport was frequently used, but where greater distances had to be covered the trader experienced pressure to use the more expensive mode.

Traders in travelling bags, provisions and soaps, Adabraka. The charge for using non-motorised transport is comparatively cheaper and the distance from Central Accra where they buy most of their goods to their store is short such that it takes no time for truck boys or kayayoos to cover with a few minutes.

Trader in pillows, roofing sheets, nails and shovels, Adabraka. According to the trader she uses motorised transport for some of the goods like the shovels, nails and other building materials because of the distance. But for roofing sheets and pillows she almost always uses truck.

Trader in foreign papers for wrapping, Jamestown. I use motorised transport most of the time for bringing papers from town (Accra) but I at times use truck especially when I take the papers from a place nearer. (The trader has two places of buying the old papers.)

Not surprisingly, given the use of both modes by the bulk of traders, there is widespread knowledge of the substantial cost differentials which exist between the motorised and non-motorised modes of goods conveyance. There was extensive comment by traders on the need to economise on cost in the context of low profit margins pertaining in petty trading.

Trader in soaps and provisions, Adabraka. According to the respondent the difference in costs between these two transport arrangements is great. Load that costs 1,000 cedis for using non-motorised transport will cost over 3,000 cedis when motorised transport is used.

Trader in soaps and toothpaste, Adabraka. Non-motorised transport is used because of low cost of transportation which can be afforded by businesses like us.

Trader in provisions and cooking utensils, Jamestown. I use motorised transport when I have enough money on me after buying the needed goods and also when I feel like taking car instead of walking to follow the truck boys while pulling my goods to the selling place. I use non-motorised transport most of the times because of its low cost comparing to motorised transport.

Trader in yam, maize and millet, Jamestown. Benefits derived from using non-motorised is that the cost of transporting goods is comparatively cheaper and this helps to get the required profit ... The difference in costs between motorised and non-motorised transport is very large. Truck charges 150 cedis per large bag of maize but motorised transport will never charge anything less than 300 cedis to 400 cedis per bag of maize.

Trader in flour and rice, Jamestown. Benefits derived from using truck are that the cost is comparatively cheaper and also goods are sent to the exact trading point unlike motorised transport where you have to incur additional cost of sending the goods into the store. The difference in cost between motorised and non-motorised transport is very large. Truck charges 150 cedis per bag of flour whilst taxi charges 300 cedis per bag of flour.

There is some evidence that traders with small profit margins are likely to use non-motorised transport on larger loads, in the recognition that larger loads mean larger transport costs and thus the switch to non-motorised transport generates a larger saving. The availability of non-motorised transport operations plays an important role in a low income, petty trading economy. It provides traders with enhanced flexibility in determining the transport costs they will incur in conducting their business. When traders are at a low point in their business income cycle, they make use of the cheaper, non-motorised mode.

Trader in tinned tomatoes, tinned fish, provisions, Jamestown. I use taxi or tro-tro to convey goods to my store most of the time when the quantity of goods is small. However, when I purchase larger quantity of goods I prefer using truck or kayayoo so as to beat down the cost.

Trader in provisions, New Town. I use motorised transport when the goods are small such that the cost will be less.

Trader in vegetables, cooking oil, Osu. Truck is used for large quantities of goods and cars (not hired) for smaller quantities of goods. According to the respondent trolleys (two wheeled carts usually pushed by one person) are used for smaller quantities of goods.

105

Where coordination on motorised transport exists then costs of that mode are lowered: however, where traders have to organise sole transport then the low cost of the non-motorised mode is more attractive. As we saw in earlier chapters, the collective organisation of motorised transport by traders is not common. The same pattern was found amongst this sample.

Trader in foreign papers for wrapping, Jamestown. I cooperate with another paper dealer at Salaga Market near Jamestown whenever I use motorised transport, so that we share the cost involved. But because she doesn't take papers from my second customer, I usually use truck alone whenever I buy from that store (the second customer).

Trader in yam, plantain, cocoyam, cassava, Osu. 'I use motorised transport (tro-tro) when we are about three or four traders sending goods to one place (Osu) so that we share the total cost involved. Other than that I always use truck or kayayoo when transporting goods to Osu ...' According to the trader the difference in cost between these two transport arrangements is not all that great when three or four traders hire one tro-tro (low cost car) and share the cost involved. But the difference is great when the cost of hiring the car is paid by one trader.

Trader in smoked fish, tomatoes, pepper, Osu. According to the trader about four of them have arranged with a particular tro-tro driver for their goods on every Monday and Thursday ... She therefore uses truck to beat down the cost of transportation when the need arises for her to go for more goods on any other day aside Monday and Thursday.

Accessibility considerations also played a major part in determining the choice of non-motorised transport. Many traders operate from kiosks, booths and premises which are located down the lanes and alleys of low income neighbourhoods. Trucks and trolleys are able to move down alleys and into compounds which are not accessible by motorised vehicles. The urban design of low income Accra is contributing to the persistence of non-motorised transport: accessing the back lanes and alleys where petty trading occurs through a motorised retail distribution system is problematic. The more flexible trolley or truck can more readily penetrate the local neighbourhoods.

Trader in pillows, roofing sheets, nails and shovels, Adabraka. The advantage of using truck is that the truck is able to enter the store from which I buy the roofing sheet or the slates and also it can enter my store without difficulty.

Trader in provisions and cooking utensils, Jamestown. The truck boys carry the goods from the market interior to the packing place and also to the exact trading point where the truck can't go.

Trader in provisions, New Town. Goods are sent to the exact trading point unlike urvans and other cars which stop some distance from you to find different people to carry the goods to the kiosk (the exact trading point).

Trader in beans, rice, groundnuts, New Town. The benefits derived from the use of truck is that it is less costly as compared to motorised transport. Also the truck boys are the same people who go and carry the goods from the wholesale if their truck can't go there. This a taxi/urvan driver would not do.

Whilst many traders indicated that they routinely traded off longer journey times against reduced transport costs, it was also the case that where greater distances were concerned they were less likely to trade time off against cost. Although, it is not possible to provide exact information on the parameters of acceptable delay from the evidence we have collected, journey times of more than an hour by truck appear increasingly less attractive to traders.

Trader in provisions, Jamestown. The only disadvantage of using non-motorised transport is that it wastes time since its operation is not as fast as that of motorised transport.

Trader in plastics, New Town. Motorised transport is more faster than non-motorised transport (truck). Urvan can use less than 25 minutes for the journey but truck boys will spend not less than an hour.

Trader in provisions, New Town. I use motorised transport when the distance from my kiosk to the place for the goods is far. For example I use car whenever I go for goods from Glamour areas (Accra). But I use truck when I buy from places nearer than Glamour like Circle areas.

Trader in provisions, soaps, sugar, Osu. I use motorised transport (taxi) at times when I want to get to the store in time for selling. However the usual way of transporting goods to Osu is by truck. According to the trader he like using truck because the cost of using truck is far below that of motorised transport (taxi).

In considering the time aspect of mode choice, traders indicated that motorised transport is not always the fastest mode. Motorised congestion generates an advantage for non-motorised transport over short distances. It reduces both the time advantage of motorised transport and reduces accessibility to trading outlets.

Trader in tinned tomatoes and cooking oil, Tudu. The main advantage gained from using the truck is that the goods come straight to the trading point (kiosk) without any problem. Motorists face the problem of parking places for loading and offloading the goods. They are also not able to get to the exact trading point which therefore requires additional cost of doing that.

Trader in provisions, Tudu. The advantages derived from using truck/trolley are that goods are sent to the trading point and at times inside the kiosk by the boys (truck boys). The same boys carry the goods from the storeroom and at times from the market interior without charging nothing for that. However, when using motorised transport (taxi) you have to find kayakaya (i.e. men porters) or kayayoos (women porters) to carry the goods from the storeroom or the market interior to the car and also from the car to the kiosk since taxis cannot go to these places.

Trader in canned fish, canned tomatoes and rice, Tudu. I use the truck only when there is congestion making it impossible for the car to park near the store ...

Trader in children's wear, Adabraka. I use motorised transport (taxi) most of the time for sending goods to my store. I however use non-motorised transport, usually a trolley (two wheeled cart) or kayayoo when there is too much congestion or motor traffic in Central Accra.

An important consideration when deciding upon mode was the escort time requirements of the respective modes. Some traders experienced a need to escort the goods carried by truck boys in order to avoid theft or spoilage; where such a need was perceived then the slowness of the mode had negative consequences for the trader's own time budget.

Trader in margarine and cooking oils, Tudu. However, some of the load gets lost if you don't follow them leading to waste of time and energy.

Trader in provisions and cooking utensils, Jamestown. The disadvantage for using truck is that you have to follow them if they are not known or if they are not regular customers.

Trader in provisions and soaps, Jamestown. The advantage for using truck is that it is comparatively cheaper but it is not comfortable at all. You will have to follow the truck boys all the way to the kiosk at Jamestown here.

In order to free their own time whilst developing secure transport arrangements, some traders entered into standing arrangements with particular sets of truck boys thus obtaining a higher level of reliability than would exist under a simple market arrangement.

Traders in toothpaste and soap, New Town. The cost of using motorised transport (urvan) is twice or thrice of that of using non-motorised transport. However motorised transport is faster than non-motorised transport. Motorised transport also saves time and energy. One has to follow the truck boys till they reach New Town if the truck boys happens not to be the traders own customers ... Yes I have my own customers, eight or nine Frafra truck boys. They have been my customers since three years ago when the number was by then only three. They go for my goods every Monday (as have been agreed upon between us) whether they see me that day or not. My customer (wholesaler) knows them and every information is given to them by the wholesaler.

Trader in wheat, rice, oats, Adabraka. The respondent stated that she has her own customers, seven truck boys, who send all her goods to Adabraka whenever she comes to buy goods. She continued by saying that it is better and safer to give goods to known people.

The use of lower cost transport exposes traders to a set of dangers, for the use of non-motorised transport in Accra is associated with an increased risk of spoilage, delay, accident, confiscation and theft. Taking the first of these, weather conditions figured prominently in traders' financial assessments of the respective modes. Using non-motorised transport in bad weather could lead to substantial financial losses: variations in weather, it seems, are likely to have a greater impact on transport organisation in a developing context than they do in more industrialised and motorised society.

Trader in gari, rice, sugar, etc., Adabraka. I use an urvan or taxi if I am transporting sugar especially. This is because of experience I've had with transporting sugar or gari by truck. It rained and I incurred a very great loss. I use a truck when I know the weather is clear and there are no signs of rains ... I've not had any bad experience in transporting loads since I started this business. Only once that the goods were beaten by rain resulting in some losses.

109

Trader in wheat, rice and oats, Adabraka. I don't normally use motorised transport. It is used only when it is raining and I don't have any good place to keep the goods. In that case I would be compelled to hire a taxi or an urvan. Non motorised transport is the main form through which I transport my goods ... I have had many bad experiences in transporting goods especially by truck. But this is due mainly to the location of my kiosk. Once a truck loaded with gari and beans had an accident in the muddy area a few metres away from the kiosk leading to spoilage of more than half of the load.

Trader in beans, gari and cooking oil, Jamestown. She uses motorised transport only when it rains making it impossible for truck to come to her trading place because of mud. Apart from this she always uses truck or kayayoo in transporting her goods from the Central Market.

Trader in rice, wheat, sugar, Osu. It once rained while the truck boys were bringing two bags of sugar to the kiosk, they failed to cover it with rubber and I was therefore compelled to sell them for less than the actual cost price.

Turning to the topic of delay, much of the literature on the informal sector in developing countries assumes that this sector is free from the trappings of bureaucracy and officialdom. In fact, the accounts of traders in Accra indicate that the informal sector is subject to a very high level of semi-official regulation. Such regulation results in substantial institutional delay, which has a negative impact on transport costs. The prospect of delay on account of officials 'investigating' the legality of the truck boys and the goods being transported pushes traders towards the higher status transport options such as taxis, which are less subject to this interference. In order to short cut the delays, traders and truck boys frequently have to furnish 'dash': they make an unofficial payment in order to be permitted to go about their business.

Trader in provisions, Adabraka. There are no difficulties with Police in transporting goods by truck, but AMA officials poses a lot of problems to us when transporting loads with truck. They demand your income tax, trading license and other documents at the time of transporting the goods, causing delayance if you are unable to provide them.

Trader in provisions, New Town. There are no difficulties with police when transporting goods by truck but for motorists yes and AMA partially yes. According to the respondent the motorists don't pay any regard truck boys as road users. AMA officials or task force also at times stop and ask many questions causing delayance etc.

110

Trader in cassava, yam, plantain, cocoyam, Osu. There are no difficulties with the police but the truck boys are most of the time asked to show their Identity Cards. If none of them is able to show one the truck in addition to the loads are confiscated by the City Council Officials which causes delay before goods are returned.

Trader in maize, rice and groundnuts, Osu. There are no difficulties with the police in transporting loads by truck but we face a lot of difficulties with the AMA officials especially the city council on confiscation of truck, when transporting loads by truck. This leads to unnecessary waste of time and delay before reclaiming or retrieving the truck and the goods.

Whilst it may have been thought that the slower mode of transport would have found more convenient conditions of operation outside of rush hours, in fact, the behaviour of the municipal authorities operated against such an efficient use of road space, as truck boys operating outside of normal trading hours were apprehended by authorities on suspicion of theft. Transporting goods on an empty road made truck boys a readier target for semi-official attention.

What emerges clearly from our respondents' accounts of low cost transport options in Accra is that there is a very high level of accidents between motorised and non-motorised transport forms. Indeed, the level is so high that it forms an explicit part of traders calculations about which mode they will use. Currently, there is substantial under-recording of the real rate of accidents and very little understanding of the consequences of such an accident rate for the organisation of trade. Of the 60 per cent of our trader respondents who had personal experience of an accident when using non-motorised transport, many of these had experienced more than one accident. The majority of accounts stressed the normality of this experience. At present, it is an experience which has no official register to record it.

Trader in pillows, roofing sheets, nails and shovels, Adabraka. There have been about three or four truck accidents but there were no casualties and no spoilage of goods. This is because they are always having roofing sheets as load whenever the truck gets accident.

Trader in children's wear, Adabraka. Yes I've had two bad experiences of transporting load. One was more or less a miracle to me. I loaded a trolley with children's wear but when I reached my store two boxes of such goods were to my surprise containing rags and waste papers. Another incident was an accident of the truck.

111

Trader in provisions, Tudu. I've had two bad experiences, one with my customers (truck boys) – an accident with a Datsun pick-up trying to escape knocking a pedestrian lost control and hit the back of the truck injuring the one driving severely and two others. Another bad experience was when it was announced one Friday on the radio that there was going to be power off. I therefore went to town to buy candles (four boxes) and gave them to a boy using a trolley (two wheeled cart) but due to congestion in the town the boy sent[2] all the candles away.

Indeed, it seems that accidents are such frequent events that our respondents can identify for us the protocols which hold for the resolving of payment of costs of accidents. The routine occurrence of accidents involving trucks and trolleys gives rise to clear expectations of where the costs are to be borne: however, these arrangements take place in a context where there is considerable hostility towards low status, non-motorised transport forms on the part of motorists and of officialdom. When an accident occurs, to get a satisfactory outcome traders and truck boys have to resolve the matter of attribution of costs there and then: involving officials will simply worsen their lot. The people on the street frequently become part of the negotiating process between the colliding parties. Collision protocols are public property and enforced by the public.

Trader in rice, sugar, provisions, Adabraka. However the spoilage of goods through accident is the owner's expenses ... Accident of the truck and loss of some of the goods are the only bad experience I have had since I started this business. According to the trader loss of goods are paid by the truck boys but spoilage of goods resulting from accident is his own expenses.

Trader in wheat, rice, oats, Adabraka. I have had one bad experience in transporting goods to my store. This was an accident of the truck with a taxi leading to the spoilage of goods and injuring one of the truck boys. The cost of damaged goods and that of the injured boy were all paid by the taxi driver since he accepted it to be his fault.

Trader in provisions, Adabraka. According to the respondent she has had several bad experiences in transporting load. Some of them are accident of the truck with cars and other road users. The spoilage of goods resulting from accident is the owner's expenses. It was only once that a driver of a VW bus paid half of the amount of goods spoiled.

Trader in yam, maize and millet, Jamestown. The bad experience I have had in transporting loads is an accident of the truck with a Benz car resulting in complete spoilage of all the goods, but none of the truck boys got injured. The cost of the damaged goods according to the police was to be paid by the Benz driver since he was at fault but I've never found him since then.

Trader in tinned tomatoes, tinned fish, provisions, Jamestown. I have had two bad experiences which I will never forget. One was an accident which resulted in spoilage of goods and damage to the truck. Another was loss of some of the goods on the way to the store. Spoilt goods resulting from the accident was borne by myself but the lost goods was paid by the truck owner.

Traders typically focus on the attitudes of other road users in explaining the occurrence of accidents. It should be remembered that the traders' account is more likely to be authentic than even that of the truck boys themselves. These traders' accounts of a transport culture which punishes the non-motorist fit precisely with the accounts provided by cyclists of this transport culture in the next section of this chapter.

Trader in pillows, roofing sheets, nails and shovels, Adabraka. Motorists are the only main problem we have when transporting goods with truck. All the three accidents were caused by motorists. Using truck for roofing sheets is not easy but motorists don't consider the truck boys in any way.

Trader in yam, maize and millet, Jamestown. Motorists don't give truck boys the equal right of using the road. Also AMA officials at times demand documents on the road.

Trader in tinned tomatoes, tinned fish, provisions, Jamestown. Motorists pose a lot of problems on the road.

Trader in soap, toothpaste, provisions, Jamestown. Motorists also pose problems at times causing delayance.

Trader in yam, maize, beans, Jamestown. Motorists cause a lot of problems to truck boys making the truck business unsafe and discouraging.

Trader in plastics, New Town. At times the truck boys complain of some drivers bad attitude towards them especially when they are crossing the main road.

Trader in provisions and soap, New Town. Only motorists creates some problems on the road especially when the truck boys want to cross the road to the other side.

Trader in vegetables, cooking oil, Osu. Motorists give a lot of problems to the truck boys. They don't regard them as equally important road users. The drivers have no patience for the truck boys though they see them exerting much energy in pushing or pulling the truck.

Trader in provisions and soaps, Osu. Motorists give them a lot of problems when transporting goods. They think not of the good services they render to traders.

Although, the majority of traders, as the comments above indicate, perceived accidents to be largely the fault of other road users, one trader commented on the reckless behaviour of truck boys. Yet another commented on the unwieldiness of trucks as a contributing factor in the occurrence of accidents. And accidents also occur between trucks and cyclists.

Trader in canned fish, canned tomatoes and rice, Tudu. Concerning bad experiences, I used to have accidents with cars and at times through careless driving of the truck driver resulting in the bursting of rice bags or falling of goods into gutters choked with dirt. However, I have not had any such bad experiences since I started using the car three years ago.

Trader in powder in sacks, Tudu. Accidents with cars are common especially when the load is heavy making controlling of the truck very difficult. Also the drivers don't have respect for the truck boys.

Trader in yam, maize, beans, Jamestown. I have had two bad experiences in transporting loads. One was an accident (a crash of the truck with a bicycle) which resulted in a serious injury of the cyclist. No damage was done to the goods and the truck.

This perception of the problem fits with earlier work into the views of truck boys themselves presented in the previous section. However, whereas the majority of truck boys discussed the difficulties involved in controlling trucks, and indeed some suggested improvements, the majority of traders focused on the attitudes of motorists as the principle reason for accidents in the interaction between the motorised and non-motorised form. The research suggests, therefore, that despite the ready availability of motorised transport within urban Accra, there is a significant and continuing demand for non-motorised transport services. Given the presence of such continuing demand, explicit attention must be paid to the needs of non-motorised transport in the planning of the transport infrastructure for urban Accra.

5.4 A trading cycle? Cultural and infrastructural barriers to petty traders' use of the bicycle

Within the transport culture of Ghana, women are greatly under-represented in the operation of even the simplest transport technology. They are not active as commercial drivers nor do they operate hand pulled trucks and trolleys, despite evidence of female ownership in both of these sectors. As we shall see in this section, the same holds true for as simple a transport technology as the bicycle. Yet the bicycle is a form of transport which could have great economic use for female traders, given the extensiveness of small volume trading (Pankaj and Coulthart, 1993). Indeed, the bicycle is widely used for petty trading by the male vendors of East Africa.

Economic liberalisation programmes have been implemented in countries across the developing world to encourage the efficient operation of markets and the reform of public sector enterprises. The subsequent changes in the ownership of urban public transport often result in an increase in fares. This has a direct effect upon the urban poor, who have to absorb such increases into their meagre household budgets if they are to continue to carry out essential activities (Mbara and Maunder, 1994). In Asia, cycling is more commonplace amongst the urban poor. The widespread use of this mode allows sudden changes in transport costs to be better absorbed. In an effort to improve the ability of the African urban poor to travel and to improve the urban transport system, the World Bank, through its Sub-Saharan Africa Transport Policy (SSATP) programme, has initiated research into urban non-motorised transport. This research, focusing on East Africa and Francophone West Africa, has looked at ways of increasing the use of bicycles by Africa's urban poor. However, the role that cycling can play within a petty trading economy has been neglected. Bicycles could be used extensively for trading purposes, given the small load characteristics of much petty trading.

In Ghana, traders are, however, primarily women. Cultural stereotypes and infrastructural dangers, e.g. the hostile transport culture in respect of non-motorised modes, work against the use of the bicycle by women. The capital requirements of bicycle purchase are beyond the horizons which domestic financial organisation places around female traders. Redesign of bicycles and cycling facilities could assist female traders in accessing more flexible travel modes and time arrangements than they currently enjoy. However, research in Accra indicates that strategies for enhancing bicycle use amongst female traders may differ between the different ethnic sub-communities of the city (Grieco, Turner and Kwakye, 1995). The communities of Nima and Jamestown have different cultural attitudes towards bicycle use: in Nima, the bicycle is seen as an acceptable mode of transport, a symbol of high status. In Jamestown, the bicycle is seen as an anachronism, a low status mode of transport, very dangerous in a motorised world and with little future. In Nima, the key strategic goal must be dismantling the cultural and economic barriers which operate against women cycling: the utility of cycling is already accepted. In Jamestown, the key strategic goal must be to establish that the bicycle has utility as a modern transport mode: promoting women's cycling inside Jamestown must be part of an overall strategy of demonstrating the efficiency and economic benefits of cycling as a modern transport form.

In depth qualitative interviews with bicycle riders, bicycle owners, bicycle hirers, bicycle sellers and non-riders in Nima, a community which is a major reception area for Northern migrants, and Jamestown, a community which is composed primarily of indigenous coastal people, in Accra, Ghana indicated a difference in cycling level within the two communities. Over 52 group and individual interviews were conducted on cycle use and cycle access in these areas. Interviewees reported not only on their own characteristics and experiences but also upon those of their households: in all the ownership/non-ownership experiences of 260 people were reported upon. This cycling study found that ownership of a bicycle, even a second hand bicycle, represents a large capital item for a low income household. The priority given to cycle purchase and use differs according to the cultural attitude towards cycling: northerners value bicycles; southerners, on the whole, do not.

Although, cycling is seen as an acceptable activity for boys and men amongst northerners, it is not seen as a fitting activity for women and girls who have reached puberty. Cultural barriers against women cycling are reinforced by religious barriers against females riding in Nima. According to one respondent, on one occasion when the Imam saw a female riding a bicycle, he preached against the practice in the mosque. Furthermore, in Nima neighbours make rather uncomplimentary remarks about females who ride. In Jamestown cycling is generally frowned upon and both boy children and girl children are discouraged from cycling by their parents and the community as a whole.

There is clear evidence in Accra of different levels of cycle ridership between different low income areas (Grieco, Turner and Kwakye, 1995): it is the differences in 'transport cultures' that exist among different ethnic communities which produce widely varying ridership and ownership levels in low-income areas. There are highly divergent socialisation practices around cycling in the Nima community, composed as it is of northern Ghanaians or those of northern extraction, as compared with those of the Jamestown community, composed as it is of primarily coastal indigenous people (Jamestown). In the north, cycling is a widespread practice amongst male adults (Pankaj and Coulthart, 1993); in coastal Ghana, cycling is rare as an adult activity. Whereas the parents of children in Jamestown frequently beat their children for cycling, the parents of Nima encouraged cycling as an activity. In Nima, many girls are permitted to cycle as children but not thereafter: however, in some households, girls are either discouraged or prohibited from cycling:

> *Male security guard, owner, 42, Nima.*
> Q: How about your children, since you have a large family?
> A: They are all females, so they can't use the bicycle.

Like most of the developing world, Accra has a very mixed road use (Gardner et al., 1989). Within this pattern of mixed road use, there is a negative attitude in the urban area as a whole towards cyclists and, our research revealed, particularly towards female cyclists. This leads to a dangerous environment for anyone cycling: they put themselves at considerable risk of death or injury. Female traders who wished to make use of the bicycle in the conducting of their business would have to justify their case in an environment where negative attitudes to the bicycle prevail, where negative attitudes to women's use of the bicycle prevail and where the purchase of a bicycle represents a large capital sum. In a low income household, the female trader bargaining for her 'right' to a bicycle has the odds greatly stacked against her; and, as we shall see in the next chapter, most low income households do indeed contain a female trader.

Due to the costs involved in ownership, cycling has to be for an economic or purposeful activity to be justifiable. As so few women appear to use bicycles as adults for economic and occupational purposes, there is pressure on them not even to acquire riding skills in childhood. The fact that bicycles cannot obviously be seen as a means to greater income earning for women is perhaps a result of the inability of current vehicle design to reflect the need for greater carrying capacity, for economic use to be viable. Many respondents, both male and female, stated a preference for existing designs that have greater load carrying capacity and offered suggestions on how future bicycle designs could be adapted to improve their carrying ability. Given the weak position of women when bargaining for access to capital within households, there is a need for schemes that enable them to purchase bicycles of current design or improved form. Bicycle loans could usefully be made part of business plans designed to assist women petty traders.

There were scattered examples of women who had overcome the cultural odds and owned a bike, such as the Nima female cycle hirer who used her bicycle as the basis of her petty trading business, or of females who wanted to own a bike in order to earn a rent from it, such as the girl child in Jamestown who indicated that if the opportunity presented itself to purchase a bike she would and hire it out for money. However, most of the economically active women surveyed saw the purchase of a bicycle as something which detracted from their ability to invest in a business. 'Spare' income was invested in trading: the opportunity cost of bicycle purchase was seen as too high.

Urban poor households have implicit principles that guide family members when seeking the family good in the survival of the household (Moch et al., 1987; Ross, 1983). These are termed 'household survival strategies' and receive a fuller theoretical treatment in Chapter 6. All resources available to the household (monetary, time-based, physical and human) are guided by these strategies. Assessing attitudes towards cycling in terms of survival behaviour points to the differential effect of high cycling cost upon different communities within Accra. In those communities that have learned that ownership and use of a bicycle can be economically beneficial, such as the northerners of Nima, who owns a bicycle and who gets to use a bicycle will depend upon the survival strategy adopted and power relations within the household. In those communities that have not yet learnt the benefit of its use, such as the coastal people of Jamestown, cycle ownership is seen as an unnecessary expense and bicycle use may prove very expensive by posing a significant risk of death or disabling injury to the principal resources the household has control over – its human resources.

Even communities which have already learned the economic utility of cycling are likely to be affected by high costs which will limit the number of bicycles a household can afford to buy. This leads to family-imposed restrictions on ownership, thus preventing use becoming widespread. Household decisions are made to restrict ownership to those within the household who have greater control over household resources, either by being able to demonstrate possible higher earnings or by having greater power. In this equation, women typically lose out on the opportunity to own cycles. Communities which have not yet learnt to accept cycle use are unlikely to experiment whilst the cost of ownership puts bicycles out of reach. Lack of community knowledge about the economic utility of purchase will mean it is not adopted by households trying to reduce risks in order to survive. Households will, instead, adopt community views on the use of bicycles which make cycling unacceptable.

Households only allow cycle ownership to those who can show that there will be some economic and occupational use for it and that ownership will generate greater income than would otherwise be the case without it (by carrying greater loads or allowing travel to work and job search over greater distances). Adaptations to improve load carrying capability of the respondents' bicycles serve to strengthen the case for ownership and cycle use within the household. However, whilst household strategies may guide household behaviour, these strategies may often not be consensual; rather, those who can command most power and resources within the household may have greater say over what is and is not beneficial economic use. Qualitative evidence indicates that use of bicycles within households is determined by the ability of the 'best off' member to secure sufficient resources, with other household members only gaining access for specific and 'emergency' uses. Many respondents, both in Jamestown and Nima, frequently lent out their bicycles though often only under the strictest conditions. Often only close family members were able to borrow it and then only in emergencies: males have more chance of being permitted borrowers than females.

> *Male carpenter, bicycle owner, 21, Jamestown.* My elder brother uses it, when I am in the house not going anywhere. Conditions given to him is that, to be very careful and repair anything that should get spoilt while using it. No one else uses it.

Some respondents did, however, use the bicycle in a revenue earning capacity, by hiring out the bicycle to those in the local neighbourhood willing to pay the hiring fee. Revenue from hiring offset the purchasing costs of the bicycle. Furthermore, once purchased a bicycle had use-value that people would pay for. Cycle hire is part of the petty trading structure and the petty trading structure could be harnessed to promote women's cycling if the cultural barriers against women cycling were dismantled. The petty trader does not require the full time use of a bicycle but needs a bicycle to be available to her for her small load restocking journeys: the petty trading structure of Accra deals in such small value/small quantity units as a matter of course. Cycle hire by the hour/s fits with the existing practices of this type of economy. Incorporating these institutional features into policies which promote women's cycling ought to be a relatively easy matter.

> *Unemployed male, 18, Jamestown.* The elder brother bought the first bicycle for him at 12,000 cedis but this present Raleigh was bought from his own personally accumulated savings from the hiring of the first one for one month.

Nearly all respondents who owned a bicycle reported that they purchased it through their savings or the resources of some close family member. The use of traditional group saving and rotating credit systems, such as 'susu', was also commonly cited (see Steel and Aryeetey, 1994).

> *Male watch repairer, 45, Nima.* Mallam Adams saved money with susu collector to buy his bicycle. He plans to purchase next bicycle through 'Group Susu' under the Group Susu system, a number of people contribute a stated amount each month or week etc. The money is then given to one member at a time. This continues till the last person gets and the process is repeated. Other people he knows also used the susu method to finance the purchase of their bicycles.

Table 5.6 shows that the purchase of a bicycle is a major capital expenditure. The average respondent reported saving for between six and nine months before purchase and this was very much dependent upon a stable financial base in the household. During this time the ever-present pressures of other, equally pressing, household expenditures must be overcome. This is particularly difficult for women who often spend most of their income on the household. Access to credit is limited and fraught with difficulties, such as legal implications if repayments are in arrears; women's credit worthiness is often weak in the eyes of formal institutions as a result of low social status and the high interest rates payable to money lenders reduce the viability of this option for women. Steel and Aryeetey (1994) claim that interest rates can be as high as 100 per cent over 9–12 months.

Table 5.6
Costs of bicycle ownership in two communities in Accra

	Jamestown	Nima
Number of owners who bought new bicycles	5	11
Average new bicycle purchase price	33,000 cedis	20,700 cedis
Purchase price as per cent of GNP per capita (US$450)	10 per cent	7 per cent
Average time saving for new bicycle	2.9 years	5.6 years
No. of owners bought second hand bicycle	10	9
Average second hand bicycle price	17,900 cedis	23,800 cedis
Purchase price as percent of GNP per capita (US$450)	6 per cent	8 per cent
Average time saving for second hand bicycle	9 months	14 months

The lack of low income access to formal credit facilities results in people diverting sums from their meagre income to informal savings collectors such as the susu (Gabianu, 1990), with the risk of losing the accumulated capital and the devastating effect that that could have on household survival.

Ewe kayayoo, 45, working at the Timber Market:
No because I am fairly old and need not involve myself in the social activities of the youth. I always keep my monies in the room that I stay

in with some relations. I have no trust for susumen because they have twice absconded with my savings.

Women cyclists who were not owners and who rode only provided leisure, enjoyment and exercise as reasons for riding. There are clear cultural barriers against women cycling for leisure; similarly, there is little cultural acceptance of female children's need to play. Girls should not be at play but rather they should be assisting adult females in household reproductive tasks from a very early age (Grieco, Apt and Turner, 1994). Lack of entitlement to play equates with lack of opportunity to learn to ride. Riding for leisure on the part of a female is not seen as a sufficiently pressing reasons to warrant large capital outlay in an income-scarce environment. Few of the respondents who did own bicycles cited such leisure use as justification for purchase. Of the male cycle owners, a large number have occupations (e.g. tradesmen, farmers) that require the carrying of goods during the working day or the need to travel to their workplace outside of the most convenient time for the use of public transport (e.g. night watchmen).

The continuing perception of most urban Accra dwellers is that cycling is a dangerous activity. The cultural values and attitudes of the urban communities within Accra influence the reaction which develops over time to the increasing level of cycle accidents. These community values and attitudes are explored to assess what effect possible policies and measures may have in altering the level of cycling safety. For households living in constant threat of dire poverty, access to resources (financial, time-based, physical and human) and the well-being of those resources are of importance. The key role children, especially girl children, play in acting as a labour resources for the household from a very early age must be considered here (Grieco, Apt and Turner, 1994; Joekes, 1994). Within communities that do not recognise the economic benefit of riding a bicycle, attempting to learn to ride as a child is not seen as acquiring life skills but merely putting important household resources in danger, for no economic benefit, in a risky traffic environment. In those communities where riding bicycles is seen as having a clear economic benefit, learning to ride as a child becomes a useful life skill. Accidents with other road users in this context do not deter the community from endorsing children learning to ride, but rather produce adaptive behaviour to reduce the risk, such as only encouraging riding by those who will go on as adults to cycle for economic purposes. Women in neither community were perceived as having a need to use bicycles for economic purposes. As we saw, in Jamestown learning to ride by girl children was discouraged and in Nima girls cycling after puberty was discouraged. However, parental opposition to cycling feeds a 'dare-devil' cycling culture amongst youth where accidents are more likely (Grieco, Turner and Kwakye, 1995). Dare devil cycling on the part of youth interacts with a disregard for cyclists on the part of motorists: cycling is viewed as a low status activity and a traffic nuisance. There were many respondents, both in Jamestown and Nima, who told of aggressive driving behaviour and pedestrian movements which led either to accidents or near misses. This aggressive behaviour was an outcome of the negative attitude towards cycling formed within the greater Accra urban community.

Northerners come from areas where cycle/other traffic interaction was more cycle-friendly. By contrast, indigenous ethnic groups of Accra are used to living in areas where this interaction is dangerous. The northern communities are more likely to ignore the risks, i.e. evidence of accident frequency is roughly the same but 'lessons learnt' are different. Salifu (1993), studying the cycle accident statistics of Tamale, Northern Ghana, points out that the increase in motorisation in this bicycle-using area of the Northern Region is having a significant effect on the level of cycle accidents. Whilst in the present, cycle use remains high as compared with other areas of Ghana, with time this cycle-friendly area may too experience a change in attitude by the community against cycling. This will have detrimental financial, environmental and safety effects upon the urban poor, unless steps are taken to protect the existing cycle population.

Improving the safety of cycling is a fundamental step in increasing the demand for cycle use amongst the urban population. As recognised by the World Bank (Pankaj and Coulthart, 1993), the segregation of non-motorised modes from motorised modes is fundamental. The provision of a dedicated bicycle infrastructure is seen as a way to reduce the risk for cyclists. However, how to enforce a right of way for bicycles within an environment of mixed road use needs consideration. The problem of who has priority in a mixed road use environment is significant when determining how to promote non-motorised modes in the developing context: consider the context and culture of the cycle/other transport interaction in Accra.

Male construction worker, bicycle owner, 24, Nima.
Q: What journeys around Accra can you not use your bikes for and why?
A: Very long journeys and on busy streets because of dense vehicles and human traffic.

Male petty trader, 38, Jamestown. I don't take it to Circle area because of the nature of the traffic and the way the taxi drivers drive around

As we saw in the previous section, mixed road use in a Ghanaian context is characterised by conflicts between motorised and non-motorised modes and conflicts amongst non-motorised modes. In Ghana, human transport (e.g. head load porters) and roadside vendors fulfil a significant economic role; cyclists do not. Correspondingly, within the transport hierarchy, human transport and vendors have more status than cyclists. Many respondents recounted incidents where pedestrians deliberately stepped out in front of the cyclist or where the cyclist was verbally or physically abused for travelling in crowded pedestrian areas or for colliding with street vendors. These experiences were paralleled by abuse from motor vehicle road users, especially taxi drivers. Other forms of non-motorised transport such as barrows and trolleys experienced the same disregard. Attitudes of junior officials are unfavourable towards non-motorised modes; respondents reported occurrences where bicycles or trolleys were confiscated for being in places of high human or vehicular traffic density. The transport environment of Accra is not friendly towards cyclists.

Women cyclists talked of the abuse they experienced from motorists. They told of being deliberately pushed off the road into the gutter by vehicles, of being shouted and hooted at, of being jeered at and ridiculed for daring to cycle on the public road. This exposure of women to public dishonour works strongly against an increase in the number of women cycling: as we saw in the last section, the fear of negative encounters with motorists – the 'fear' of traffic – is sufficient to prevent women from easing their own burden by moving loads off their heads onto wheels. To prevent this negative interaction with traffic which so dishonours women, segregated facilities for cycles and trucks are necessary: without segregated facilities, cultural factors will continue to militate against the use of non-motorised wheeled transport by the female petty trader.

There are clearly cultural aspects involved in rendering cycling safe. In China and much of South East Asia, there is mass cycling behaviour and safe road space for cyclists is determined by sheer weight of numbers. In the UK the pressure group 'Critical Mass' organises mass cycling events to 'claim back the road'. In the Netherlands and Germany, cycling is a respected means of behaviour and is provided for within the transport system (Tolley, 1990). Positive measures for the provision of bicycle infrastructure and its efficient enforcement may effect some change in the Accra transport culture towards cyclists. As people perceive that, as a result of these official actions, there is no longer an official endorsement for their own negative attitudes, cycling may become more acceptable and thus safer. Increased safety will,in its turn lead, to increased acceptability and the virtuous spiral can begin.

Given existing community values and the mixed road use characteristics within Accra, simply providing an infrastructure for cycling does not guarantee that it will be used for this purpose. Respondents painted a picture of conflictual interaction of pedestrians with cyclists, motor vehicles, pedestrian street sellers, kerbside vendors and people living on the street. Where there is a collision over use of road space cultural attitudes currently favour vendors' rights against cyclists' rights. There is significant potential for invasion of dedicated cycle infrastructure by vendors and other non-motorised road users. Motor vehicles have the natural advantage of being able to enforce their share of road space; solitary bicycles do not!

If there is, as yet, not enough cycle demand in Accra for the bicycle to be able to maintain a right-of-way in competition with other human activity by sheer weight of numbers, how are the cycle lanes which are currently planned for Accra going to be protected from becoming yet more space for street sellers and pedestrians (Pankaj and Coulthart, 1993)? If cycling were safer then there would be more bicycles to use the dedicated infrastructure, but if the risk of constant interaction with other road users is seen as a safety problem, then, clearly, there is a need for some form of enforcement of any newly-constructed cycle lanes. Extra enforcement needs to be introduced and paid for. Conspicuous signing indicating bicycle priority needs to be put in place. In the most congested locations, such as the central market areas, where all forms of human transport are competing for limited space, only the construction of alternative provision for pedestrians and street vendors will begin to ensure cyclists have priority.

Ownership of a bicycle represents a significant investment for an urban poor household. Reduction of the purchase price of bicycles makes it easier for household members to justify ownership. It is not enough simply to accommodate a suppressed demand by reducing bicycle costs, as this will merely replicate the current gender and cultural divisions. There are significant variations between communities within Accra towards bicycle ownership and these will not be overcome through purchase price reductions alone. Within those communities that accept cycle use, the cost to the households of earmarking valuable resources for bicycle ownership should be made easier; the lack of access to credit for the urban poor hinders efficient organisation in transport provision. Demand must also be induced within other communities and sections of the population. Explicit consideration must be given to how to render the bicycle more economically and occupationally useful, in order that people can justify the large call on resources necessary within a household to purchase a bicycle. Cycle use must be promoted within communities with limited acquaintance of the bicycle and to promote its use by women: sustainability should be accompanied by equity.

Household members are major economic resources within an urban poor household and, as motorisation increases even in those communities that accept cycle use, it will become increasingly difficult to justify the risk cycling places on such human capital. Segregated infrastructure is required to preserve the existing levels of cycle use and allow its promotion in other communities. The special features of mixed road use in Ghana and the overall negative attitudes towards cycling require consideration in the designing of infrastructure. The potential for vendor and pedestrian invasion of cycle facilities, the costs of enforcement and role of signing require explicit consideration in any scheme. It is not sufficient to build cycle paths or to persuade a substantial section of the public to use cycles on the main arteries of the city. The implementation of a dedicated infrastructure for bicycles may require a significant level of enforcement for success, as a result of the negative community attitude towards cycling and the prevalence of the invasion of road space by the informal trading sector. Other road users need to be educated on their behaviour toward cyclists. In the absence of an appropriate infrastructural policy that considers behavioural as well as engineering factors, the admirable goal of sustainability will inevitably be subverted.

5.5   Conclusion

As we have seen, non-motorised transport persists in a context where prevailing official values operate against its safety. Other road users, in line with the official and professional perceptions of the outdatedness of non-motorised transport, discriminate against users of the mode in such a way as to maximise danger. Where collisions occur, this has negative consequences for the general flow of traffic. Given the current high level of accidents and as non-motorised transport is unlikely to disappear, there is a need for rethinking on the ways of permitting it to move safely and separately from the main traffic. In order for non-motorised transport to make its fullest contribution to the transportation of goods and to the economy in the petty trading structure of Ghana, it is necessary that the harassment of truck boys by officials, as evidenced by our respondents' accounts, be discouraged. Similarly, other road users must be educated to see the value of this transport sector and required to respect its safety.

   Much of the discussion, such as there is, about the future of non-motorised transport assumes that this mode of conveyance is transitional: however, the evidence from Accra suggests that this is not the case. Increased congestion as a consequence of increased motorisation generates conditions conducive to the persistence of non-motorised transport, for in such conditions non-motorised transport is faster than motorised transport over short distances. Similarly, the existence of an extensive petty trading structure which depends upon the provision of low cost transport supplied by the non-motorised transport sector, coupled with the physical design of the trading districts which necessitates the use of smaller vehicles than that suppliable by motor transport ensure that the trucks and trolleys of Accra will outlive the existing policy makers' antipathy towards the mode. There are few reasons, then, to suppose that non-motorised transport is a transitional form. As it seems unlikely to disappear it must be recognised as part of the existing transport structure and brought within the scope of urban transport planning in the developing context. It is our recommend-ation that transport planning for the city build in appropriate facilities for the efficient operation and development of this sector rather than simply try to squeeze this sector out of existence.

There are a number of measures which could usefully be adopted to improve the operation of non-motorised transport. Firstly, the semi-official and the informal interference of authorities with this mode of operation should be discouraged. Such interference, our evidence suggests, may dissuade traders from making use of the mode as a consequence of the negative effects such interference has on the reliability of their trade. Secondly, segregated road space could be made available for such trucks and trolleys, especially in the central trading districts: this would help provide the non-motorised sector with a more positive image and thus reduce harassment it presently experiences from both motorists and municipal and other authorities.

Similarly, if the promotion of cycling as a sustainable mode of transport for the Third World is to be gender equitable, attention should be paid to ensuring the access of females to this mode. In Ghana, the scale of the female petty trading sectors, with its small load requirements, could provide a fertile ground for a sustainable non-motorised transport policy. Gender barriers to cycling in all communities mean that if mass non-motorised transport is promoted and women continue to have very limited access to bicycles, women will be pushed back even further on to their own two feet. The promotion of cycling should be designed so as to alleviate and not intensify this. The success of a sustainable transport policy for Ghana is dependent on effecting a change in behavioural attitudes towards cycling amongst both population and municipal official-dom as well as upon the construction of appropriate segregated facilities.

Notes

1   A tribe from Burkina Faso.
2   By 'sent', the trader either means that the truck boy either spoilt or absconded with the goods.

126

Binkabi
(been KAH bee)
From the saying, 'Do not bite one another'. Symbol of harmony and unity.

6 Female domestic financial responsibilities and household survival: Travel strategies in a developing economy

Jeff Turner

6.1 The activity approach and survival networks: coping strategies amongst the urban poor

In low income groups, women's access to capital has to be negotiated through the household; the profits from their trading get absorbed in household budgets and their time and travel patterns have to be scheduled to meet the survival needs of the household. The household is the major agency determining individuals' time, travel patterns and access to transport resources. This chapter uses evidence collected from 54 households in Accra to describe the relationship between household organisation and activity patterns in a developing context. The 54 Accra households provide a good first entry into the complexity and varied range of household structures which exist in Ghana. Our focus is on the survival strategies of the urban poor, with a special focus on female headed households. This chapter reports on the ways in which the urban poor adapt to their own poverty and to unreliable public transport services by task sharing among extended family units. Life among the urban poor of any city is characterised by a continuous struggle for survival (Abrams, 1980; Apt and Katila, 1994; Chinn, 1988; Ross, 1983). It is a struggle constantly threatened with failure through disease, premature mortality, unstable employment and economic disaster. Surviving threats such as losing time off work through accidents or losing valuable money through meeting customary obligations around birth, death or marriage (Bevan and Sseweya, 1995) or corruption can only be overcome by having access to resources: financial, time-based, informational, human and cultural. In this uncertain environment, low income households are forced to substitute social resources, i.e. the help of kin, for absent financial resources (Grieco, 1995). As individuals and households, the urban poor within the

Plate 8   Small scale facilities: the equipment for petty trading

developing world are characterised by a lack of the financial resources needed to allow them to cushion the impact of uncertainty. As a result, they must, as a matter of survival, widen the social area over which they can gather resources when the need arises. In Africa, the extended kinship system plays precisely this function (World Bank, 1994a).

It has been widely suggested that urban poor households, far from being helpless and disorganised as suggested by conventional accounts, adopt strategies of behaviour on how to access much-needed resources in the long term (Ainsworth, 1992; Ardayfio-Schandorf, 1994; Chinn, 1988; Hareven, 1982; Moch et al., 1987; Whipp, 1987). Successful strategies allow them to overcome potentially disastrous events where these arise. To survive, a household must recruit or reproduce a sufficient membership to perform a range of economic activities, maximising the number of people who generate income for the household. There are other activities that members of a household need to perform that are not income generating, especially in a context where there are considerable infrastructural deficiencies (Benneh et al.,1993). The collecting of water, the obtaining of fuel, the disposal of refuse, queuing for services in conditions of overall scarcity – these tasks all fall heavily upon the time budgets of the poor urban household. Time is a valuable commodity in such circumstances and all these activities need to be organised and coordinated within a household to minimise the amount of hard earned income spent carrying them out.

A successful survival strategy must facilitate the performance of this portfolio. One way this pressure of time is accommodated is by having a large supply of human resources within a household to provide flexibility. Taking this perspective, the level of fertility amongst the urban poor may be viewed as an important element in their household survival strategy (Joekes, 1994). Children and older members can be seen as resources to be used to allow those with highest potential to maximise their income for the household's benefit (Grootaert and Kanbur,1995; Johnson, Hill and Ivan-Smith, 1995). For example, where a transport system is costly – forcing the poor into low cost modes, such as walking – or unreliable – thus generating substantial variability in travel times – children are used as substitute labour to compensate for these travel and transport uncertainties. This has the consequence of rendering children less able to carry out activities such as schooling (Odaga and Heneveld, 1995). Viewing children as resources in the developing context, rather than as the responsibilities which they are viewed as constituting within the conventional Western activity frame of analysis (Hillman et al., 1990; Jones et al., 1983; Jones, 1989) has importance for understanding the travel and transport organisation of the household. In Ghana, children's labour is typically used to support women's performance of a range of household and economic tasks: children, especially girl children, substitute for their mothers and older female relatives even in the conduct of trading tasks where this older personnel is routinely subject to travel and transport delay.

131

The public transport system in Accra has been characterised for many years by informal sector provision, despite attempts by successive governments to develop and maintain publicly organised stage-bus services (Fouracre et al., 1994). As we have already seen in Chapter 2, this provision is based on a range of vehicle types, from minibuses to lorry-type 'mammy wagons' to taxis (Grieco et al., 1994). However, the service provision does have problems, as detailed in Fouracre et al. (1994). They point to the poor quality and high cost of the service to the user. The poor quality of service is exemplified by lengthy waiting times for travellers and long in-vehicle travel times. Our own research indicates that travellers can wait for as long as two hours in the afternoon off-peak period for a vehicle to fill up and depart the Central Market district termini, i.e. the 'lorry parks'. The practice of buses and taxis waiting at lorry parks until full makes journey times unreliable and life difficult for passengers waiting along the route. Increasing congestion causes long in-vehicle travel times and adds further unreliability to journeys. Furthermore, there is a large volume of substandard vehicles operating in the informal public transport system with the consequence that vehicle break down en route is a frequent experience.

In order to understand how household organisation impacted upon transport use and, correspondingly, how transport organisation impacted upon household functioning, the research attempted to capture an equal number of nuclear and extended households in order to identify differences in household organisation, roles and travel activity patterns within these households. Within the category of extended households, interviews were sought with polygamous as well as monogamous households. In the event, 25 interviews were obtained with extended households and 29 with nuclear households. Eight interviews were obtained with extended polygamous households. 12 of the extended households were female headed. Seven of the nuclear families were female headed. The survival strategies of female headed households in Ghana are of particular interest as recent surveys have indicated that female headed households are emerging out of poverty faster than conventional households (World Bank, 1995).

Samples were primarily drawn from two communities in Accra, the first being an area inhabited by poor migrant households, Nima, and the other a low income area which houses the traditional people of the city, Jamestown. Four households were interviewed from Russia, a low income area within Accra city and two households were interviewed from Madina, which is a low income surburb of Accra. Interviews with these six households were undertaken in the early stages of research in order to establish a framework on local household organisation. In the event, a comparison between Nima and Jamestown proved to be the most effective basis on which to organise the household research. Nima is a major reception area for migrants from the North of Ghana whereas Jamestown is characterised by the high percentage of residents indigenous to Accra, the Ga people (Kilson, 1974; Grieco, Turner and Kwakye, 1995). In typically large households, the practice of fostering children to obtain their household labour, hiring domestic servants and doorstep petty trading by elderly women are three notable strategies for relieving middle age adults from transport stress and under-provision, and enabling them to be wage earners. As resources, rather than responsibilities, children fetch and carry, and attend school in shifts. From a transport activity or survival network approach, these elements can be viewed as key strategies in the organisation of travel and transport in a developing economy. In Ghana, as in most developing countries, comprehensive data recording the parameters of household travel behaviour is unavailable. Consequently, the materials presented here are indicative rather than conclusive. Nevertheless, these indicative materials have consequences for the planning of public transport in developing cities for women and the urban poor.

6.2 A trader in every home: domestic anchors, domestic business

Working from home has long been recognised as an economic and employment strategy adopted by low income women in their child rearing years (Allen and Wolkowitz, 1987). In Western societies, attention has fallen upon the home based garment industry with its elaborate outwork structure. Home based work in the West has long been a domestic extension of the factory system. Home working in Ghana takes a very different form: typically the home worker employs herself. She is a petty trader working on her own doorstep to enable her to take care of children, earn a living and ensure the safety of her goods and property. The formal and even the informal economy offers little hope of employment by another. The domestic financial responsibilities of the Ghanaian woman impose a life long requirement for her earning: household survival is a consequence of her ability to generate the income necessary for the support of offspring and dependents. In Chapter 1, we saw that the classical anthropological and the emerging economic literature recognises the high level of spousal separation in Africa, and in Ghana in particular. Detailed studies of how such spousal separation operates in terms of the time budget and travel functioning of the household are largely absent. Our own investigations of female headed households reveal a keen awareness of the importance of constructing sustainable household employment and travel portfolios on the part of low income women. In addition, and in contrast to the understandings in much of the literature, in co-resident polygamous households women continued to have major financial domestic responsibilities. Spousal separation serves to reveal how strong female domestic financial responsibilities are: polygamous co-residence, given the way in which the majority of household surveys have

133

been conducted, has served to conceal the level of economic activity of multiple wives. Indeed, the presence of a second wife often leads to a heightening in the economic activities of the first. There is an extensive array of different household arrangements present in our data: however, the following examples serve to give some indication of this range:

A local description of a household in Russia (a low income area of Accra). The number of people in this house is 18. This comprises mother (64 yrs), son (38 yrs), daughter (34 yrs), daughter (28 yrs), daughter (25 yrs), daughter (24 yrs), son (18 yrs), son (14 yrs) and daughter (11 yrs). Ranging from the ages nine, eight, eight, six, five, four, four, two, and eight months baby are all grandchildren. In this house, there is a mother who has children and who in turn have children of their own. The eldest son who acts as household head has two wives but does not stay with them (the wives). Likewise, the daughters also do not stay with their husbands. They have separate houses and so their husbands have been remitting them.

10 member polygamous Fulani household living in Nima. Yes. Since the second wife trades at home she is always present to take care of young children. Her trading is preparing and selling of food from home.

Head of Busunga household of 60 members living in Nima. (On the occupational structure of the household.) My two wives, Adisa and Zenabu sell cooked food here in Nima. Two of my sisters do business in cloth and other items between Accra and Lagos. The other women sell petty items around the house. One of my brothers is a painter who works on private jobs and another is a watchman. The rest of the adults are unemployed. Of course, the children are still in school. The two old ladies are too old to work. I am a retired painter myself. I used to work with the Ghana Civil Aviation Authority. I retired in 1981, Mallam Alidu, 74 years old, another brother, is a retired driver.

Within this pattern of spousal separation and female domestic financial responsibility (Lloyd and Brandon, 1993), door step trading is a routine feature of Ghanaian economic life (Apt et al.,1996). Its prevalence is reflected in the weakness of commercial distribution systems and accommodated by the extensiveness of the petty trading system. Doorstep trading is rarely undertaken by men. Within our sample of 54 households, covering 580 persons, 84 per cent of homes had one or more female traders present in them. This fits closely with the findings of Elizabeth Ardayfio-Schandorf (1994) who reports that over 60 per cent of Ghanaian urban households are supported solely upon the earnings of women and with those of Lloyd and Brandon (1993) 'who find that in Ghana, a woman was the primary source of economic support in a significant number of reported male-headed households' (Handa, 1994).

The case of the seven member monogamous Kotokoli household living in Nima. My wife is always present because she sells food in front of the house. Based on the fact that my wife trades just in front of the house, she is always around. However, if she has to go somewhere, she does it at weekends when the eldest son is at home.

Trading on the doorsteps of Russia (a low income areas of Accra). Both mother and 34 year old daughter are not working but 25 year old daughter sells in front of the house. That means there is always someone in the house to take care of whoever is sick.

Many households contained more than one trader and one household of 47 persons contained 13 traders, five of whom traded upon their own doorstep. The research into the activity patterns of low income Accra households revealed a relationship between the extensiveness of doorstep petty trading and the availability of domestic 'anchors'. The presence of a member of the household trading on the doorstep provides a fixed point around which other household members and the household as a whole can schedule its set of activities. Respondents stressed the importance of these arrangements: household scheduling is an outcome of transport and travel strategies which explicitly identify the function of 'domestic anchor' though respondents do not themselves describe the function in these terms. Doorstep trading is a planned activity, not simply an outcome of local circumstance. Women discuss the choices they make in order to preserve domestic continuity and the smooth running of the household. The prevalence of doorstep trading amongst the sample indicates that there is a weaker separation of home and work in developing countries than that which exists in developed countries (Apt and Katila, 1994: Apt et al., 1996). This weaker division between home and work is associated with a lesser number of trips by the household as a whole. The merging of domestic and economic responsibilities by trading from home is, within the sample, primarily a female pattern. There were only two cases of males who traded from home, one of a teacher who ran his school from the home and a number of cases of retired males who also served as domestic anchors. As the evidence collected demonstrates, there is a need to recognise that differences in the economic and social structures of developing countries, as compared with developed, result in different activity patterns and thus different patterns of urban mobility.

Household size is another factor which needs to be taken into consideration. Our sample revealed households which are significantly larger than Western households. The unweighted average household size within the sample is 10.7 persons. These findings are not only at variance with Western statistics on household size (Jones et al., 1983) but also with the published statistics on Ghanaian household size which give the average urban household size as 4.3 members (Ghanaian Statistical Service, 1992). It is interesting to note that the household size reported for Cote d'Ivoire, the country adjacent Ghana, is significantly higher than that found by official sources for Ghana. The Cote d'Ivoire Living Standards Survey (1993) reports an Ivorian national average household size of between 8.31 and 6.32 members between 1985 and 1988. Fostering, polygamy and strong sibling bonds are major factors in explaining the large household size. All three institutions are widespread within Ghana (Oppong, 1994).

Table 6.1
Household size in urban Accra

Household size	Frequency
1–5 members	17
6–10 members	25
11–20 members	8
20 and above members	4
Total number of households	40

Our findings raise the question of what constitutes a household in the Ghanaian context, and indeed in the African context (Clark, 1989: Handa, 1994; Lloyd and Brandon, 1993). Valuable guidance can be gained from respondents' own accounts. Our interviewer, speaking in the respondents' mother tongue put the following question to the household of a northern chief living in Nima, a household which the head of household described as being composed of 60 people:

Q: Do you think as many as 60 people (of you) can and should be considered as one household in an urban setting of this nature?

A: Apart from any children and wives, all other person in this house are related to me by blood. We come from either the same father or mother. The children of such brothers and sisters certainly are my children too. In addition to this my brothers and sisters consider and treat my own children also as their own. In fact, there are no tenants in this house.

Q: Apart from the blood relationship, what other things bind you together as one family or household?

A: In our preparation of meals, we do things collectively. As the head of the household, it is my objection to the entire good to provide at least one meal each day. This I normally do for supper. For breakfast and lunch, however, the children rely on their individual mothers. Even then, our oneness is still manifested. Each mother tries to provide not only for her own children but also for the children of other mothers and brothers.

Large households are aware of the scheduling flexibilities their household size provides them with and describe these in terms of transport and travel strategies. The head of large northern household explicitly discussed the benefits of household size and structure in terms of the provision of domestic anchors which could provide for child care and household security whilst the bulk of the household travelled on its daily or longer term business:

A: Because of our large number, we have the advantage of often having somebody left beside to cater for the younger ones and to ensure the safety of the home.

In Ghana, the customary obligation to attend funerals is a very strong one. The presence of family parties and not simply family representatives is routinely required, despite the considerable distances that may be involved for migrant households. The social scale of the activity can be elicited from the language the households themselves use to describe attendance at funerals:

A: Normally, we send a delegation to attend on behalf of those of us here in Nima.

Large household size permits the meeting of this responsibility without exposing the home to danger: a 'delegation' is sent, guardians are left behind. The home is left in the custody of the females, who are often doorstep traders. Greater household size permits both routine and crisis commitments to be met simultaneously. Low income economies, with their widespread daily requirements for small, regular purchases automatically provide trading niches which can be harnessed by women whose responsibilities and commitments require them to earn whilst at home. Petty trading fits the purchasing abilities of low income areas whilst simultaneously meeting the child care needs of low income women. The income base and the child care needs of low income areas exist in a symbiotic relationship. Similarly, large household structures appear to meet the survival needs of the urban poor better. The next section further investigates this issue.

137

6.3   Child's play: the economic and domestic responsibilities of children

Conventionally, within transport studies, household activity analysis has focused upon the role of adults as escorts and guardians of children's security in the developed world (Jones, 1989; Hillman et al., 1990). The data collected from the household interviews conducted for this study indicate the importance of children as the securers of the domestic environment as opposed to being made secure by the domestic environment. Within the interviews it was repeatedly indicated that it is the presence of a family member in the home which is the security requirement, independent of the age of the family member. Children are regarded as viable substitutes for adults in ensuring the security of the home. The interview material indicates that in the developing context, children acquire social responsibilities at much earlier ages. Similar findings have been obtained by Johnson, Hill and Ivan-Smith (1995), Joekes (1994) and Grootaert and Kanbur (1995). In order to understand the activity patterns of children in the developing context, a change of perspective is necessary. Whereas in the developed world, children are viewed largely as domestic responsibilities, within the developing world, children are considered largely as domestic resources. This has consequences for households' time and travel budgets which have not yet been considered in the literature. The view of children as resources occurred repeatedly within the interviews conducted.

> *The case of the nine member polygamous Chamba household living in Nima.* Normally, the children are made to stay with the house while the wives travel and work to earn income for the household.

In understanding how children come to play such a significant role in ensuring the continuous presence of a family member in the home, attention should be paid to the school shift system which makes a major contribution to children's ability to perform this function. In a number of interviews, it was indicated that the school shift system formed the basis for the allocation of 'time of day tasks' amongst the household's children:

> *The case of the seven member female headed Samiir (Benin) household living in Nima.* Any of the children at home assists. Fortunately, the children do not go to school at the same time because they belong to different shifts ... Also the children belong to different shifts at school so someone is at home at any point in time. Apart from Mother who trades from home, the children's school shift defines who stays at home. If any one has to travel, he or she does it when others are at home.

Where a family is able to harness the benefit of the school shift system and achieve a distribution of its members across the system then schooling and household tasks can be combined. In cases where families do not have the option (it is the school not the parent in Ghana which determines which shift a child is to be placed on), schooling may be sacrificed. There is an increasing recognition that the household task burden of the girl child in Africa represents a major barrier to her education (Ainsworth, 1992; Odaga and Heneveld, 1995; Beijing Declaration, 1995). Detailed studies are still lacking; in this respect, the case evidence collected in Accra indicates the importance of synchronising household and community scheduling of activities.

Not only do children play a critical role in securing the domestic environment, they also play a crucial part in the management of domestic sanitation. Defined as domestic resources, children play a central role in refuse disposal including the disposal of human excrement. The consequent health and environmental dangers attending this practice require further research. In addition to playing a central role in the disposal of waste, children also play a central role in the fetching of water. The infrastructural deficiencies of the developing context impact heavily upon the activity patterns of children.

The case of the 16 member extended female headed Ga household living in Jamestown. The children of the household empty chamber pots, sweep, wash dishes, and fetch water.

The hygienic performance of sanitation tasks typically involves children walking substantial distances to official dumps: sanitary infrastructure is rarely available in the immediate vicinity of low income residences with travel times to authorised dumps often taking as long as 20 minutes (Dankwa et al., 1994). In practice, many children reduce their travel times by unauthorised dumping of refuse and excrement close to home (Benneh et al., 1993). In order to undertake their tasks, children were frequently required to start their day at dawn. Certain tasks such as disposing of refuse and excrement were typically undertaken at the very beginning of the day in order to conceal illegal dumping. In order to fit all the activities of the working day into childhood, children were required to lengthen their waking day. Within Western analyses, it has been widely recognised that women 'rob the night' in order to accomplish the tasks their two roles impose upon their daily lives. In developing countries, there is a need to undertake similarly comprehensive studies of the time and travel budgets of children (Ainsworth, 1992).

The case of the 16 member extended female headed Ga household living in Jamestown. When they wake up early it doesn't affect their schooling.

The majority of respondents indicated that the tasks performed by children did not interfere with their schooling as such tasks were assigned to children outside of school hours. However, there was little discussion of the impact of these tasks on children's alertness in the classroom. Despite parental assurances to the contrary, other studies indicate that the performance of household tasks by children does have an adverse impact on school performance, most particularly in the case of girls (Odaga and Heneveld, 1995).

> *The case of the seven member monogamous Kotokoli household living in Nima.* Undertaking household jobs does not interfere with children's schoolgoing. Jobs are assigned in such a way that it will not interfere with children's schooling. Unfinished jobs are abandoned when it is time for children to go to school.

Where there was discussion of the impact of children's task loads on school performance and attendance, respondents stressed that such loads were a necessary part of household survival. The social and economic responsibilities of children in the developing context are not confined to duties inside the family, for children frequently provide domestic services on a commercial basis for non-family members. The purchase of children's services for the fetching of water and the disposal of waste often occurs on a spontaneous basis and is used to compensate for the delayed arrival of the household member who is normally responsible for performing these domestic functions.

> *The case of seven member polygamous Fulani household living in Nima.* Sometimes, tasks are left awaiting their (the women's) arrival. However when we realise they are getting too late we rely on services provided by children in the neighbourhood for a fee.

In addition to performing tasks connected with household or neighbourhood sanitation, children are also required to assist in the petty selling and trading activities of their family elders. This is in line with evidence from other recent studies which indicates that Ghanaian children frequently carry considerable financial responsibility for their education (Asomaning et al., 1994; UNICEF, 1994).

> *The case of the nine member monogamous Ewe/Hausa household living in Nima.* The children are too young to work but they can assist in taking care of the home to allow us, their parents, to engage in our economic activities. They look after the home in our absence. They can also assist my wife to sell.

In large households, children can represent a substantial labour force. Children are used as a form of distribution system: they are sent out from the house to sell the goods in the local neighbourhood. They walk the neighbourhood to make contact with the customers for their goods. The selling of bread typically takes place in this way. The lesser honour of children and their social directability allows them to be used in semi-illegal activities such as hawking goods at the road side: activities which, if performed by adults, are more likely to result in prosecution or official harassment (Humphries, 1981).

> *The case of the 47 member extended Ga household living in Jamestown.* The children help parents to sell. They sell iced water or hawk petty items. When some go to school, some have to stay and help their mothers sell their wares. Children who sell are influenced by money and it affects their schooling, but they do because that is the only (way) we parents will be able to fend for them.

The data collected indicates that children are a key resource in organising household accommodation of changes and unreliability in transport provision. Children perform this function both as members of households and as bought-in providers of services. On the evidence collected, there would seem to be an impact of children's household activity roles on their schooling: however, no one simple relationship appears to hold. As schooling has to be paid for, the non-performance of these household activity roles by children can have negative effects on household income and thus preclude the schooling option. In conclusion, it should be noted that the domestic task load of low income children in urban Ghana involves them in a high level of local mobility. Transporting refuse to the dump, peddling goods locally and carrying water and fuel wood all generate a high number of local short trips for children. These arrangements serve as a contrast with the recorded experience of Western children (Hillman et al., 1990)

6.4 Fostering, family structure and activity patterns: flexible household boundaries

Household activity analysis has been instrumental in highlighting the impact of household structure on travel patterns and travel behaviour. As the work of Jones et al. (1983) indicates, household structure changes over time, e.g. with position in the life cycle, and consequently household patterns also change. Within activity analysis – an analysis which has typically been conducted on Western data - these life cycle stages have been taken as largely unproblematic. Detailed studies of household organisation in Accra, Ghana (Turner, 1994) and in other West African locations (Ainsworth, 1992) indicate that African households do not share the same life cycle stages. One reason for this is that whereas Western households recruit primarily through marriage and birth, West African households also recruit extensively through the fostering of children. Another element entering the equation is the existence of the ancestral home (Kilson, 1974: Woodford-Berger, 1981): rights of residence to family members are inalienable; consequently, family members depart and rejoin the ancestral household according to changes in their personal circumstances. The Western equation of separate nuclear household with separate residential space over which the nuclear family has unambiguous control does not fit the circumstances of many West African communities. The joint family structures which develop around the West African ancestral home are typically multi-generational and, therefore, do not exhibit the life cycle stages of conventional activity analysis. Nevertheless, policy analysis typically ignores the differences in household structure which exist between the developed and developing world; this disregard of difference has consequences for the effectiveness of the implementation of a range of policies stretching from cost recovery in health to the design of appropriate vehicles and transport systems.

Our interviews conducted in the in depth household studies of travel organisation revealed a range of differences in household structure as between Western and African society. A key difference lies in fluctuating household size and membership. Fluctuations in household composition are a common feature of African urban life, with households expanding and contracting as the medical and educational needs of their rural kin are met by their accommodation in urban space (Ainsworth, 1992). Fostering children of other family members is a common practice in Ghana (Goody, 1978), with such children often occupying the ambiguous location of domestic resource and domestic responsibility (Ainsworth, 1992; Asomaning et al., 1994). This pattern is evident within the sampled households.

The extensiveness of such fostering arrangements makes its contribution towards the creation of substantially larger households and correspondingly more complex household activity patterns. Cases A and B below are presented as examples of the complexity of household structures captured by our research. In fact, these do not represent the most complex structures encountered: in Jamestown, we encountered a household which contained 47 members; in Nima, we met with a household which contained 60. Presenting the information on the latter in an easily decipherable form is no easy matter: indeed, it is impossible to fit the information on one page of text, hence the choice of cases A and B in order to give some feeling for the complexities involved. Consider the complexity of scheduling common activities for a household of this size: equally, consider the range of back-up or substitute labour this provides for the performance of any specific activity or task.

Case A: Extended family structure (ethnicity: Fantes), Jamestown

	Gender	Age	Occupation	Position in the family
1	M	72	Pensioner	Head
2	F	62	Lotto staker	Wife
3	F	36	Trader	Daughter
4	F	34	Trader	Daughter
5	M	32	Fisherman	Son
6	M	30	Fisherman	Son
7	M	29	Fisherman	Son
8	F	27	Seamstress	Daughter
9	F	26	Trader	Daughter
10	M	25	Lotto staker	Daughter
11	M	18	Fisherman	Son
12	F	2	Not schooling	Grandchild
13	F	3	Not schooling	Grandchild
14	F	5	Pupil	Grandchild
15	M	7	Pupil	Grandchild
16	M	9	Pupil	Grandchild

Case B: Extended family structure (ethnicity: Kotokoli), Nima

	Gender	Age	Occupation	Position in the family
1	M	45	Driver	Husband/head
2	F	35	Petty trader	Wife
3	M	21	Unemployed	Son
4	M	19	Unemployed	Son
5	F	8	Pupil	Daughter
6	M	90	Unemployed	Wife's father
7	F	60	Iced water seller	Wife's mother
8	F	28	Foodseller	Wife's sister
9	F	4	Pupil	Wife's sister's daughter
10	M	13	Student	Wife's sister's son
11	F	22	Apprentice Seamstress	Wife's sister
12	M	7	Pupil	Wife's sister's son
13	F	4	Pupil	Wife's sister's daughter
14	M	2		Wife's sister's son
15	F	19	Foodseller	Wife's sister
16	M	4	Pupil	Wife's sister's son
17	M	20	Student	Wife's sister's son
18	M	17	Driver's mate	Wife's sister's son

The fostering of children by their grandparents is a customary practice in Ghana. Such an arrangement provides children with the benefits of adult supervision and the elderly with the services provided by the more agile (Apt and Katila, 1994: Ainsworth, 1993). A number of households within the sample contained grandchildren and siblings' children without the presence of their parents. Typical examples were: i) a ten member polygamous Chamba household living in Nima which consisted of a polygamous nuclear family of seven members plus two nephews and a 14 year old maid servant; and ii) a six member monogamous extended Ga household living in Jamestown which consisted of a three generational female headed family of five members including two school age nephews. These arrangements free the middle generation to pursue economic activities (Grootaert and Kanbur, 1995). It also works against the prospects of the elderly being found in single generational arrangement as is found in contemporary Western society. The presence of children to perform errands reduces the number of trips the elderly are required to make in the meeting of their survival needs. The evidence is of children travelling to the market areas in order to obtain the stock required by their elderly trading grandmothers. Such an arrangement reduces the exposure to travel discomfort which would be experienced by the elderly were they to travel on the crowded, congested informal public transport system of Accra.

Fostering was not simply a feature of two generational households but was also a feature of three and more generational households. Even where parents are present inside a household, the supervision of grandchildren by their grandparents inside that household is a conventional arrangement and frequently stretches to children being deemed the financial responsibility of the grandparent. The internal financial organisation of the Ghanaian family is now widely recognised as being distinctive in respect of the separation of the internal household economies of males and females and often of generations (ODA, 1994)

> *The case of 16 member three generational Fante household living in Jamestown.* Responsibility for child care is with my wife because when she is around she does everything and takes care of the grandchildren to enable her children to carry out their businesses.

In Ghana, like much of West Africa, the line between fostering and the hiring of child labour is not easily drawn (Ainsworth, 1992). The social arrangements around girl servants can be viewed as an extension of the fostering structure. Girls are sent from poor rural households to their urban relatives or home townspeople to provide domestic services (Oppong, 1994) under the social description of 'fostering'. Recently, with the development of the African platform for Beijing, attention has fallen upon the role of girls as household servants in Ghana (FAWE, 1995). Currently, research is being undertaken to establish the scale of girl children's incorporation in domestic service, for whilst it is generally recognised as being extensive, no source of comprehensive data on the topic yet exists (NCWD, 1995). Whilst the scale of girl children's domestic service is not yet known, our research indicates that this service presently provides substantial domestic flexibility for Ghanaian households of all income classes. Maidservants are to be found even in low income households. These girl servants fulfil the function of domestic anchors, thus permitting other family members greater time and activity flexibility. The pervasiveness of girl domestic servants in urban Ghana raises the issue of time ownership in respect of household organisation and flexibility. The purchase of a maidservant's services can be viewed as the purchase of the essential commodity of time: she is completely directable by the household, lives in and has no effective freedoms.

The case of the five member monogamous Akan household living in Nima. When my daughter is late then the meals are prepared by the maid servant. This leads to the late preparation of meals and too much work for maidservant. The maidservant steps in to perform the tasks of members who are late or delayed. By the nature of her work, the maidservant is always at home. She is instructed to stay at home always.

The existence of house girls within a household, as with the spontaneous purchase of the sanitation services of neighbourhood children, increases the flexibility available to the household. The low cost, e.g. low wages, and general availability of domestic help in developing contexts has consequences for the activity patterns of households. Such domestic help can compensate for the consequences of delay in a context where there is great variability in journey times. Within the data collected, there were a number of instances of the employment of house girls. It should be remembered that the research has confined itself to low income households and a substantially larger number of households using house girls is likely to be found within the urban professional classes.

Although this study did not collect detailed evidence on how long individuals had been members of their present households, the information on fostering and child care responsibilities indicates that the composition and size of household in this context are more fluid than is conventionally assumed. As the cases presented above illustrate, there is considerable cultural flexibility surrounding the construction of the urban Ghanaian household. This cultural flexibility around the restructuring of households in the African context clearly requires further investigation. It clear that researchers investigating household size using Western household models have misunderstood Ghanaian household structure (Oppong, 1994; Clark, 1989).

6.5 About town: ethnicity and urban mobility

Although the sample of households is too small to make any definitive statement on the differences in household activity patterns as between migrant and indigenous local communities, the data appear to indicate that the migrant community is more mobile within the urban area than is the indigenous community. The indigenous Ga community of Jamestown appears to be less mobile than the recent migrant community of Nima. Whilst all 20 of the Nima households exhibited significant levels of urban mobility (i.e. at least one member involved in daily travel), seven of the Jamestown households possessed a lower level of urban mobility.

The case of the four member extended Ga household living in Jamestown. Lateness or delay does not affect the household because we or I just sit by some friends in front of sea view and sleep in the night. None of us travel: we do not have anywhere to go and do not have money so we do not travel. Travel delay does not affect me because I do not do anything, I just sit and chat. These days there is nothing to be done so it is even difficult to get money for transport. Only God knows how we are able to cater for ourselves and the children.

The case of the six member female headed Ga household living in Jamestown. (On who travels most.) Aku but she just travels to Mamprobi because we have an Auntie there: Aku has to go because our aunt is quite old and can not handle some things very well. We do not even travel because we have nowhere to go. It doesn't happen to us because we are always at home except when I have to buy something for my business.

Respondents stressed the links between employment and travel and education and travel. The greatest familiarity with mobility is demonstrated in the educational and employment mobility experiences of the urban migrant sample. It can be argued that migrant groups have the necessary mind set for search and travel in the urban context. The two cases of children being educated outside the locality were found within the migrant sample.

The case of the nine member monogamous Basaari household living in Nima. (On who travels most.) My wife and children. My wife because of nature of her trade – she is a fufu (cooked food) seller in Accra Central and the children because they attend school at Nkrumah Circle. Women now need to travel more than men because they are becoming more active economically.

146

The case of the seven member female headed Samiir (Benin) household living in Nima. (On who travels most.) The first son because he attends school at Kaneshie which is quite far.

The case of the seven member monogamous Kotokoli household living in Nima. (Who travels most in your household? Who needs to travel most in your household?) My husband and eldest son. My husband needs to travel most because he trades at Accra Central to earn income for the household's upkeep.

The case of the 18 member monogamous extended Kotokoli household living in Nima. (On who travels most.) My husband who is a driver and my sisters who sell food. We are all economically active – my husband, myself and my sisters.

In both indigenous and migrant communities, there was strong evidence on the economic activity of women and of the mobility requirements which were associated with such economic activity. The majority of economically active women captured by the sample were traders and thus were required to travel to obtain goods and frequently to dispose of them.

The case of the 15 member female headed Ga household living in Jamestown. (Female head of household kenkey (cooked food) seller: Who travels most in your household? Who needs to travel most in your household?) I do. I have too. Yes when I have to go and buy some ingredients. For my business during weekdays and in the mornings.

The case of the nine member polygamous Chamba household living in Nima. (On who travels most.) Women. Women because their activities demand travelling to procure items for their trade.

Thus whilst there is evidence of employment-related travel occurring within the indigenous Ga community, it is a more prominent feature of the migrant household accounts of their travel behaviour. Within Accra, the role of Northern males as night watchmen in the high income residential areas is common knowledge. This pattern was also encountered within our own research, with Nima males also having the most access to bicycles to undertake the lengthy journeys which the antisocial timing of their occupation and the location of their job required. One factor suggesting different attitudes to and different levels of urban mobility between the indigenous community and migrants to Accra is that, whereas migrant households mentioned bicycle ownership and use, indigenous respondents did not. This confirms earlier investigations into the differences in travel and transport culture between these two low income communities (Grieco et al., 1994).

147

The case of the seven member monogamous Safalba household living in Nima. (On transport difficulties.) There are times when it is difficult to get a vehicle to one's destination. However my husband uses the bicycle mostly.

The Ga community has the urban advantage of possessing its family or ancestral homes in Accra, e.g. Jamestown (Kilson, 1974; Apt et al., 1995), whereas migrant groups do not. These ancestral homes are concentrated in particular areas of Accra. Family members have customary rights on ancestral homes and the expansion of population without a compensating expansion in the property base of this community is a factor which may go some way towards explaining the household size and composition found within this community. These arrangements ensure the continued adjacency of relatives and their immediate social contacts and thus lessen the need to travel to perform social functions outside of the community. The Ga localities are seaboard communities and obtain a living from the ocean. For migrants, the picture is very different. Accommodation has to be paid for and thus necessitates a stronger employment base: furthermore, the location of these migrant communities gives no ready access to natural resources on which a livelihood can be constructed. Similarly, although some kin members are to be found within the same urban locality, other kin members are to be found in different urban localities and many kin members are still to be found in the home town. Participation in kin based social functions is a key feature of Ghanaian social organisation, most particularly, funerals and naming ceremonies for children ('outdooring'). In a context where there are strong social pressures to attend such social functions, the geographical separation of kin increases the volume of travel undertaken by kin; thus migrant households undertake a higher volume of social travel than indigenous groups. Evidence on the links between migration and increased travel to meet social responsibilities is not provided by northern migrants alone, for comments from members of Ga communities from the greater Accra region indicate similar social obligations and considerations.

The case of the six member monogamous extended Ga household living in Jamestown. We hardly travel but if there is the need it depends on what we are going to do. If it is a funeral and it is closely related to my mother she will go and vice versa. I always do the work and my mother stays at home.

Clearly, the findings can be viewed as no more than indicative, but it is sufficient to suggest that any investigation of the urban mobility patterns of low income households in the developing context would be well advised to take account of indigenous/migrant differences in the propensity for search and travel.

6.6 Conclusion: household organisation in the developing world – policy considerations

Whilst household structure is significantly different in the developing world to that of the developed world, many of the tools used for policy analysis fail to take such differences into account. For example, the definition of what group of family members constitute a household is no easy business in a context where polygamous marriages are pervasive. Similarly, in a context where it is conventional for the partners to an operative marriage to live in separate accommodations, conventional approaches within household analysis are deficient. Yet another feature of the developing country urban household which falls outside of the scope of the conventional Western approaches is the fluctuations in household size which result from the more open boundaries of family membership. Fostering in Ghana precisely generates such fluctuations in household size. In the case of migrant households even greater fluctuations are likely to result from the role such households play as reception institutions for new migrants from their home areas.

Both the scale of and the fluctuations in household composition between developing and developed households can be expected to have their impact on role definitions and activity patterns. The data collected during this study did not directly attempt to measure the fluctuations in household size and composition: however, this is clearly a possible direction for further research. The data collected did indicate the presence of schooling children in non-parental households and this would seem already to indicate a different pattern of household organisation to that which presently exists in the western context. The cultural flexibility around the restructuring of households in the African context clearly requires further investigation.

Two main findings emerge from the data collected. Firstly, the petty trading structure of Ghana enables women of the household both to trade and to act as domestic 'anchors'. The acceptance of doorstep trading is key in this arrangement. The performance of this economic role is buttressed by the existence of ancestral homes and multigenerational living arrangements. Secondly, children are central to the domestic and economic organisation of the household. Children play a significant role in ensuring the continuous presence of a family member in the home and frequently substitute for adults in this capacity. The school shift system appears to make a major contribution to children's ability to perform this function. Whereas in the developed context children are typically viewed as a domestic responsibility, in the developing context children are frequently viewed as domestic resources. Correspondingly, children play a central role in refuse disposal including the disposal of human excrement. The consequent health and environmental dangers attending this practice require further research.

In conclusion, it is readily seen that existing deficiencies in transport services and infrastructural provision impact upon the time budgets of children, especially girl children, with negative consequences for their access to education. It is now widely believed that restrictions on the education of girl children have serious negative consequences for economic growth and development. Transforming the activity patterns of Ghana's children may prove as important as the construction of schools and other facilities in finding a robust path to social and economic development.

Gye Nyame
(jee nyah MAY)
Literally means, 'only God',
suggesting that the gods, not
humans, make important
decisions.

7 Stepping in and losing out: Bread winning and educational loss amongst Ghana's school age girls

Vida Asomaning, Margaret Grieco, Yaw Dankwa and Nana Apt

7.1 Time, task and educational loss: the economic life of Ghanaian girls

A woman's work is never done: and, correspondingly, girls' tasks are never ending. This chapter focuses on the consequences of family labour requirements for girls' education. It examines the contribution that transport organisation makes to this educational loss. An understanding of the constraints on girls' time is of major consequence for educational policy in a context where the low enrolment of girls is a major policy issue. Long and unreliable waiting times have substantial impact on household organisation, most particularly on the scheduling and activities of school age girls. The labour of school age girls is used to compensate for the time lost by the trader when using the transport system, with clear and obvious negative effects on the education of girls. Recent studies of primary education in Ghana reveal that a high percentage of Ghanaian girls disappear from the classroom in their primary school years. These girls do not return to the schoolroom. In Ghana, girls are more likely to drop out of school than are boys. Previous understandings of these gender disparities in primary education participation rates have assumed that girls leaving the schoolroom are simply absorbed into the performance of household tasks within the family. This chapter, in contrast, explores the employment pressures and occupational training processes, the social expectation and the survival needs which result in girl children leaving the Ghanaian schoolroom. It argues that the pressures to pursue gainful employment, especially in respect of trading, fall upon the shoulders of the Ghanaian girl child more heavily and earlier than they fall upon her brother. It then suggests alternative approaches to education which better fit with the life of the working girl child.

Plate 9: Child's play: girl with head load

7.2   Home based learning? Family labour and travel flexibility

The use of family labour is important in providing traders with flexibility in making travel arrangements and organising transport. Such flexibility is of great importance in a context where the stocking or restocking of businesses cannot be accomplished from a distance by reordering goods through the mail or by phone and where the delivery of goods by wholesalers to small traders is not a routine arrangement. The stocking and restocking of the business involves the trader him- or herself in making the journey to the wholesalers or other points of purchase. Our materials show a strong pattern of the use of girl child labour in operating petty trading outlets whilst their elders engage in the purchasing of the goods for sale, a finding which fits with other materials collected in Ghana on the early occupational socialisation of girls (Sowa, 1994). There are a number of family help patterns which emerge from our respondents' accounts of their arrangements for ensuring that their businesses keep trading whilst they travel to Accra to purchase the goods for stocking it:

* mother/daughter pattern, in which the daughter is often a schoolgirl;
* mother/son pattern, where son is a schoolboy;
* daughter/mother where both are adults;
* adult siblings;
* in-laws.

In considering these different arrangements, it is important to note that the family can provide the trader with considerable flexibility in her travel arrangements. This is an important consideration in a context where many traders are making several trips a week into Accra to restock and some traders make the journey every day. There are, however, some tensions in these arrangements which have to be considered: for example, the youth of a school age daughter allows a mother to direct the activity of her offspring and ensure that the business is covered. However, precisely the youth of the daughter may generate problems in ensuring that the customers get the correct service so as to remain loyal. Both the age of the helper and the relationship of the helper/s to the trader have their implications for the trader's travel flexibility and consequently for the trader's transport choices. Although there is evidence of male support, the predominant pattern appears to be that of female support.

Girls are socialised into the trading occupation as early as primary school age in Ghana. Two patterns of occupational socialisation are evident: a) girls remain in school but assist with trading after school or take occasional leave from school when necessary; and b) girls leave school to assist their mothers and other female relatives in trading on a full time basis.

Female trader in yam at Madina. The trader's daughter sells the goods in her absence; the girl runs shift at school so the trader makes sure her going to Accra coincides with her morning shift. The trader does not feel the need to hurry back because the daughter is mature enough to handle the goods in the mother's absence.

Female trader in vegetable oil at Abeka. She leaves the stall in the hands of her daughter who is a school girl. When daughter goes to school she does not make any special arrangements – 'so in that case all that I do is I leave the house early enough so that by 8.00 a.m. I am at the station and then the cars leave immediately they get there.'

Female trader in yam and plantain at Madina. The shop is catered for by my daughter who goes to school on shift.

Female trader in rice, provisions, canned minerals at Madina. I arrange with my daughter to keep the shop when she comes back from school.

Female trader in rice, provisions and soap at Madina. This trader started trading with her mother at about 12 years of age; they still trade together. The daughter is now 32 years of age.

Female trader in rice, gari, yam at Teshie. This trader started trading at ten years of age. She began with fish and turned to rice. She was selling fish with her mother and now she is selling rice on her own. Now her sister assists her in her trading business by taking care of the stand while she goes to purchase new stock.

Female trader in vegetables at Abeka. Respondent has been trading since she was eight years old.

There is a clear pattern of occupational succession in the trading sector of Ghana where mothers in their middle years typically hand over their trading business to their adult daughters (Sawyerr, 1976; Apt and Katila, 1994) such daughters typically having spent some time supporting their mothers in their trading activity before this business handover. Subsequent to such business handovers, mothers typically continue to trade on their own but at a lower level of activity and on a smaller capital base. From the evidence collected here, it is clear they also continue to act as support for their daughters in their trading activities. Three generations are, thus, frequently involved in the trading exchange of task and time between household members.

Male trader in rice only at Mallam-Atta. My mother keeps the shop.

Female trader in plantain, fish, tomatoes, spices, oil at Burma Camp. When she is in town her mother and sister are in the stand. Any time she leaves to buy her goods she wants to return quickly; thus she takes the taxis as mentioned.

Female trader in rice, groundnut, beans, oil at Teshie. The mother stays behind and sometimes she stays when her mother goes. These arrangements don't affect her decision on transport; she is in no hurry.

Female trader in vegetables in Abeka. Mother takes over the stall when she is away buying wares for the stall.

Female trader in textbooks and stationery at Accra Central. My mother or sister takes over the sales whilst I am purchasing the wholesale products.

Sisters are also a key component of the time and task support system. The comments of some of the respondents indicate that the support provided is not solely that of adult sisters, but school age sisters are called in to assist their trading elders. The larger household size and the greater number of siblings found in the Ghanaian family as compared with Western structures is clearly playing its part in enabling the adaptation of the small entrepreneurial community to transport difficulties in the developing context.

Female trader in yam at Burma Camp. Her sister's daughter sells her yams while she is gone. She likes to come back quickly but the cost does not change for her.

Female trader in provisions at Madina. Her small sister takes charge of the store. She never gets worried and therefore takes normal transport.

Female trader in provisions at Malata. A younger sister stays in the stall. The trader manages to go by the taxi when she is restocking.

Female trader in cloth at Makola. My younger sister takes over whilst I am out to buy the goods wholesale.

There is some evidence of schoolboys assisting in the trading activities of their parents: however, this is the exception rather than the rule in terms of respondents' comments. Brothers are also mentioned as a source of support to traders in organising the restocking of their outlets: however, this is mentioned much less frequently than mothers, daughters or sisters. Evidence from every quarter indicates that the task burdens of the African girl child are substantially greater than those of her brother.

157

Female trader in provisions at New Town. I ask my son who is a schoolboy to keep the shop whenever I go shopping; when he is supposed to go to school in the morning I wait until he comes back before I go shopping.

Female trader in provisions and silver pans at Madina. I have brother who normally keeps the shop when I go shopping in Accra Central.

Female trader in rice, soap, provisions at Madina. I have a brother who keeps the shop whenever I am in town buying goods.

Male trader in rice, sugar, flour at Madina. I have a brother who keeps the shop when I am away purchasing wholesale products.

Female trader in oil, onions, paste, ginger, spices at Madina. Her brother sells her goods while she is gone.

As we saw in Chapters 1 and 6, in the Ghanaian context it cannot simply be assumed that spouses share economic responsibilities. Traditionally within Akan culture, women had separate property rights and entitlements, with husband and wife often possessing their own separate houses (Apt, 1995). Similarly within Ga culture, husband and wife frequently inhabited separate residences. These customary arrangements around separate property persist in the trading culture of Ghana. Twumasi (1979), in his study of women traders in Ghana, discovered that most of his sample were married by customary rite but were living alone with their children. On the evidence collected to date, sharing a business with a spouse is the exception rather than the rule. Flexibility as between spouses is less frequent than flexibility as between female family members.

Male trader in soap, rice, cooking oil at Nima. I arrange with my wife who manages the store until I come back from town.

Female trader in cloth, shoes, jewellery, hair goods at Madina. Her husband manages the stall while she is gone; there is no special arrangement; they work together; sometimes she goes to town and sometimes he goes to town. It does not affect the transport at all; she is in no hurry since they work together.

Female trader in stationery and provisions at Burma Camp. Sometimes her husband buys her goods when she goes to town her sister stays to sell her goods. She takes the tro-tro; she doesn't feel she has to return quickly because her sister is there.

Female trader in rice, flour, sugar, oil, tinned fish at Malata. My small child and at times my husband manage the store in my absence.

Male trader in building materials/ cement at Accra Central. My wife takes over the sales in my absence to buy the goods at the wholesale point.

There is some evidence of in-law involvement in helping traders to provide the necessary cover for their retail outlets when absent because of the requirements of restocking: however, this is relatively infrequent in the case of our sample. The preference for relying on own blood kin increases the burden upon own daughters and girl folk: the use of daughters as trading 'lieutenants' is not simply to be explained in terms of the unavailability of other labour but is to be understood in terms of training and equipping a daughter for the economic and domestic financial responsibilities of adult life. Traders cannot simply rely on any member of their family to take care of their retail outlet whilst they are in Accra obtaining stock. Choosing the right member of the family to take over is a salient consideration. However, the appropriateness of replacement labour is primarily determined by the established customary roles.

Female trader in flour and rice at Nima. I arrange with a relative who keeps the shop until I return from town. The choice of members of the family to staff my stalls depends on how trustworthy that person is; I do not just pick anybody

For those who do not have female kin to train, support or depend upon, the absence of such family proxies means reduced travel flexibility and the closing of their shop or the hiring of help. The hiring of labour and the closing of shops have clear consequences for the profit margins of the small businesses which characterise trading in Ghana.

Female trader in soap and provisions at Mallam-Atta. I close the shop since I don't have anybody to care for it.

Female trader in provisions at Madina. Since all my family members are students and workers I close the shop.

Female trader in provisions at Madina. I close my shop because I don't have a helper.

Female trader in soft drink at Accra Central. I buy goods and then go in for the transport to convey them to the sales point. I make no arrangement with family members, but rather with other people who are paid after the services. I usually make my trips in the morning to

159

buy the goods. I normally go in for a higher quality transport (taxi) to convey the goods so I do not face any problem with that.

Nevertheless, for some traders the use of family members to tend the store does not come without its constraints and costs. Where traders try to confer upon their daughters both the benefits of school and learning their trade, scheduling journeys can generate substantial time pressures. The desire to provide girl children with both paths of opportunity leads, for some traders, to the adoption of higher cost, more reliable and swifter forms of transport.

> *Female trader in oil, onion, paste, ginger, spice at Madina.* Yes, she wants to hurry to take over selling herself (from her brother); she comes quickly because of shortages; thus she would pay more for faster transport.

> *Female trader in plantain, fish, tomatoes, spices, oil at Burma Camp.* When she is in town her mother and sister are in the stand. anytime she leaves to buy her goods she wants to return quickly; thus she takes the taxis as mentioned.

For others, however, family labour is used primarily because it provides a considerable degree of flexibility where other activities are deemed to be less important. In some households, school for girls is viewed as a diversion from the real business of life: children, trading and the upkeep of the household.

> *Female trader in rice, provisions, canned minerals at Nima.* This does not affect my decision on the type of transport I take because my daughter takes very good care of my shop.

Viewed from an activity approach, the travel patterns of traders in a transport context where short journeys can take a lengthy time require considerable coordination at the household level, most particularly coordination between school age girls and adult female traders of the same household. A responsibility for household synchronisation is part of the socialisation of the girl child in Africa. Women grow up depending on the help of their female kin in organising their dual worlds.

7.3   Girls' own stories: trading pressures on their time

In Ghana a high percentage of girls disappear from the classroom in their primary school years (UNICEF, 1993). Girls' departure from the school room is connected with ensuring the early exposure of girls to work discipline in a nation where women are the predominant source of household income and economic support (Hyde, 1993). The occupational socialisation of girls is more important than that of boys and thus takes place earlier and more systematically (Sowa, 1994).

Gross enrolment rates for primary school in Ghana were 83.5 per cent in 1991/2, 45.5 per cent of which was female. Since 1991, however, local authorities and communities have introduced new fees, as part of cost recovery efforts, which have had a dramatic effect in reducing new entrants to Primary 1 and increasing the rate of drop out at higher grades (UNICEF, 1993/4). The overall percentage of girls enrolled in primary schools has remained steady since 1989/90. However, the overall percentage of children dropping out of school was higher for girls (8 per cent) than boys (6 per cent) in 1992. Disaggregating the existing data by regions reveals an even more dramatic level of gender inequality. The variation between the south and the north of the country is marked, for whereas in Accra, the major urban centre of the south, only 4 per cent of girls dropped out of primary school, the corresponding figure in the north in 1992 was 20 per cent. Moreover, enrolment figures by sex and grades in basic and senior secondary education show that the percentage of the enrolled which is female gets progressively lower at each level (UNICEF, 1993/4). Regional disparities and disparities within regions, and even within districts, in respect of enrolment are considerable. Whereas in the Greater Accra and Central Regions, the gross enrolment rate is over 95 per cent (including private schools) it is only 43 per cent in the Upper East Region. Gender disparities are greater in those regions with low enrolment rates: the three northern regions have a combined girls' participation rate of under 40 per cent as compared with the national average of 66 per cent. The evidence is clear: northern girls are more likely to be absent from the classroom than their northern brothers and more likely to be absent than their southern counterparts.

It is the pressure on young Ghanaian girls to become wage earners which explains their disappearance from the schoolroom. As Chapter 4 signalled, there is a growing body of material in related areas which indicates the extensive involvement of the girl child in income earning whilst in her primary school years. Research conducted by Apt, Blavo and Opoku (1992) examined the experiences of street children. Girls gave accounts of being placed with both kin and non-kin households as domestic labour in their primary school years. Girls from rural households were placed with urban families as domestic labour. Local informants readily provide examples of households which contain girl servants, with such servants sometimes being kin to their employers (Apt, 1994). The true statistics on the use of girl children are socially disguised by the widespread practice of fostering out children. As we have already seen in Chapter 6, 'fostered' may mean little more than food and shelter in exchange for labour with no provision being made for attendance at school (Goody, 1978). Apt et al.

161

(1992) identified a range of occupations in which primary school age children were engaged: load carrying, iced water selling, petty trading, guarding goods and property, child minding.

A second source of evidence on why young Ghanaian girls depart the schoolroom, is provided by the Department of Community Development[1] which has, through its routine encounters with women and girls in rural areas, become aware of the trade in rural young girls as house helps in urban areas. Where girls are sent as house helps to urban households, parents receive the payment for their services. Such girls have little or no opportunity for a return to the school room.

In earlier chapters, we reported on the relationship between gender, low income, trading and travel in urban Accra. Our research revealed high levels of girl child employment and migration within the kayayoo occupation. Girls of eight years old reported being sent by their parents from the rural areas of the north to Accra to work as porters where they live with older sisters, relatives or other home town contacts. In the previous section, the reliance of female traders on the family labour of school aged girls emerged as a widespread pattern. What emerges from these separate sources of evidence is that girls are not removed from the schoolroom simply because of the costs of education but rather are taken away to generate the income for family survival. Girls' education bears a large opportunity cost.

In order to provide insight into the household processes which result in the early occupational socialisation of girls and their corresponding removal from the schoolroom, ten case studies of working girl children were selected from our gender, trade and transport research. In addition, as the research on transport organisation did not directly address the educational issues now being considered, ten new case studies of girls who were working on the street were assembled. Ten girl child workers between the ages of eight and 12 were randomly selected in trading areas of urban Accra and directly interviewed about the reasons for their non-attendance at school and about their future educational prospects. These 20 case studies have been brought together and organised into occupational groups in order to provide important contextual detail on the educational/occupational circumstances of Ghana's working girls.

Out of school, into work: girl kayayoos

Case 1: School, an uninteresting experience: the perspective of a seven year old

She is from Savelegu in the North, is ten years old and is a kayayoo in the Cocoa Marketing Board area. She left school at seven years old because:

To me going to school was very boring, I preferred to pick colanut instead.

She left school to engage in income earning activities. She has no brothers. Of her two sisters one finished Class Six at 12 years old and one stopped school at Class One. On her employment as a kayayoo and upon the need for welfare intervention, she remarks:

The loads that we carry are sometimes too heavy for us and thus we needed some help to enable us to survive.

Case 2: Sent from the far North to Accra: an eight year old kayayoo

She is eight years old from Wa in the North. She is of Wala ethnicity. She works at the Tema station area and left school at seven because:

Daddy was not too prepared to pay for my schooling and so I stopped.

Within a year of leaving school in the North she was sent to Accra to work as a kayayoo. She has no expectation of ever returning to school:

I have no hope of going back to school because I cannot stop my trading activity since it is my only source of income.

She has one brother who is at the moment ten years of age and in Class Four at Wa and one sister who is three years old and thus too young to go to school.

Case 3: Binto, an eight year old head load porter

Binto is eight years old and has lost the hair from the middle of her head through load carrying. She is from Savelegu and works with her elder sister as a kayayoo. She does not know who paid for her journey from Savelegu to Accra but the decision that she should become a head load porter was that of her mother and her sister. She has been head load carrying for four months. She sleeps with her sister in a large wooden shed with many other women and children amongst whom are several kayayoos of her own age group. Binto has little autonomy in respect of whether she works as a porter or how she works as a porter.

No its my sister who tells me what to do ... I can't tell (about the management of her money) because I am not old in the business to know. I give it to my elder sister who takes part to pay for my susu and adashie[2] contributions. My sister decides how much should be saved and handles all money matters. I can't tell how much is saved;

163

but maybe my sister knows better. It is my sister who handles the money so she knows. My sister normally buys some dresses and sandals for me and keeps the rest.

Binto knows that money and goods are sent back to her mother from her earnings but she does not know how much, what or how often.

I can't tell but I do hear my sister sending parcels through people who visit from our village to mother. I can't say how regular it goes but I know she sometimes sends parcels home.

Binto has no direct contact with her mother either physical or written.

It's my elder sister who does that but my mother occasionally sends her regards/greetings to me through these people who visit Accra and also the migrants into the business.

Binto has been told there is no choice but to work as a kayayoo.

There is no other work my sister tells me, she says this kaya work is more lucrative.

How does Binto feel about her job and her future?

No I do not derive any satisfaction (from the job). It is a difficult task. But I enjoy being with my sister in Accra. Maybe upon return home she would buy something big and precious for me.
Yes the negative sides are that I have lost contact with my biological parents and siblings. I am the last born child of my mother's eight children. I also have to wake up very early to start work. The positive side is that my elder sister buys clothes for me.
My wish is to return home and join my family. Yes I am anxious to return home as soon as my sister releases me to go and I have any reliable person to take me along.

Binto's health has been badly affected by the job.

I have fallen sick three times since I started doing this work. My sister buys some drugs for me to take from the chemist. Normally I feel very cold, have a warm body temperature and headaches. I can't tell but for me it's mostly headaches. The others we live with, some take their children to the clinic when the sickness is serious but mostly they also buy from the drugstores to treat themselves and their children. Yes the major problem is my inability to have enough relaxation. And forcing myself to carry very heavy loads; even when I am tired.

Case 4: Self-financing education: the Northern cola nut picker, aged 9

She is now ten years old, she is from the north and she works in the Makola market area of Accra as a kayayoo. She left school at nine years old because of the financial costs. Until she was nine her education was paid for by herself and her mother. She picked cola nuts for sale in order to obtain the fees necessary for her education. She has no intention of returning to the schoolroom because:

> There is no money in the classroom.

Having struggled to meet the cost of schooling, having failed, having migrated without parental company and having entered at such a young age such an arduous occupation, this child is no longer motivated to participate in formal education. She has two brothers neither of whom went to school, both of whom are now in Accra but she does not know where. She has two sisters neither of whom are school age.

Her earnings are managed for her by an older kayayoo who has taken her 'as her sister'. She would be interested in participating in evening classes for working girl children provided that she does not have to pay anything.

> So far as I won't pay any money I think it will help me very much.

Case 5: Heavily loaded and far from home: an 11 year old female porter

An 11 year old girl kayayoo gave us an account of her life. She is a Kotokoli from Northern Togo whose parents now live in Jasikan in the Volta area. She operates as a porter at the foodstuff market and was 'invited' to Accra by her sister who is herself a kayayoo. She lives with her sister in a shed at the back of the market. They share this accommodation with eight other kayayoos. Her total earnings for a day are between 2,000–2,500 cedis,[3] out of this the girl kayayoo saved an amount of between 1,500 to 2,000 cedis a day and this money is kept by her sister. For a normal carrying trip she received between 50–100 cedis. Asked what she intends using the money she is saving for she replied she will use it for personal items such as clothes, footwear, etc. She had been in Accra in order to do this job for only three months at the time of interview and intended staying for only three more months. Then she wished to return to her parents in Jasikan.

Case 6: Money not education: the philosophy of the 12 year old kayayoo

She is 12 years old, comes from Sandema in the North and works as a kayayoo in the Agbogbloshie market area. She left school at eight because:

I lost interest in school, I just wanted to make money.

She has no brothers and one sister 'who has never been to school although she is ten years old'. She requests that any help given to her be monetary and not in the form of education.

Case 7: The refugee from the war zone⁴: a 12 year old kayayoo

She is aged 12 and comes from the northern region. She left school at 12 years old and in Class Five to come to Accra as a kayayoo. She carries loads in the Railway Station area. She does not consider herself as really having left school:

I haven't really left school, I fled from the war torn zone and now do not feel like going back.

She has one sister who is not of school age and six brothers all of whom are at school apart from the eldest, who is 20 years old and learning to be a fitter. She intends going back to school:

I know it (education) helps one in everything one does.

She would like to have the opportunity to attend evening classes:

It will help me a lot.

She reports that she moved to Accra with three of her female friends, two of whom stopped school at Class Three and one of whom has never been to school. On her present life, she has this to say:

It has been a hard time living in Accra.

Case 8: Foster child or forced porter? The shaping of occupational decisions

A 13 year old girl from Savelegu near Tamale had no say in the decision which resulted in her entering the occupation of head load porter.

It was my paternal cousin's decision (that I should become a porter). I moved in to live with her after her (i.e. cousin) aged mother who was fostering me decided there was not much activities at her home and so I should join her daughter (i.e. cousin) who is a petty trader and sells scarves (head gear), veils, blouses (i.e. tops) and other petty items in some of the towns and villages in and around Tamale (i.e. Walewale, Yendi, Tanule, etc).

This cousin brought the then 12 year old girl to Accra to enter the kaya business as a way of generating enough working capital to promote her cousin's business. She lives in overcrowded accommodation in Tudu with her cousin's friend and in the company of her girls and women from her home region. Her elder sister had preceded her in the kayayoo business but was now married and back in the North. Her mother had ten children of whom only one had been to school. She saves through the susu system and also with a group of colleagues. She regularly sends money to her cousin in the north for the financing of her business and also sends money to the paternal aunt who fostered her.

> I regularly send part to my cousin at home and use the remaining amount to buy my personal belongings. This is because my cousin also told me I could buy those items I feel will be pressing when I am married in the future which I do. I also send occasional gifts to my paternal aunt (i.e. cousin's mother). I even sent her 4,000 cedis less than a month ago now.

This kayayoo does not seem to have considered the option of keeping her earnings solely for her own use but views her cousin as entitled to a share of her earnings. This understanding of the situation as acceptable is no doubt supported by the frequent visits her cousin makes to Accra to collect monies and impart news of home. Despite the proportion of her income taken by her cousin, this kayayoo views her time in Accra as an opportunity to earn sufficient income to finance her marriage and a career in petty trading. She expects to return home in the next year and start trading in the villages. She expressed her intention of trying to prevent her juniors from entering the kayayoo trade:

> The work is too tedious; and again it is only people who have not been to school, who have dropped out of school, who engage in this business. I shall do my best to assist other younger relatives and future children and generations to abstain from the job (if I ever have enough income to do so).

Case 9: Earning to learn, the hope of a better occupation in the future

A 15 year old Kotokoli girl who worked as a kayayoo in the Makola market area had very definite ideas about what to do with her earnings. She is saving so that she can get enough money to buy a sewing machine and go back to Jasikan to her mother to learn how to sew. Her mother (40 years old) sells kola nuts and she thinks that her mother can afford to pay the cost of her seamstress apprenticeship out of this trading activity. She saves 200–300 cedis daily with the 'susu collector'[5] and saves 400 or 500 cedis daily on her own. This kayayoo worked in Accra, travelled back to

Jasikan and returned to the kayayoo trade in Accra. She and her sister entered the kayayoo trade eight months previously.

Case 10: Sponsored to work, family investment in the kayayoo trade

A 16 year old kayayoo from Tamale in the north discussed the financing of her journey from Tamale to Accra in order to undertake the kayayoo trade. She and her mother financed the journey between them. It was her understanding that the journeys from the north to Accra were self-financed for most of the adults whereas most of the journeys to employment of the young kayayoos were financed by their parents or distant relations. She believes that the majority of kayayoos are between ten and 45 years.

She saves with the susu collector and also in a group with her colleagues:

> I save on daily basis of 500 cedis with the susu collector and 300 cedis on a monthly basis with ten colleagues of mine.

Some of these savings are sent home to her mother, some of her savings are reserved for the purchase of the goods which she must take into marriage:

> I send at least 5,000 cedis monthly to my old lady (i.e. mother). But when I have more than enough, I send it earlier or even twice in the month. I buy certain valuable items such as wax prints, ceramic bowls, sauce pans and other household items. To keep me in readiness for marriage in the future.

Her mother in Tamale sends her 'junior sister' down to Accra to discuss financial issues with this kayayoo and to carry some of the household items which have been purchased back home. She views the kayayoo trade as affording a decent income but wishes to give it up in one year's time when she hopes to return home, marry and engage in petty trading. She is clear about the negative aspects of being kayayoo but sees it as a way of acquiring the necessary income to finance a more pleasant career.

Out of school, into work: housegirls and petty traders

Case 11: The Teshie housegirl

At the time of interview, the respondent was 21 years old and earned her living as a bicycle repairer and hirer. Although a resident of Accra, she is from the northern community living in Nima – a community where northern practices are prevalent (Grieco, Turner and Kwakye, 1994). It was in the course of her account of how she learnt to ride a bicycle that the fact that she had been employed as a house girl at 13 years old emerged.

> I served as a house girl with this nuclear[6] family; caring for their younger child and other household duties.

In the course of this employment, the house girl was surreptitiously able to learn to ride by using the cycle belonging to the daughter of the family. Indeed, her access to this bicycle provided her with the knowledge base necessary for a new direction for future employment,

> It happened that, one day while my mistress was away at work her daughter's (bicycle) broke down while she was using it. A part in the bicycle called the centre pin got broken and I used some part called the Allen key to repair it. For the second time another part ... came off and was missing. So I used an empty milk container to design a similar part to fit it into the bicycle and she was able to use it perfectly. Since then I gained confidence in technical skills and management of the bicycle, so I started using my mistress's daughter's bicycle anytime they were away at work.

The respondent does not tell us whether she had been employed as a house girl before working for this nuclear family: she does tell us she returned to her parents after. She explains that her parents were not favourable towards her cycling in the first instance as they viewed it as interfering with her income earning,

> Though initially, they did not encourage my riding, especially my mother for the fact that she wanted me to assist her sell her cooked food. But later they both encouraged me to ride, especially my father, who now even plans to apprentice me to bicycle/motor trade to enable me to polish up my skills. My mother too later agreed because I use the bicycle to run errands for her to aid her prepare her cooked food for sale.

This girl was able to set up as a bicycle repairer/hirer when she was provided with the capital to purchase a bicycle as a reward for carrying a critically ill person on her back to hospital. From the interview data, it is clear that this is a highly intelligent girl who was not only deprived of schooling but commenced employment earlier than is legally permitted by the laws of Ghana.

Case 12: Household servant and trader's assistant: 12 years old in Nima

An interview was conducted with a 55 year old female trader who, although married, lived separately from her husband[7] with her five children and her domestic servant of 12. All five children were at school. The trader sells soaps, sugar, teabags, etc. The trader is of northern ethnicity and although we do not have direct information on the ethnicity of the 12 year old girl, it seems probable that she too is northern. The 12 year old girl servant has the dual responsibility of attending to the running of the home and of hawking her employer's wares around Nima and Maamobi everyday. The trader, who pays the school fees for her five children, has recruited the cheapest form of reliable labour in the 12 year old female servant.

Case 13: Nuniah, the grand-daughter househelp

Nuniah is 14 years, has no education whatsoever and serves as a house help to her grandmother, Ramatu, who is a trader in rice and raw beans at the Nima local daily market. Ramatu herself is 45 years old and is the head of her family. She lives as a lodger in a large extended polygamous household in Nima with her two school age children and her 14 year old housegirl/ granddaughter. The two school age children are both girls and enrolled in school at Kanda. The oldest is 14 and thus ages with her house girl niece, the youngest is ten.

Case 14: The harassed vegetable trader: seven years old in Accra

She is seven years old, she is Fanti in ethnicity and she sells vegetables in the Railway Station area of Accra for a living. She is very worried about the way the city guards molest the traders and about two months ago her wares were seized from her by the guards. She left school at seven years old because:

> There was no money to pay my fees.

She has no brothers. Of her three sisters, the eldest sister went up to middle school, the sister below her stopped at Class Six and the sister below her stopped at Class Two.

Case 15: Helping my mother, the pressure to earn: eight year old fruit seller

She is eight years old and left school at six after completing Class One. She works as a fruit seller at Makola market. She is Ga and comes from Accra. She left school because:

> I didn't like sitting in the classroom because I felt it was boring. To crown it all sometimes the money I was given for transport and food wasn't enough and I had to walk all the way to Bubuashie and back.

Her school fees were paid by her mother:

> Mum (paid the school fees), because daddy does not work and so he claims he has no money for me.

She has one sister not of school age and six brothers, four of whom are of school age and are enrolled, with the eldest brother presently training to be a fitter. These brothers contribute towards their school fees by running errands and doing some small trading. She has no intention of going back to school:

> It was boring and I wouldn't like to stop my trading because this gives me money to help my mother. She is also a petty trader.

On the prospect of attending evening classes, this young trader did not feel she would be able to afford the time:

> I continue with my trading activities at home in the evening and thus would not get time for any classes. These monies are very important to us.

Her contribution to family income is substantial in Ghanaian terms:

> Most of the money I earn goes to my mother, I earn between 18,000–22,000 cedis per month.

On the problems of schooling when poor, she had this to say:

> Schooling is good but if you do not have money it is very difficult and sometimes it makes me unhappy that even when I was sitting in the classroom I could not concentrate. I envy those who came to school with packed foods and well dressed.

Case 16: The sweet seller: nine years old and no clothes for education

She is now ten years old, lives in Accra with her parents, is of Ga ethnicity and sells sweets at Kwame Nkrumah circle.[8] She left school at nine years of age because:

> Money was the problem, my school uniform was torn and there was no one to buy me one and it was difficult to go to school in such a state, friends made fun of me.

Her sisters and brothers are too young to be at school. On her own educational ambitions, she is realistic about her ability to pay but

171

nevertheless she has not lost interest in education. Were evening classes to be available to girl workers then she would like to attend:

If classes are free, only in that case then I would like to be part of it.

Case 17: The iced water seller: aged ten

She is ten years old, lives with her parents in Abeka, Accra and works in the same area selling iced water. She dropped out of school at nine; one of her sisters left school at 14 years, the other stopped at age 11 in Class Five. Her brother is still in school at Class Four. She was taken out of school because she 'was not doing well' there and her 'mother felt she was just wasting her money'. Despite her circumstances she has nevertheless retained an interest in education and would like to benefit from any classes that are organised for street girls. Her concern is more with esteem than literacy or numeracy:

I would go to any classes that are organised for street girls because I want to be a lady.

Case 18: Boys' education, a legitimate claim on the male purse

She is 11 years old, she is from the northern region, lives in Nima and works as a trader in food items in central Accra. She left school at the age of nine in Class Three.

I stopped school because I wanted enough time to do my trading activities.

She has three sisters only one of whom is of school age: this sister is nine years old and is presently still at school. She also has a brother of the same age who is also at school. When she was at school, her fees were paid by her mother and herself. Her brother's fees are paid, however, by her father, mother and brother. Her girl friends also stopped school at Classes Three and Four respectively.

Despite having contributed to the payment of her own school fees in the past, she has no intention of returning to school:

At the moment, I don't have any interest in school.

Even were evening classes to be offered, she would not be interested in attending:

It will be wasting my time.

Her main focus is how to succeed in trade:

> Because I am very young, I need to struggle with the older ones in order to survive.

In school/into work: schooling and working at the same time.

Case 19: Selling bread, a schoolgirl's contribution to household income

Maria is the daughter and granddaughter in a large northern polygamous extended household. She is a senior secondary school student at Kanda: however, after school she also works as a trader selling bread in order to supplement the household income.

Case 20: Measure for measure, a schoolgirl's petty trading in milk

A young female cyclist from Nima told of the way in which she financed learning to ride a bicycle and how she finances the use of a bicycle for her leisure:

> I learnt to ride at age 11 years. I learnt to ride a bicycle just in Nima, Accra. As part of my labour activities after school, I sell Nido powdered milk in bits to children in the neighbourhood (Nima). I make profits of about 300 cedis on each container I finish selling – out of this amount of profit I set aside 20 cedis to hire the bicycle to learn to ride. This is how I initially financed my riding.

There are issues which emerge repeatedly in the course of respondents' accounts of their entry into work: the existence of little autonomy in occupational choice or timing of commencement, the obligation to donate or remit a substantial part of income to parents and other senior relatives, the separation of children from parents at an early age. The next section synthesises the evidence from these various case studies, identifies the key themes emerging and analyses the consequences of such evidence.

7.4   Contributing to family survival: the pressures on girls to earn

The case studies illustrate that the early occupational socialisation of girls has negative consequences for their educational attainment. Girls are routinely present in the workplace. The occupational socialisation of girls takes place very early indeed. Girl children as young as seven years old have a clear sense of their earning responsibilities, both in respect of meeting their own survival needs and those of their families (Case 3). The

173

language used by these girl children to describe the pressures which lead them to seek a means of livelihood so young is indicative:

There is no money in the classroom.

There is clearly a relationship between the early occupational socialisation of females and the non-enrolment in or the drop out of girl children from formal education (Hyde, 1993). Girl children are taking on the full set of occupational tasks performed by adult women whilst still in their primary school years. The expectation that young girls will participate in economic activities is an entrenched cultural norm which is consistent with the much remarked upon predominance of women in the trading structure of Ghana. The strength of women's economic role as traders in Ghana has knock-on effects for the education of girl children, as a lengthy formal education is not viewed as necessary for participation in this task (Hyde, 1993; Robertson, 1984). Educational capital is not viewed as leading to enhanced earnings: teachers, on account of their low salaries and poor conditions, are often viewed as possessing a low status (Apt and Grieco, 1994a). Women's responsibility to earn works against girls being provided with the opportunity to school. Both the structure of the Ghanaian family and the division of economic responsibilities associated with this family structure play an important part in determining the restricted access of girl children to formal education.

In the majority of cases presented here, the working girl children have had an experience of formal education. Earning in order to contribute to the financing of their own education is a common experience on the part of Ghana's girl working children: however, such earning is rarely sufficient when undertaken on a part-time basis to provide them with the necessary capital for education. Within our case studies, there are a number of examples of girls who started out trying to finance their schooling through their own earnings but who failed in their attempt. Ironically, many of these working girls are remitting substantial amounts of income to their parental homes which is used to finance the education of their brothers (Case 2). As Peil (1995) notes, in Ghana in the 1980s households that could not afford to send all their children to school continued to send boys and, on our case evidence, working girl children helped to finance this preferencing of male children in the educational stakes. The exile of girls from their local areas and parental home appears to be part of a survival strategy which generates and frees resources for the education of males (Case 2). As we saw in Chapters 1 and 6, the economic organisation of the typical Ghanaian family is significantly different to that of the Western household. It is common for fathers and mothers to operate separate households even where a marriage is still operative. Corresponding to such separate households is the institution of largely separate budgets (Robertson, 1977; Hyde, 1993; ODA, 1994).

Peil's statistical evidence, previous research by Robertson (1977) and our own in depth ethnographic evidence indicate that fathers are reluctant to bear the burden of paying for children's education. Even where fathers do contribute towards the education of their children, they are more likely to do so for boys than for girls. Once again girl children's own accounts of why they dropped out of school provide clear awareness of the reluctance of male parents to finance the education of girls (Case 2). In Case 18, for example, the father is contributing to the education of the boy child but not of the girl children. Systematic research is required to establish how extensive such a practice of gender preferencing is.

Why are boys are preferred in the educational race as compared with girls, especially in an economy where the informal trading sector is dominated by female labour? One possible explanation might be that whilst it is the case that most males will not find employment success in the formal sector, those who do find success in the formal sector are more likely to be males than females. Whilst investing in male education does not necessarily produce substantial rewards for the investors, there is nevertheless a prospect that it will. There is an opportunity lottery – but the prizes can only go to males. An alternative perspective is that, given the lesser economic burdens attending the male role in Ghanaian society, the labour of boys is expendable. The opportunity cost of girls' time at school is higher than the opportunity cost of boys' time at school (Hyde, 1993; Robertson, 1984) because girls are culturally defined as key earners in the household. Clearly, girls are not removed from the schoolroom simply because of the costs of education but rather are taken away to generate the income for family survival.

The obligation of girls to earn affects educational experience and attainment in more than one way, it can result in the withdrawal and non-enrolment of girls in school or it leaves them fatigued with a corresponding reduction in their attention in the schoolroom. Reduced attention can result in poor performance and thus to the withdrawal of the girl from the schoolroom. Such a process is compatible with the statistical data collected which shows the gradual withdrawal of girls from the schoolroom as they get older. The pressures to earn generate a situation in which girls are gradually 'cooled out' of the educational structure by the combination of poor performance resulting from fatigue – a poor performance undermining the social justification for remaining within the education system – and the economic calculations they must make as to whether the benefits of education are equal to the cost they must pay for it by their own increased physical effort and earning. Very young girls are 'forced' by their social and cultural circumstances to face this dire and, in many other societies, specifically adult calculus. Children who pay for their own education through their own occupational earnings are likely to assess the benefits and performance characteristics of such education more critically.

175

Ultimately, girl children have little control over whether they attend primary school or not. The survival needs of the household, in a context where women are the key economic agents of the family and their occupational responsibilities commence early, are determining girl child drop out rates. However, girl children themselves internalise the cultural norms which require their physical, emotional and educational sacrifice and frequently present the outcome of this socio-educational cooling out process, i.e. their departure from the schoolroom, as if it was either their own decision or the only possible decision. The deficiencies of the Ghanaian primary school education (Apt and Grieco, 1994a, 1994b) furnish them with a battery of readily available justifications (Case 1, Case 6). Quite what part of the drop out equation is provided by a poor experience of education and what part by the necessity of earning is not clear even from the drop-outs own accounts. Would an improved classroom experience improve the retention rate of girls in education or would the survival pressures and occupational expectations of the society still result in the departure of girls? What is clear is that the majority of girl children have experienced a taste of the disciplinarian, poorly resourced and frequently linguistically unintelligible Ghanaian classroom (Apt and Grieco, 1994a, 1994b)[9] and, as their own accounts graphically demonstrate, find the experience boring, costly and irrelevant. Undoubtedly the experience of education itself helps households produce the compliance of their daughters in entering the arduous world of earning overly early.

Much of the research on child labour has concentrated on the exploitative aspects of the situation[10] (Grootaert and Kanbur, 1995): however, one recurrent message emerging from our case studies is that girls involved in earning view this as a base for social esteem both in terms of their present contribution to their households needs and in terms of their ability to construct a better future. They contrast the social esteem that can be obtained through earning with the lack of esteem they experienced in the education system. Working provides them with greater autonomy than they experienced in the schoolroom, though less than that enjoyed by their senior relatives. They look forward to a future where they will enjoy the increased autonomy that comes with age: however, they also seek in the present to harness part of current earnings to ensure the material quality of that future. For example, a particularly interesting feature of the Teshie housegirl's account of her life (Case 11) is the way in which the working girl child was able to harness the resources of the employing family in order to expand her own skill base. Proximity to a wealthier household opened up her view of what was possible. Not every house girl has the confidence, sharpness or opportunity to make the transition from household drudge to small business woman that our bicycle repairer made: however, the case cautions us against too readily imposing the 'victim' description on the lives of working girls. On the other hand, there are, indeed, cases where these early occupational experiences appear to have produced a strong sense of fatalism in the girl worker (Case 3).

The infrastructural inadequacies of the developing context and the perception of children as household resources promote the use of children for domestic tasks such as water carrying and refuse disposal. Similarly, where much petty trading is conducted from the doorstep of the home, children are also used to protect the home from theft and to ensure that trading continues in the absence of adults by remaining in situ. In the absence of hired child help, these tasks are frequently performed by own girl children. The presence of hired child labour frees own children from these tasks and permits their schooling. Our case studies (Cases 12 and 13) support the understanding that the presence of hired child labour enables own children's school attendance. The attendance of a child at school is frequently dependent upon the availability of another child to perform those household tasks which are culturally deemed to be children's work. Households who wish to school their own children frequently foster children (Case 13) from amongst their own relatives in order to provide a source of such substitute labour. However, some girl children are engaged in the parallel activities of trading and schooling and survive the 'cooling out' process (Cases 19 and 20) despite the pressures and fatigue of earning and its consequences for educational performance.

Northern girls predominate in our case studies of girl workers, most particularly girl workers who are out of school. Certain common features emerge from these cases. There is a clear cultural expectation that young northern girls will be involved in earning. Where these girls are from rural areas, such earning is likely to separate them from their parental homes and from any prospect of schooling; where these girls are of northern ethnicity but originate from urban areas earning and schooling are more easily combined. In the case of northern girls, the separation of child from parents is not deemed abnormal, for as we have seen in Chapter 6, the practice of 'fostering' children out is widespread within Ghana. There is little or no expectation that the fostering out of children weakens the parental claims on the child's affection and it is this social expectation of separation which allows children to be dispatched to the urban area to earn yet remain within the same social and familial context.

The sending of young girls to the south to work is not just a matter of family decision-making and of having family connections which will support and protect the child in the urban location; it is also a matter of financial investment in this particular family human resource. Although rural families in Ghana typically have good access to foodstuffs and the indigenous forms of shelter, they have little access to cash income. Raising sufficient cash income even to pay the fare of the outward travelling girl worker represents a substantial amount of financial effort and organisation. In addition to providing the fare, families sometimes provide the departing girl workers with money to purchase the head pan she will use as part of her portering trade. As we have seen through our case

177

studies, very young girls are being financed by their parents to travel from the north to Accra to undertake employment as kayayoos. These are not runaways but human resources in which the family has made a financial investment in the expectation of receiving in return remittances from the urban area. Girl kayayoos, as we have seen, do not choose their occupation for themselves nor are they generally in the circumstances in which they can decide to leave the occupation for themselves. Their occupation is a family decision; their employment is a family survival strategy; their income is a family resource. The family is operating an economic portfolio with the parent/s in the north being responsible for the provision of the household's housing and the production of foodstuffs whilst the exiled girl children in the south are generating the cash income necessary for, amongst other things, health care, clothing and education.

The income from the earnings of kayayoos is not, however, simply absorbed into the family budget, for part of this income is used to invest in the future of the girl child who earns it. As we saw in Chapter 4, many of these young girls see employment as a kayayoo as a way of getting the goods which are necessary for their marriage together. Typically they talk of obtaining the income necessary to finance their future occupations as seamstresses or traders after marriage. Marriage means children and children are largely supported on the income of women. Gaining access to local gainful employment as a married woman is the social goal to which these girl workers aspire, many expressing the desire to protect their own children from having to enter the occupation of kayayoo. Staying in the classroom does not generate the income necessary for meeting these social goals; rather it precludes the accumulation of the necessary capital to ensure that these goals can be attained.

The girl kayayoo is thus earning to meet the income needs of her family and to obtain the income necessary to meet the status goals of her own future. Recapturing girls caught in this complex social web for the classroom is likely to prove a difficult policy task, for it is a task which requires the unpicking of an elaborate set of interactions between material needs and cultural expectations and norms. In the next section, we assume that the pressures for the girl child to work and at a substantial geographical distance from her home will not change in the foreseeable future and we therefore make policy recommendations which are concerned with improving her situation as opposed to eradicating it.

7.5 A better occupational childhood: the need for alternative education

If rural Ghanaian girls are absorbed so early into the world of work, then there are consequences for the provision of girls' education. For example, organising education so that girls could depart and reenter easily would prevent any departure from the classroom on the account of a family's pressing income needs spelling the end of the education for the girl called upon to be the income provider. Provision should be made which permits girls to drop back into school as and when circumstances allow. Indeed, the evidence is that in the case of the kayayoo trade, girl children leave the parental home for a more of less defined period of earning, after which they return to the parental home before embarking upon marriage. This pattern would support a dropping back into school if girl kayayoos had an experience of education which encouraged them to view education as worth investing their savings in. For example, a scheme could be developed which permitted girls who were working to place some of their savings[11] in educational schemes which would entitle them to reenter education when they returned to their home area or would be refunded if that was their preference. As one of the key problems of access to education in rural areas is the lack of the necessary cash income to participate, such a scheme would provide rural girls in urban employment with a mechanism for getting over this barrier when they returned to their home areas.

Similarly, permitting girl children to join adult evening literacy classes may be a necessary step to ensuring girls receive education when they are obliged to become wage earners so young. The timing of education, i.e. evening classes, can be organised so as to permit young girls to attend school when their economic tasks were over for the day. Our interview with girl child workers and the experience of the Department of Community Development, which already has some practice in bringing together young girl workers with adults on functional literacy courses, suggest that there is considerable demand for such a programme.

A corollary of the study of why young girls leave the schoolroom must be the design of educational provision which enables them to gain education outside of the conventional schooling arrangements. The earnings of Ghana's girls seem likely to figure as a major part of the occupational structure for some time to come: the provision of education for those in this category must take place within a new format. Recognising that Ghana's girls are already involved in the world of work requires that the curriculum they follow reflect their occupational status (Freire, 1970). The need is for a relevant education. Business education and bookkeeping provided on an evening basis may do much to help the missing gender acquire its literacy and could do much to render the functional literacy programmes, which have so far floundered, effective educational contributions.

Recognising that young girl workers have had little opportunity to experiment with their creative capabilities nor have they had much space to develop their own decision-making facilities even though they work and earn as adults leads us on to the issue of what precisely a compensating educational programme should provide. A first base must surely be that of creating the forum for the development of self-esteem and self-awareness.

179

Indeed, the development of self-esteem and self-awareness in children who are experiencing such economic exile may be a very necessary first step to creating an interest in numeracy and literacy. Many of these girls talk of having letters from home read to them by others or of being dependent on word of mouth for news of their family's well-being. The separation of these girl children from their parental context generates the conditions for literacy to be a relevant dimension of social experience; it provides a mechanism by which they can check on how their contributions are benefiting their own folk. The self-esteem to embark upon acquiring literacy is as likely to be the major barrier to experimenting with access, not lack of interest. To focus purely on numeracy and literacy and to neglect self-esteem is to misunderstand the situation of the working girl, a child who is frequently exposed to verbal abuse on the part of customers and stigmatised on account of the linguistic and other cultural differences which are the product of her separation from her home area – a separation which is inherent in the pressure to earn sufficient income to marry within her local community.

In considering how education should be delivered to working girl children, it is important to appreciate that many of these children are of no fixed abode. Although when in the urban area they are part of stable social groups, the group as a whole has no legal residence of its own but rather rests nightly in facilities which belong to others and which are used for business by day, such as market sheds. There is a need to provide some form of secure facilities where girls who wish to school in the evening can leave their materials and the products of their educational activities in safety. Indeed, given the urban homelessness of these rural girls, the educational facility could serve as an important location for and source of identity. In the absence of such a facility, working girls have no place in which to display the products of any creative talents which they possess.

There is a need to think about the development of forms of education which do not rest upon the premise that the child exists primarily in a world of leisure. In order to provide an appropriate mode of education for the working child, the child's adult occupational role must be recognised. Earning is one of the few sources of immediate esteem open to these children who must bear the tedium and the arduousness of portering the wealth of others. A relevant content which provides such children with knowledge of alternative ways of life without destroying their social and economic relationships with their families and which is provided in a forum and at a time suited to their working activities is an educational imperative. Removing child labour through regulation is not an option: an alternative educational format is.

7.6 Conclusion: schooling for life – a business education

This chapter has linked the low primary school female enrolment rates to the economic role played by women and girls in Ghana. It has stressed that female drop out rates are not explained simply by costs of education, but rather it is the opportunity cost of the female earnings foregone which explain the lower enrolment rates of females as compared with males. Girls are to be found at the centre of a web of economic and domestic responsibilities which militate against their school attendance. The economic pressures to drop out of school are compounded by the present unattractiveness of the low income school room experience in Ghana. Girls are likely to retain their earning role for the foreseeable future in Ghana. As our case studies demonstrate, there is a need for more extensive research into the linkages between gender, education and early occupational socialisation in the developing context.

It is increasingly being recognised that child labour is a feature of developing countries which cannot be eradicated through any simple form of legislation (Grootaert and Kanbur, 1995). Legislation frequently intensifies the burden upon the working child, creating the circumstances in which complaints about conditions cannot be articulated without the access to means of livelihood being lost and in which bribes frequently have to be paid to minor officials in order for the earning child to continue working.[12] One consequence of this understanding must be the search for a different form of educational delivery to that which existed historically in the West. Providing free universal education and regulating for and enforcing universal attendance is not an option for many societies. In the absence of free education, fees will clearly act to discourage certain categories of pupil; even with free education, where survival necessitates children working and where enforcing the attendance of children at school by Government is not affordable, then enrolment is likely to suffer.

Whilst all possible policies to obtain the greatest level of enrolment possible should be followed, at the same time it must be recognised that there is a need for alternative, supplementary and lower cost forms of education. Educating working children through an evening, rest day, i.e Sundays, and national holiday format lessens the cost to the individual and her family and by so doing removes an important barrier to the access to education. Accepting that children are working permits the designing of educational provision which meets their needs; insisting that universal education is the only and the best way of delivering knowledge simply closes off their access to education.

Schooling in knowledge which never receives practical application in the lives of these young earners is from their perspective a waste of their scarce resources. Schooling in activities which can increase their income or permit the better management of their lives is a different prospect. As a first step in designing appropriate alternative educational provision for

181

working children, there is a need to consult both the children and their communities in creating a relevant curriculum. Children who earn should determine what they learn. In the next chapter, we move away from the earning or learning dilemma of the girl child to a consideration of the relationship between trading and old age.

Notes

1 Interview with Department of Community Development officer, May, 1994.
2 Adashie is a local rotating box credit saving system. for further information on rotating box credits see Ardener (1964); Besley et al. (1993).
3 Earnings in the kayayoo trade on a good day are approximately 2,000–2,500 cedis daily. Earnings per load carried vary but younger girls appear to earn less per load carried than adult women: whereas an 11 year old girl reports earning roughly between 50–100 cedis per load carried, adult women are reporting between 200–500 cedis per load carried. Yet both adult women and young girls are reporting the same daily earnings. If these preliminary findings are true across the head load carrying market it implies that younger girls are making more carrying trips per day than their adult counterparts.
4 Ethnic conflict took a war form in the northern region in February, 1994. Whilst interviewing adult female porters, the researcher observed that a large proportion of the kayayoos at this point in time were young northern girls. The presence of these girls tied in with the timing of conflict in the north.
5 For a description of the 'susu' system see Gabianu (1990).
6 Interview was conducted in one of the northern languages: the interviewer has used 'nuclear' family in translation because the respondent herself was distinguishing between extended and nuclear families. This is presumably because in extended families child care is readily available; in nuclear families where both parents are working it is not.
7 This is a common arrangement in Ghana where polygamous marriage is widespread and husbands and wives do not necessarily share accommodation. Associated with this separation of accommodations is the separation of responsibilities, with the economic responsibility for offspring falling largely upon women.
8 This is a local area in which the presence of traders is discouraged and enforcement officers are often over-zealous in the conduct of their duties.
9 Teaching takes place in English frequently without the safety net of teacher and pupils sharing the same mother tongue.

10 See Grootaert and Kanbur (1995) for a review of this international literature.
11 The savings of girl kayayoos are in local terms relatively substantial and the majority of such girls are involved in well-developed informal savings schemes.
12 'Child miners: no simple way out', *The Economist*, 26 February 1994, p.54.

Fihankra
(fee HAHN krah)
Literally means, 'a house which is safe'. It represents the floor plan of an Akan house. Symbol of security and peace.

8 Protected by their past, working for their future: Doorstep trading and elderly women

Joanne Koomson, Norman Williams, Nana Apt and Margaret Grieco

8.1 Multigenerational living: a multigenerational business

Even when they are elderly the pressure is upon women to continue contributing towards their keep: consequently, elderly women feature strongly within the practice of doorstep trading. Female traders frequently gift their business to their trading daughters when their own health begins to fail, often somewhere in their mid to late 40s, and commence at that point to trade on their own doorstep. Both daughter and mother frequently share a home as a consequence of customary household arrangements. Mother and daughter effectively swap places. The mother now becomes the domestic anchor providing the functions of childcare, food preparation and ensuring the security of the home as well as participating in the petty trading economy. This chapter makes a contribution to the literature on the role of the extended family in providing social welfare in the absence of formal social insurance systems.

Ghana's female traders 'gift' their working businesses to their daughters or other junior female relatives as a means of providing for their old age. This occupational gifting customarily ensures the aging trader social and economic support in her later years. However, the gifting of the working business to a daughter does not spell the end of the woman's trading career. As she gets older the Ghanaian trader scales down the level of her business activities, frequently ending up trading on very little capital on the doorstep of her home. This 'career' structure provides the aging woman with a strong economic and social definition amongst her kin and facilitates her active integration into the household unit. Continued trading inhibits social marginalisation. 50 elderly women traders were interviewed about the practice of occupational gifting within the trading community and asked whether they themselves had experience of this arrangement. The key finding is that, although the practice is still widespread, it is in

187

decline. This chapter moves from this finding to the consideration of alternative ways of ensuring the active integration of elderly women into the contemporary African urban household. From a travel and transport perspective, doorstep trading allows the aged to remain economically active with diminished mobility requirements and permits the household to use this same diminished mobility of the elderly as a domestic anchor enabling the enhanced mobility of other household members.

8.2 Occupational gifting and occupational insurance: a Ghanaian recipe

Ghana, like much of the developing world, has a weak formal social security structure (Apt and Grieco, 1994). Aging females in Ghana attempt to provide for their old age by transferring property, in this case occupational property, to their female offspring or younger female kin. Amongst Ghana's female traders there has been a well developed practice of transferring 'going businesses' to daughters and younger female kin. These informal practices of women in the developing world parallel the operation of formal security systems in the developed world, yet they have received little or no sustained policy attention.

Alongside these practices of property transfer, there exist traditional domestic or residential arrangements which render the ancestral home or 'family house' inalienable (Apt, 1995; Woodford-Berger, 1981). The role of the 'family house' or 'ancestral home' has little or no equivalent in Western culture; as a consequence, analysts have failed to recognise its importance as a source of support for the elderly and indeed for the poor. It is a source of support which it is likely to be substantially eroded as a consequence of urbanisation and migration. Already the elderly members of migrant communities in Accra are disadvantaged in that their ancestral homes are located in the rural areas outside of the city (Woodford-Berger, 1981), whereas elderly females of the indigenous Ga community continue to have access to this inalienable source of urban shelter (Kilson, 1974). Access to a 'family house' in the urban area provides elderly women with premises from which they can trade, even where such premises are simply those of the doorstep.

For Ghana's female traders the transfer of a 'going business' to a daughter does not spell the end of her career in trading but is rather associated with a reduction in the volume of business traded and a change of location from central marketplace to family doorstep. Elderly female traders are frequently assisted in obtaining replenishment of their small doorstep trading capital by their trading daughters or daughters for whom they perform child care services. These economic exchanges between the generations can usefully be viewed as an informal insurance system which has been concealed from analysis in these terms by an over-concentration on the social and affective aspects of kinship.

As we have already seen, the importance of female traders in Ghanaian economic structure has been widely acknowledged for a considerable time (Cutrufelli, 1983; Gabianu, 1990; Garlick, 1971; Little, 1973): however, little attention has been paid to the various stages of a woman's trading career from schoolgirl helping in her mother's business to elderly woman trading on the family doorstep (Twumasi, 1976). Furthermore, the interrelationship between domestic responsibility and the economic role of Ghanaian women has been largely ignored (Oppong, 1994; Lloyd and Brandon, 1993; Ardayfio-Schandorf, 1994). Studies of women's place in the household have largely ignored their place in the economy, whilst studies of women's place in the economy have largely ignored their place in the household. Yet it can be strongly argued that it is the character of female financial domestic responsibility which determines the presence of women in the economy (Ardayfio-Schandorf, 1994). That these domestic financial responsibilities of females continue into old age is demonstrated by the commonplace involvement of elderly women in doorstep trading. Indeed, it is the weight of these financial responsibilities which places pressure on older female traders to transfer business to the young and active as a means of managing their future.

Whilst evidence collected in previous research indicated that Ghanaian females invested in their daughters as a way of providing for their own old age (Katila, 1994; Apt and Katila, 1994), this evidence came solely from the accounts of younger female traders. In order to gain the views of the elderly, ten elderly females engaged in doorstep trading in five low income districts of Accra (Adabraka, Jamestown, Osu, Madina, Nima) were interviewed as to why and how they came to be doorstep trading.

8.3 Keeping busy: a working old age

Three major factors contribute towards doorstep trading on the part of elderly women in urban Ghana. First, there is considerable competition for central trading locations. This competition results in a pressure upon older women who either own or hold the tenancy of central premises but who are no longer healthy enough to operate at peak performance to surrender such premises to younger, healthier and more active close female kin. There are clear inheritance practices in respect of the tenancy of market kiosks and stalls, etc. The donation of a prime trading space to a daughter is sometimes associated with an exchange of trading locations between the two, the daughter previously having occupied the doorstep of the family house. The surrender of the market location is, however, very frequently associated with the movement to doorstep trading, whether a daughter has previously traded there or not. Moving out of the market does not signal the end of a trading career.

Secondly, the weak regulation of the commercial sector plus low income levels of developing societies create the opportunities for doorstep trading. The petty trading structure of Ghana provides the elderly with a scale and pace of commercial involvement which is commensurate with their physiology and a capital base which is correspondingly in line with lessened physical and economic activity. Put simply, developing societies contain opportunities for the active involvement of the elderly which are unavailable in industrialised societies (Derricourt and Miller, 1992).

Thirdly, in explaining the commonplace occurrence of elderly women trading on the doorstep, attention has to be paid to the 'family house' or ancestral home. Of the five districts sampled, three (Adabraka, Jamestown, Osu) are areas in which the indigenous Ga community either predominates or has a considerable presence: two (Madina, Nima) are areas in which migrant communities predominate. 'Family houses', i.e. ancestral homes, in Accra are primarily a feature of the Ga community and not surprisingly doorstep traders within these communities primarily lived in 'family houses', with only 11 out of 30 traders living in rented accommodation. In the migrant areas, ten out of 20 traders were living in rented accommodation. Whilst living in a rented house does not preclude doorstep trading, it seems probable that family houses are more hospitable venues for doorstep trading in that the elderly female has a customary entitlement to occupancy. Furthermore, it seems probable that the transferring of business from mother to daughter is an outcome of the inalienability of the mother's residential status in the ancestral home and the limited access of daughters to sources of accommodation other than that of the ancestral home. A mother may have transferred her business to her daughter but she would continue to remain within the same household and thus enjoy a continuing share of the benefits. The family house is part of the social equation which permits the investment in offspring by simultaneously securing the position of the elderly trader in the household as a family member and providing a new trading location, the family doorstep.

Residence in a family house, given the inalienable entitlement of family members to share in this accommodation, is not surprisingly associated with the presence of extended family composed of several generations (Woodford-Berger, 1981). The traditional property arrangements support multigenerational living and multigenerational living is an important source of support for the elderly in a context where formal social welfare provision is weak.

70 year old widowed Ga trader with three trading daughters. She stays with her daughters and their children in her own house (meaning 'family house').

63 year old divorced Krobo trader with two trading daughters. She lives in a family house with one daughter and one granddaughter.

70 year old divorced Ga trader with three trading daughters. She lives in a family house with one daughter and her grandchildren.

56 year old widowed Ga trader with no trading daughter. She lives in her own house left to her by her father with some of her children.

However, whilst the family house may offer additional insurance, living in rented houses is also associated with the presence of extended family and several generations. The customs and practices of the ancestral home may be carried over into rented accommodation.

61 year old married Akan trader with trading daughter. She lives in a hired house with her daughter and grandchildren.

80 year old widowed Ga trader with trading daughter. She stays with her daughter and grandchildren in a hired house.

Kilson (1974) identified the customary practice of separate female and male households amongst the ethnic group indigenous to Accra – the Ga. Boy infants and children are housed with the females until they reach puberty, when traditionally they would join the male households. The information collected in the course of this research into occupational gifting indicates that these patterns of separate male and female households are still to be found in urbanised Accra (see Tables 8.1 and 8.2). Other patterns of split households also occur; within the Akan matrilineage system, a husband may sleep in the house of his matrilineal kin whilst his wife remains in the ancestral home of her own mother (Woodford-Berger, 1981). In a number of communities, married women frequently live separately from their husbands and are typically responsible for the organisation of their own financial world. Even where women do live with their husbands, their economic contribution to the household frequently exceeds that of the male (Lloyd and Brandon, 1993). Indeed, it is these financial domestic responsibilities which frequently propel women into their slower paced second trading career on the doorstep.

In exploring this practice of 'occupational gifting', it became quickly apparent that the social definition of elderly operated by Ghana's female traders was substantially different to that which would hold in a Western society. Doorstep traders reported themselves as elderly at around 50 years old with the handover of business to offspring frequently taking place at around this time of life. It should be noted that this social definition of elderly reflects the lower life expectancies within the society as compared with the developed world and the low levels of well being experienced by women traders in the performance of their occupation.

Table 8.1
Accommodation arrangements of respondents by district

	Living with female kin	Living with male and female kin	Living with husband	Living alone/ with housegirl	Total
Adabraka	9			1	10
Jamestown	7	2		1	10
Osu	5	1	2	2	10
Madina	5	1	2	2	10
Nima	6			4	10
Total	32	4	4	10	50
Percentage	64	8	8	20	100

Table 8.2
Marital status of respondents by district

District	Single	Married	Divorced	Separated	Widowed	Total
Adabraka		4	1		5	10
Jamestown	1	4	1		4	10
Osu		2	4		4	10
Madina	2	3	3		2	10
Nima	1	3	1	1	4	10
Total	4	16	10	1	19	50
Percentage	8	32	20	2	38	100

Table 8.3
Ethnicity of respondents by district

District	Ga	Akan	Krobo	Ewe	Nzema	Northern	Other	Total
Adabraka	4	6						10
Jamestown	6	1	1	1			1	10
Osu	7	1		2				10
Madina	2	4		2	1	1		10
Nima		4		3	1	2		10
Total	19	16	1	8	2	3	1	50
Percentage	38	32	2	16	4	6	2	100

Table 8.4
Age group of respondents by district

	45–50	51–60	61–70	71–80	81+	Unknown	Total
Adabraka	1	4	4		1		10
Jamestown		5	3	2			10
Osu	1	2	5	2			10
Madina		2	5	3			10
Nima	1	1	4	1		3	10
Total	3	14	21	8	1	3	50
Percentage	6	28	42	16	2	6	100

How widespread is the practice of occupational gifting amongst female traders? Although, our sample is only large enough to provide a preliminary indication of the extent of the practice, 18 of our 50 respondents (36 per cent) had donated either capital, premises or business to their female offspring or younger female kin.

61 year old divorced Ga trader. She donated her market stall to her two daughters who took over her former trading activity.

58 year old widowed Ga trader. She did not give any financial help to her daughter but provided her with the premises for trading.

65 year old divorced Akan trader. When I became too old to go to the market my daughter took over from me. She now takes care of the shop in the market (Makola). I only do petty trading because I do not want to be idle. She used to come to the market with me when she was very small so she knows everything about the business that is why she stepped into my shoes.

83 year old widowed Akan trader. I helped my daughter set up her trading business. She used to help me in baking so I gave her some of my savings to use for trading.

63 year old divorced Krobo trader. She has been trading for a total of 30 years but only for five years on her doorstep. She was formerly selling cloth in the market but now sells plastic plates, cups, bowls. She has two daughters and one granddaughter who are traders. She donated her business, premises and initial capital to her daughter and granddaughter.

73 year old widowed Kwahu trader. When I was trading at Makola I made sure I arranged for all my daughters to acquire stalls at the market. I also gave them the capital to start their trading.

68 year old divorced Ewe trader. She donated her market stall to her daughter when she stopped going to the market.

45 year old widowed Fante (Akan) trader. I used to do some trading in the past at the spot where my daughter is now trading at Kaneshie but when I went bankrupt I stopped but kept the space so when my daughter wanted to trade I offered her the premises.

Although occupational gifting is still practised in the present, there is evidence to indicate that it was far more extensive in the past. A number of elderly traders indicated that whereas they had received their businesses or assistance in setting up their businesses from elder kin, they had not, in their turn, passed on such business or assistance to their own female offspring or younger female kin.

53 year old married Ga trader. Her mother and sister are traders. She inherited her trading space from her mother who is also trading on the same spot. She has a daughter but her daughter did not become a trader.

Amongst those elderly traders who have transferred of their business to younger female relatives, many have moved from major trading role to minor one. 39 of our 50 respondents (78 per cent) indicated that the movement to doorstep trading represented a significant reduction in their level of economic activity. A reduction in level of activity was also frequently associated with a change in the types of goods traded and lessening of travelling activity.

83 year old widowed Akan trader. Formerly I was a baker. I was making bread for distribution. Now I sell handkerchiefs and napkins ... I was trading on a large scale in the past but now it is on a minor scale.

The expectation that advancing years would be associated with a reduction in the level of trading activity rather than complete retirement was widespread amongst these elderly traders. Ill health was taken as a signal to reduce the level of trading activity not as a reason to stop: doorstep trading permitted a lower level of physical activity and lessened the need for physical mobility. They viewed their own situations as typical for women rather than as unusual.

60 year old 'single' Ga trader. She was formerly selling wasted plantain by the roadside but was advised against it by her doctor so she now sells vegetables on her doorstep.

54 year old married Ewe trader. I handed over my business which had been given to me by my aunt to my daughter when I fell ill. She now takes care of the business in the market. I only go there from time to time.

71 year old divorced Akan trader. I was trading in the market until I fell ill. Then one of my daughters who was unemployed offered to help me by keeping the shop for me. When I recovered I was advised not to do strenuous work so my daughter took over. She was later joined by her daughter.

56 year old widowed Ga trader. She has been trading for one year now on her doorstep. Was formerly selling kenkey but her doctor advised her to stop. Now sells provisions, sweets, plastic ware etc.

Apart from illness being a signal that the time was right to transfer the greater volume of business activity to a daughter, the costs of health care also have their consequences for elder women's ability to preserve their capital for trading purposes.

69 year old divorced Ga trader. She was formerly selling shoes in town but fell ill and used up most of her capital for hospital bills so when she got well she had to buy some provisions for sale on her doorstep.

Social and domestics costs associated with increasing age such as the financing of the funeral of a deceased husband also take their toll of trader's capital. In Ghana, the social obligation to have a large and lively funeral is not readily escapable and considerable pressure is exerted upon the widow to expend her capital even though there may be little hope of restoring such capital thereafter.

54 year old widowed Ewe trader. She was formerly selling provisions and onions but after her husband died she used most of the capital for the funeral so she now trades in dried meat and fish. Was formerly trading on a maximum scale. Now trades on a minor scale.

Whilst for the majority of our respondents (80 per cent) doorstep trading represented a change in venue and in the types of goods traded rather than a change in type of economic activity per se, for ten of our

195

respondents (20 per cent), it was indeed a change in activity. Trading was seen to be more commensurate with the energy and status of old age than most other economic activities.

> *64 year old married Ga trader.* My daughter decided to encourage me to sell petty items because I am too old to farm now and I get bored at home. I do the trading and we share the profits.

Respondents' accounts support two distinct explanations of doorstep trading by elderly women. The first explanation focuses on the social inclusion of the elderly: doorstep trading provides elderly women with a social identity and social role which contributes towards their wellbeing. The second explanation is one of continuing and substantial economic pressure upon elderly women to earn. Although these explanations may fit well together when an elderly woman enjoys good health, an economic pressure to earn can adversely affect an elderly woman's well being when she does not enjoy such good health. Not surprisingly, some respondents simultaneously described doorstep trading as an important mechanism in social inclusion and as a forced economic choice.

> *83 year old widowed Akan trader.* At the moment what I am doing is just to keep me occupied so that I will not grow weak. It is not enough to provide for my needs. I have to depend on my children and most of them are not gainfully employed. This makes life very difficult for me. Right now I am staying with my daughter in a one roomed apartment and it is very crowded.

Some traders focused solely upon the participatory benefits of doorstep trading.

> *60 year old widowed Ga trader.* I was formerly trading in provisions at the Makola market. I still sell provisions at home. I stopped trading at Makola because too many people were beginning to sell provisions therefore people were not buying my things. I decided to sell a few things on my doorstep because I didn't want to feel lazy at home. I am o.k. with the quality of my life. My daughters send me money regularly and I trade only because I don't want to be bored at home.

> *63 year old divorced Krobo trader.* Her daughter encouraged her to do some petty trading so that she wouldn't be bored at home.

> *54 year old married Ewe trader.* My daughter suggested that I do some petty trading to keep myself occupied at home.

196

A number of respondents commented on the role played by their daughters in encouraging them to undertake doorstep trading in order to prevent them being bored. However, ensuring relief from boredom was not the sole reason for encouraging aging mothers to undertake doorstep trading as daughters were also concerned to enable their mothers to finance their own upkeep or at least make contributions to it.

> *Elderly northern widowed trader who does not know her age.* Her daughters set her up in business on her doorstep so that she would be able to cater for herself and would not be bored.

Many of our elderly female traders discussed doorstep trading simply as an economic activity which constituted an undesirable burden or chore. Elderly traders were viewed as being at a substantial disadvantage as compared with younger, more active female traders. Doorstep trading was viewed as essentially less rewarding than market trading. However, it may well be the case that these very same traders would continue in their doorstep trading for reasons of social inclusion if the compelling economic pressures were removed. What is not in doubt is that some elderly women trade on the doorstep simply to make or contribute to their living costs.

> *48 year old married Akan trader.* Life is difficult because everyone is selling and the young women are more energetic so people prefer to buy from them. they have a larger capital and can buy more quality goods. We old women can only afford to buy the cheap things so many people don't buy from us. This makes life difficult for me. I have been trading here for four years but I have not been able to save much. It is my younger sister who takes care of all the household needs and I can't contribute much because I don't make enough money ... Right now I am not making much from my trading. I would be happy if I could get my goods at a cheaper price so that I can make a little profit. If I am able to make more profit it would improve my situation.

> *74 year old widowed Ga trader.* My house is in need of repairs. My kiosk also needs repairs. Life is very difficult. I am on my own and I have to do everything for myself. This often makes me tired. Since I have no children I have nobody to depend upon so I have to continue trading in order to survive.

> *60 year old widowed Akan trader.* Life is not easy. I have hypertension so I can't be very active. I have to depend sometimes on other people to do my trading for me so that I can get some money for my upkeep. I wish I could find a way of doing something that would bring me money but which will not need me to go up and

197

down and get tired. I also go wish my son was in the position to take care of me completely.

83 year old widowed Akan trader. I think if I could get enough money to expand my trading it will improve my situation because now I have to depend on my children and they do not give me enough. I would like to make enough so that I can depend on myself.

65 year old divorced Akan trader. Life is not as good as it used to be. Things are expensive and the cost of living is too high. I would like to have enough money so that I stop trading and relax in my old age.

62 year old divorced Nzema trader. I do not make as much as I used to but since I do not have anybody to support life is not that bad for me. I don't think I need much to improve my situation but I would like to relax completely and be looked after by my daughter if she can afford it.

60 year old 'unmarried' northern trader. She goes to buy the items herself from the market. 'Life is not easy. I often fall sick and I am always tired. My sister is an invalid so I have to take care of both of us and pay all the bills. This makes life difficult.' She would be grateful for a loan to expand her business.

Some of the elderly women traders are not simply trying to generate the income necessary for their own living needs but also have the responsibility for supporting their children, including their adult children and their offspring. A mother's role to support children extends to adult children and their children.

70 year old widowed Ga trader. My life is very difficult. One of my daughters is crippled. Her husband does not take care of her and their children. I have to take care of them as well as myself. The responsibility for feeding the whole household lies on me. This makes life difficult. Sometimes my leg hurts so I can't go and buy the fish. Right now I owe somebody 5,000 cedis because I couldn't sell the fish at any profitable price. I am getting old and I need to relax but I can't do that because if I relax my children and grandchildren will go hungry. I wish my children could take some of the load off my head so that I can have some peace in my old age. There should be somewhere that old people can go and rest and leave the problems in the home behind them in their old age.

53 year old married Ga trader. I would be happy if my children could get good jobs so that they can take care of me. If they have good jobs I wouldn't have to sell to support them.

65 year old married Ga trader. Life is not so good because at my age I should be resting but I have to work because my husband is not working. I still have one daughter in school to look after. However I have no complaints.

68 year old 'single' Ga trader. Life is not easy for me at all. Both of my daughters are unemployed and they have children. I have to look after the whole household with no help from anyone. I pay the school fees of my grandchildren and provide food for the whole family. This makes life very difficult for me.

Apart from the low level of earnings associated with doorstep trading, elderly women report two other major associated sources of difficulty or discomfort. These are the difficulties in the transportation of goods from the suppliers to the doorstep and the long hours which must be spent attending the trader's kiosk or trading table. For traders who receive no support from kin in transporting their goods, the transportation of trading items is indeed a cumbersome, tiring and time consuming business. Even for younger traders, organising the transportation of their trading items is an uncomfortable and tiring business in a context where goods are not distributed to retailers by wholesalers but retailers must travel to the wholesalers to obtain their goods. For elderly female traders, the transport conditions of urban Accra must provide a very tiring task load indeed.

68 year old widowed Akan trader. She obtains her stock from retailers at Makola and transports them home by taxi or tro-tro. 'Life is difficult. I often have to do all the carrying myself and I sit at my stall all day, this makes me tired.'

70 year old married Akan trader. The standard of living is very poor. I often get tired because I have to go to the market to buy the things myself I also have to sit in front of the house to sell the wares myself. If I could get a loan to expand my business or a pension that would provide for me for the rest of my life it would improve my situation.

Elderly separated Akan trader who does not know her own age. I used to buy my goods myself from the market and transport them home but I've had arthritis for some time now so I have to depend on hired help. Life is not easy at all. My capital is running out because I can't go to the market myself. I can't depend on the people

199

I hire to buy the goods at a reasonable price so I can make some profit. I have to pay a lot of bills and this makes life difficult for me. My children do not help me because they are not gainfully employed. If I could get a loan to expand my business it would improve my situation or any other form of work like being a nanny or nursery attendant.

The evidence collected on occupational gifting and its relationship to doorstep trading indicates that there was a strong customary relationship between these two arrangements. However, in the present, it appears that whilst doorstep trading is likely to continue and strengthen as an economic activity performed by elderly women, the practice of occupational gifting appears to be weakening. The implications of any such weakening in the practice of occupational gifting will be considered in Section 8.5. The following section considers the ways in which household needs constrain elderly females to trade on their doorsteps and the benefits which accrue to household organisation from the conversion of the doorstep into commercial space by elderly traders.

8.4   Holding the fort: elderly women as domestic actors

Our research into household organisation and its impact on travel behaviour revealed that in the majority of households view the presence of a family member in the home at all times as an important security requirement. By trading on the doorstep, elderly women perform this important security function, rendering the other members of the household free to go about other activities elsewhere. Elderly women thus perform the important role of domestic anchor – their presence provides a fixed point around which other household members can plan their business. In the absence of such an anchor coordinating the activities of the household becomes an altogether more complex task.

Apart from performing this security function for the household, elderly women are also important providers of child care services. Previous research in Ghana (Goody, 1978; Apt and Katila, 1994) indicates the extent to which the elderly are involved in the provision of child care. It is not uncommon for grandchildren to live with and be brought up by their grandparents. Whilst none of our elderly traders was in the position of being 'foster parent' to their grandchildren, the majority were providing child care services for their daughters. Clearly trading at a market or at a distance from the home would prevent or greatly limit the ability of these elderly female traders to provide child care services for their daughters. By trading on the doorstep, they can continue to trade whilst at the same time providing child care services. By choosing this option, elderly women enable their daughters to trade in the more profitable venues of the central

200

markets and other high volume business areas.

> *83 year old widowed Akan trader.* I also look after my daughters' children when I am healthy.

> *60 year old widowed Ga trader.* They however bring their children to her to take care of before going to see the market.

> *68 year old widowed Akan trader.* I only look after their children.

> *80 year old widowed Ga trader.* I look after her children and cook for the household.

> *54 year old widowed Ewe trader.* Did not give any help to her daughter in her business but takes care of her daughter's child for her.

> *Elderly separated Akan trade who does not know her own age.* I was not able to give my daughters any help with their trading because I wasn't making much money when I was working. The only thing I do for them is to keep their children for them from time to time.

> *67 year old married Ewe trader.* I help my daughters by doing the cooking whiles they are away from home and take care of their children.

> *62 year old divorced Nzema trader.* I also take care of her children for her and do some of the cooking.

These elderly female traders perform the important function of child care whilst simultaneously generating the whole or part of the income necessary for their own upkeep. Providing child care support is often combined with the preparation and cooking of household food, a task which is time-consuming, given the dependence on solid fuel for cooking purposes and the nature of the Ghanaian diet. In analysing the relationship between the elderly and child care, it is, however, important to note that children also play an important role in providing care for the elderly. Previous research (Apt and Katila, 1994: Apt, 1995) indicates that where grandparents would otherwise be living alone their grandchildren are often placed with them as a source of social support and to provide domestic services such as water carrying, provisions shopping, refuse disposal and household cleaning. It is commonplace for children to assist with petty trading and elderly women, by trading on the doorstep, have ready access to the services of their grandchildren as a source of labour.

72 year old 'single' Nzema trader. When I came home my daughter advised me to do some petty trading on the spot where she had been trading in front of the house. In a sense we exchanged positions. I sometimes go to the market to buy the things myself or when I am not well my daughter sends me one of her children to come and take care of it for me.

They can rest from their doorstep trading more readily than would be the case if they were trading in the commercial centres. Access to children's services permits rest periods to be built into the trading day. Our elderly female Ghanaian traders also indicated that their grandchildren were involved in transporting their goods for them.

60 year old widowed Ga trader. She obtains her stock herself from Accra central. She brings it home by taxi with the help of some of her grandchildren.

68 year old 'single' Ga trader. Her grandchildren help her by carrying her goods from the market to the house for her.

70 years old widowed Ga trader. She obtains her stock from wholesalers in Accra Central. She has to depend on one of her grandchildren to do her shopping for her.

70 year old widowed Ga trader. Although, she has not received any financial help from her daughters, Her grandchildren some times go out to purchase the fish for her … 'I go to the beach myself when I am fit to buy the fish and then transport it home in a taxi or a tro-tro.'

The importance of children in providing intergenerational support to the elderly within the household is aptly demonstrated by the arrangements that the elderly who have no such child kin have to make for substitutes.

67 year old widowed northern trader. I have a little girl who stays with me. She goes to the market to make my purchases for me. She carries them home herself. Life is not all that bad. I am able to make a living by my trading. My main worry is how I'll cope when I grow older. I have no children and the little girl living with me is not a relative, if she decides to leave I will have no one to look after me in my old age. I would be grateful if I could get the assurance that I will have someone to take care of me during my old age. This would make my life a bit easier.

The availability of girl children who work as household servants, whilst it clearly has many negative aspects, provides the elderly who have no kin available to provide those domestic services necessary to survival in urban areas in developing countries with an important source of support. House girls are not simply to be found in wealthy households but are also a feature of domestic life in low income households (Grieco et al., 1994b), most importantly those of the solitary aged. Housegirls are used by the solitary aged as substitutes for the services provided by child kin. These services are essential in an urban context which, because of infrastructural deficiencies, requires physical agility for the performance of routine household tasks (Dankwa et al., 1994). The absence of pipe borne water and the absence of domestic sanitation generate household tasks for the elderly of the developing world such as water carrying and refuse disposal which have no Western counterpart. The old require the assistance of the active young to provide these services. In this context, the positive aspects of the interaction between child household labour and the low income aged clearly require consideration in any policy designed to improve the quality of either social category. Elderly females who themselves had not yet acquired the services of a house girl also identified the benefits of and the pressures to adopt such a strategy.

> *72 year old 'single' Nzema trader.* Life is not so good. Things are expensive. Because I live alone I often get tired. I have to prepare my own meals. The trading business is also not very profitable. I don't get many customers. If I could get someone who will stay with me permanently it would improve my situation. The person could take care of me and my trading.

Whilst some traders saw the solution to their problem of acquiring the services of the agile young, given the absence of available kin, as being the hiring of a live-in house girl, others hired the services of children for specific tasks.

> *64 year old married Ga trader.* Sometimes my daughter goes to the market to buy the items, sometimes I go myself. When I go myself I hire a 'kaya' girl to send the things to the station then I take a taxi.

It is clear that the involvement of the elderly greatly assists the functioning of household in urban Ghana: however, it is equally clear that membership of a multigenerational household provides the elderly with important services and resources. Children both provide resources to and receive resources from the elderly, the elderly both provide resources to and receive resources from the young. The trading doorstep is an important aspect of this intergenerational exchange.

8.5 Supplying working capital for doorstep trading: a daughter's obligation

Domestic support of elderly female traders is not confined to the services provided by the very young, for elderly female traders derived significant support from their adult offspring. The majority of traders only mentioned female offspring as a source of financial and social support. It should be noted that in general the level of support by offspring is likely to be under-recorded as individuals are disinclined to say that they are in receipt of help. Even so, 50 per cent of the elderly female traders indicated they received either financial or other some other form of help from their female offspring in establishing or operating their business. One important form of assistance was the provision of trading places or premises:

> *83 year old widowed Akan trader.* The place where I am sitting right now was given to me by my daughter. She also helps me from time to time with some money ... My daughter goes to buy the things for me from town because I am not healthy enough to go to town myself.

> *54 year old married Akan trader.* She received financial help from her daughter in her trading activities. Her daughter gave her the premises where she is now trading.

> *71 year old divorced Akan trader.* My daughter helped me by maintaining the shop when I was ill. She also encouraged me to start petty trading and offered me the space on her doorstep. My daughter makes all the arrangements to obtain my stock for me. When she travels she arranges with a taxi driver to bring them to me. My life is not bad. The only problem I have is tiredness since I have to sit behind the goods in front of the house. My daughters take good care of me.

> *72 year old widowed Ewe trader.* She received some money from her daughter about three years ago when she lost most of her capital (100,000 cedis). Her daughter also allows her to use the space in front of the house to put out her foodstuff.

> *68 year old 'single' Ga trader.* The children help her financially. Her daughter also encouraged her and gave her the space to trade.

Apart from the provision of premises, daughters were also involved in the provision of trading capital. In some cases, such involvement was confined to the provision of the initial trading capital.

61 year old divorced Ga trader. Her daughters gave her money to add to her own savings to start her new business.

54 year old married Ewe trader. She bought the goods for me to start the petty trading.

56 year old widowed Ga trader. Her daughters contributed towards the capital she used in starting the present business.

In other cases, the elderly traders received repeated financial assistance from their daughters in order to enable their trading activities. For some traders, this represented a regular source of assistance.

52 year old divorced Akan trader. My daughter is not a trader but she often finds me money to add to my capital.

65 year old divorced Akan trader. My daughter helps me by giving me money to purchase the sweets for sale.

68 year old married Akan trader. She receives regular financial assistance from her children to purchase stock.

For others, financial assistance in replacing trading capital or purchasing stock was more intermittent.

Elderly married northern trader who does not know her own age. Her daughters give her money to add to her capital from time to time.

63 year widowed Ewe trader. My daughter sends me some money from time to time to help me purchase more wares.

45 year old widowed Akan trader. My daughter remits me occasionally.

Daughters also undertook the purchase and provision of stock for their elderly trading mothers. By obtaining the trading stock for their mothers, daughters relieved these elderly female traders from many of the discomforts involved in travelling to purchase and transport stock.

60 year old widowed Ga trader. Her daughters help her with her trading capital and sometimes purchase her goods for her.

80 year old widowed Ga trader. My daughter buys things for me to sell.

63 year old divorced Krobo trader. She obtains her stock through her daughter and granddaughter who purchase them for her from Makola. 'Life is not very bad for me because I have my daughter to depend on. I gave my business to her because I know she can handle it and take care of me. I personally do not need anything but I only pray that my daughter is able to maintain the business and take good care for me in my old age.'

69 year old divorced Ewe trader. My daughter bought the clothes and toys for me to sell so that I won't be bored at home. My daughter arranges for my stock to be brought to me when she goes to the market. She has someone who helps me bring the things to the house. The quality of my life is not bad but it is not very good either. At first I was in charge of the business but now I have to look up to my daughter. She treats me well but it is not the same as if I were in charge myself.

70 year old widowed Akan trader. Her daughter travels to the hinterland to bring her the fruits which she sells. Her stock is obtained from the hinterland. 'My daughter together with other traders hire a vehicle and go to places like Akosombo to buy the fruits. Life is difficult. Often we incur losses because by the time fruits get to Accra they are getting rotten.'

67 year old married Ewe trader. I often feel tired because of my age. I do not make much to be able to cater for myself and the smaller children. My sons often have to send me money. My daughters buy me the things when they go to the market. They bring it home in a taxi or a tro-tro. I would be grateful for a loan. I'm tired of the hard work involved in the trade and I would like to direct into something else.

62 year old divorced Nzema trader. My daughter encouraged me to do petty trading and offered me the space in front of her house where she had been trading previously. My daughter purchases my goods for me when she goes to the market.

68 year old divorced Ewe trader. Her daughter made it possible for her to continue trading by giving her some money and foodstuff to sell in the house. She obtains her stock from the hinterland where her daughter travels to buy the foodstuffs (she was doing this work previously). Her daughter hires a vehicle together with other traders to go to the hinterland for the foodstuff.

Whilst it seems that daughters' financial involvement in elderly mothers' trading is presently still strong, it may very well be, given the evidence that doorstep trading is continuing but occupational gifting is weakening, that daughters' financial support for mothers' trading will weaken with modernisation and urbanisation. There was some indication amongst the elderly female traders that such a process had already begun.

53 year old married Ga trader. Whilst she herself received assistance in setting up her business from her mother, she could provide no such support to her daughter. Her daughter in her turn is providing minimal support for her mother. 'My daughter is a seamstress and cannot get enough money to feed herself and her family so she does not send me much. I have to depend on my trading.'

58 year old widowed Ga trader. Although she provided her daughter with the premises for trading and although her daughter lives with her in a family house, she does not receive any trading help from her daughter.

Elderly widowed northern trader who does not know her own age. She buys the things herself from the main market. 'Life is hard now because prices are high. I cannot make any profit. My daughters also do not help me often because they have their own families to cater for. I have arthritis so I can not move around often.' She would be grateful for loans to expand her trading.

For example, there is some indication that the movement away from the traditional Ga community's arrangement of separate male and female households towards more Western style nuclear households (Kilson, 1974) will adversely affect the intergenerational relationships which were associated with traditional accommodation patterns and, thus, leave older women exposed to a more hostile economic environment.

55 year old married Ga trader. She didn't offer her daughters any help in their trading. They were set up by their husbands. Her daughters do not offer her any help in her trading.

70 year old divorced Ga trader who was formerly in salaried employment. She did not offer any help to any of her daughters. They all set themselves up with the help of their husbands. Her daughters did not offer her any help, although one of her daughters lives with her in a family house. She started selling the fish with money from her pension and personal savings.

One factor which may offset the decline in occupational gifting and operate to preserve the situation where daughters provide mothers with trading capital is the role played by the elderly in child care. By providing the capital for doorstep trading, daughters are able to tie the elderly trader to the home and thus ensure her availability for child care. However, it should be noted that, whilst amongst the elderly female traders there were indeed many who received assistance in exchange for child care, there are cases of elderly traders who did provide child care but received no such assistance.

> *54 year old widowed Ewe trader*. She has one daughter who trades. She did not give any help to her daughter in her business. Although she provides child care for her daughter she does not receive much help from her daughter.

> *Elderly separated Akan trader who does not know her own age*. I was not able to give my daughters any help with their trading because I wasn't making much money when I was working. The only thing I do for them is to keep their children for them from time to time. My daughters do not help me in any way.

From the evidence collected it is clear that there is an exchange of financial assistance and of other services between the generations in urban Accra: however, it is equally clear that many of these relationships are currently under renegotiation. Whilst, many elderly female traders who have offspring are in receipt of financial and other forms of assistance, such assistance appears to be weakening with the majority of elderly female traders being under considerable economic pressure to continue their earning into advanced old age.

8.6 Conclusion: a welfare policy for Africa, supporting indigenous institutions

It has been argued that the prolonged economic activity of elderly females generates many benefits at the level of social involvement and self-esteem. However, it has also been indicated that such economic activity is often arduous and experienced as a matter of simple economic necessity. It was suggested that the lower levels of commercial regulation in developing countries provide greater opportunities for the integration of elderly women than those holding in the West. It was recognised that tighter regulation of business on the part of the governments of developing countries are likely to adversely affect these opportunities for the economic integration of the aging and aged. The modernisation of the economies of developing countries, with its present concentration on improved tax systems and revenue collection levels, is likely to generate such regulation of business. In streamlining revenue collection, attention should be paid to the likely social welfare consequences of displacing elderly females from their current trading niches on the family doorstep.

It has been suggested that the traditional accommodation arrangement of the 'family house' ancestral home provided a cornerstone in the development of the customary occupational gifting practice amongst women. As mothers and daughters shared in the inalienable right of residence in the family house and as the customary practice was for both to exercise that right, the transfer of business took place within the same household unit. As the customary practice becomes eroded through the development of more Western style household structures and mothers and daughters live in different houses, the transfer of a business no longer represents a transfer within the same household but represents the transfer of resources out of a household. Occupational gifting thus becomes less efficient as an insurance mechanism for the aging female trader. There is a need for housing policies and other social policies which recognise the impact of accommodation on informal social welfare arrangements to be developed. Clearly, the issue of multigenerational housing requires to be directly addressed as part of social welfare policy in the developing context. Practically, the construction of any new housing should incorporate multigenerational facilities and trading facilities within its development goals. Building doorstep trading space into new schemes helps elderly females support themselves.

The key finding of the research is that although the practice of occupational gifting is still widespread, it is in decline. The traditional insurance arrangements are under pressure and there is thus a need for donor agencies to consider the benefits of providing loans to the elderly in order to enable their continued trading. Whilst contemplating the continued employment of the elderly in arduous occupations may be very uncomfortable, as the formal welfare system of developing economies are unable to support their elderly in complete leisure, helping the elderly to support themselves is the most realistic social welfare goal. In the absence of innovative thinking in this area, the imminence of a social welfare crisis in respect of the aged has to be faced.

Finally, it has been argued that there has been a traditional three way balance between the generations in which the old provided child care services which benefited the 'working generation', the children provided care services for the aged which similarly benefited the 'working generation' and the 'working generation' provided financial and material support for the young and old. In this balance, there was a customary provision of domestic services by the young to the old. As family structure changes and infrastructure remains deficient, the old will have increasingly to seek these necessary services outside of the family. The use of non-kin to perform such tasks generates important questions around the acceptability of domestic child labour. In developing policies which protect the child, given the traditional interchange between these two age categories, policy makers will have to take considerable care not to damage the old. Weakening family ties may very well be associated with an increase in the use of child labour in the form of house girls. In order to protect both children and the aged, in their bid to modernise economies policy makers must also focus on supporting the traditional informal insurance arrangements. Not to do so may result in an economic social welfare burden which outweighs the business benefits.

This chapter examined the practice of occupational gifting amongst Ghana's female traders. It identified the important role played by elderly females in household organisation and the transfer of resources and 'repayments' made by their children to the elderly. It identified the institutional factors which facilitate the practice of doorstep trading by elderly women. It concluded by identifying the benefits which result from occupational gifting, and from the accompanying practice of the transfer of resources to the elderly from their offspring, in terms of the care and social integration of elderly women.

Epa
(eh PAH)
Handcuffs, the symbol of the law and slavery. Indicates that the law does not always respect persons.

9 The traders' tales: Biographies of Ghanaian female traders

9.1 Setting the story: common themes and common background

This chapter provides a description of female traders' occupational histories and life circumstances in their own voices. The life stories of both young and old traders were collected and are presented below, with the voices of the oldest traders speaking first. The traders tell of the uncertainties they have experienced in their trade – perceptions of these female market and petty traders as economic villains and social enemies have erupted at various stages in Ghana's contemporary past. In these periods of hostility towards female traders, capital, premises and goods have been seized or destroyed. Graduating from small time trading to bigger business has traditionally been a dangerous course for women. Understandable hesitation about maximising economic profit has resulted, with the consequence that the graduation of female entrepreneurs from the informal to the formal sector is rarely sought. The trader biographies presented here provide substantial insight into these economic hesitations which have, of course, considerable significance for economic development.

As the traders tales indicate, even under normal trading conditions traders are subject to a range of extortions from a host of petty officials. In what is formally a free market, traders have to obtain 'licences' to conduct various purchasing and selling activities. In addition to the financial pressures imposed upon them from petty authorities, traders also experience considerable social claims on their trading capital from their kin. Tales of female economic and domestic financial responsibilities are typically accompanied by tales of the foolhardy and outrageous social and economic behaviour of men.

213

9.2   Social claims on female trading capital: Felicia's royal sacrifice

Felicia is 71 years old and of royal stock. She is a Krobo and is illiterate.

My parents are both dead long ago. They were very old when they died. They were typical rural dwellers with very little link with the big towns. In all, they gave birth to seven children. However, my mother used to boast that she gave birth to and breast fed 12 children. So I reckon four of her children died before us. They died mostly of measles at tender ages.

With the exception of the female child before me and myself, all the children had standard four level of education. I started primary school, when I was in class three, I stopped because my father wanted me to marry his nephew who was far older, ugly and a drunkard. You are now lucky. In those times, we had lessons under trees, sitting on the ground. We tied a half piece cloth round our necks as our uniform. We called it 'collar'.

Well, my father was a 'Dadematse'[1] and had large farm lands. My mother was princess of the Odumase Krobo royal house. She converted to Christianity hence her Christian name. So, you see, I am a royal. Actually I am a sub-queen mother. Coming back to our story, when I quit school, I helped my mother in her cooking oil industry. My father had oil palm plantation so my mother used to extract palm oil and another edible oil extracted from palm kernels. It was a very lucrative business. We usually sold the gallons of cooking oil on Fridays at the Asesewa market.

When I was about 20 years, I had already had my first child, a boy who died of measles. It was to be a long time before I had my subsequent children. When my mother was about 60 years, she became totally blind because of constant eye contact with smoke and heat prevalent in palm oil production. Naturally, I was very much afraid of also getting blind. I therefore left Seseamang, our village near Asesewa to Akosombo.

Akosombo was then a fast developing town because of the ongoing construction of the dam. The town was a haven economically for people from the corners of the country. I was then a young woman in my late twenties. I settled down at Akosombo by selling oranges. I met a young, handsome, tall and well educated man. We got married and over the years had six children. We are still married despite difficult problems he gave me.

Around that time, that is when Nkrumah was our leader, Akosombo Textile Limited was being set up. My husband, a bank officer, helped me to buy a license to receive supply of textiles for retailing. Unfortunately, I had to sell my license to raise money to pay a huge debt incurred by my brother. He over-borrowed to lead a bourgeois life. This destroyed my plans of ever becoming a textile distributor. I went into foodstuffs. I had a regular truck with which I travelled to Sefwi, Techiman, Begoro and many other food producing centres to buy plantain for distribution in Accra.

By this time, I had my third child so I had to be at home more often to care for them. Lucky, my mother sent a cousin from the village to help with the children. I noticed that tomatoes were selling fast so I branched into the tomato trade. I must say that since then, tomatoes have been my very life. I buy tomatoes from Ada in the Greater Accra Region, Akumadan, Derma, Tuobodom and Tanoso, all in the Offinso district of the Ashanti region for sale in Accra.

Trade used to be good and brisk until E.T. Mensah became the head of AMA. He came with many problems and pains. Even before this man came with his bad luck, we had our own problems. Some are motor accidents and the perishable nature of tomatoes all of which cause great financial loss to us. E.T. Mensah came to 'regularise' trading activities. That is, he and his favourites every day move their trucks into the interior to buy. They allow us to buy once in two weeks. You can just imagine the results of this scheme. You see, I gave money to farmers to produce tomatoes. The situation is that I can't cart all the tomatoes on the farm in just one trip. What happens to the rest? They simply rot.

Initially I tried to treat E.T. and the people he works for with the contempt they deserve by disobeying their rules. On two occasions, I went to buy tomatoes without their so-called permission. They seized my trucks, sold the goods and kept the money. I sued them, even petitioned to the First Lady. Nothing came out of it. These people, that is E.T. and our queen mother have friends in high places. They get richer and richer whilst our capital dwindle due to the so-called twisted way of allocating permits for tomato purchase and sales.

What make my blood boil is that I have registered my business with the Registrar General's Department and I pay my income tax to the Internal Revenue Service regularly. Why on earth can somebody prevent me, a registered businesswoman, from carrying on with my legitimate business. It is very frustrating how our so-called queen mother even teams up with them to exploit us.

Well, about two years ago, I finally got sick about how small children like those operating the 31st December Women's Movement are turning my world upside down. This movement receives huge money from the queen mother periodically. I am so disgusted by their hypocrisy. In the olden days, things were not like this. I have, as you people with big English say, retired. I now sell assorted foodstuffs like, yam, plantain, cassava, pepper, tomatoes and others in front of my house. I find this very peaceful, profitable and it gives me the rare opportunity to see my lovely grandchildren grow up.

Looking back, I can say that so many things have changed. I moved together with my family from Akosombo when my husband was transferred to join the Ghana Commercial Bank High Street Branch in Accra. That was I think a little over a year before the 'Anifa nifa'2 think about our roads. There were just a few of us in the tomato trade. Right now, there are so many people everywhere. I think most of them are ghosts. And I can't understand why nowadays the sun is so hot. I wonder what kind of world my grandchildren will grow up to meet!

9.3 West African female traders: a culture of resilience – Auntie Babie's story

Auntie Babie is 65 years old. She is a Ga-Adangbe and is single. She had two years primary schooling. She trades in cooked groundnut and fresh corn. She also petty trades in food items on a seasonal basis. She undertakes her trading in front of her house, her family house in Madina, a low income suburb of Accra.

When I was a small girl I sold kenkey for my mother and she also sold fire wood. She went to the village to bring them. We were staying in Accra-New Town-Lagos Town. She also sold maize in bags. During orange seasons, we went to road (villages) to bring oranges so I learnt trading from my mother. This was after my first menstruation.

I left school at standards two and then joined some people at a stone quarry in Achimota. I was carrying stones there. But one day the quarry collapsed, I was a bit grown. This killed 18 people. My master then left the place to Nsawam.

I went to do petty trading in Accra for some time after which I went into the sale of cloth at Makola. As at that time I had married. My husband was married to two other women, making us three wives to one man. I was in good business. Life in Ghana was not like it is now. There were good stores in Ghana. I remember when I was young, there were stores like Ghana house, Bombay Bazaar, UTC, CFAO Bataah with only whites selling in them as owners. British and French whites. Syrians and Lebanese.

I had no problem with my marriage. My husband gave me the chance to trade. He was an Ashanti. We stayed in Lagos Town. I had three children.

I sold cloth at Makola for a long time and one day Rawlings came to power. Makola was broken down and I lost my business. Later my husband died. I had traded for a long time and had nothing to do apart from trading to support myself.

I then went to sell turkey-tails at Circle around the Orion Cinema. At that time too I went to Tema to bring fish and fried it for sale. One day Salifu-Amankwa also came on. They said we were doing 'kayabole' at the circle, in fact I was grown, I think. They carried us to Burma Camp and we were beaten seriously both men and women, including children and young people. This had given me much sickness till now. Headache and others. I have hypertension too this time.

I stopped this turkey-tail and fish business during that time. My children had completed school, one learnt typing and the other catering. One is now travelled.

My mother built this house and my father built another house at Madina Old road near the No. 3 school. I remember those days when my father was building. We came to carry water and stones for the masons. Monkeys could come to drive us away. The whole of Madina was a forest. There was no water. Water and sewerage people came to fix a pump near the market area.

Let's go back to our market problem. I think every parent must teach the children how to trade so that even if you do whiteman's work you can still trade to add to your income. This time I am staying in my own mother's house. I do the petty trading I sell everything and my children also give me money. I have a small farm at Mempeasem. I stay with two grandchildren. In those days we had better materials to wear. You see something they broke Makola down and Makola is now back.

9.4 Underpaid by family, forced to trade on her own: Comfort's tale of a female child's economic responsibilities

Comfort is 57 years old. She is a Krobo. She is divorced and illiterate.

My parents hailed from Somanya in the Eastern Region. They had seven children and one is long dead. I am the first born child of my parents.

It got to a point in my parents' life when their marriage became unworkable. My mother left our home at Somanya and came to live with her sister in Accra. I stayed with my father and helped him on his farm. The sad thing was that, whenever I asked him for money, he refused. I hence left him and joined my mother in Accra. I was then about 12 years old.

My aunt, that is my mother's sister was in the chop bar trade. She and my mother became partners. So I, when I joined them, I became their assistant. I was in this position for nearly ten years after which I left my people I began my small trade. I started by using my savings from the chop bar trade to retail vegetables like tomatoes, pepper, garden eggs and okro. I used to hawk. My initial capital was five pounds (10,000 cedis). I carried on like this for 12 months in Accra at Korle Worko.

I left my mother and aunt because I was not happy with the salary they paid me. My mother later left my aunt and set up her own chop bar at Madina. She suggested that I sold palm wine and local gin alongside her fufu trade. I agreed. But I left very soon because my wages were not enough. I began following the train (railway) route to Achiase to buy palm nuts and cassava for sale at Kantamanto. Because of the seasonal availability of the foodstuffs, trade was not brisk. After about six months,

I stopped. I went into selling palm wine at Airport Junction in Accra.

I got a fellow girl to help me sell the palm wine. This girl ran away with my money. This forced me to rejoin my mother at Madina in her chop bar business. It was around this time that I met the father of my children. I had three children with him. After my third child, I took over the chop bar trade from my mother and though it has it own problems, I am still in it. Currently, I sell to the students and workers of the University of Ghana. Our major problem is the high cost of cassava. As for plantain, it is beyond our means. This has adversely affected our ability to expand. Just recently, we were buying a medium size tinned tomato that we use in soup preparation for 2,500 cedis. We now buy it at 5,000 cedis. Yet when we adjust the quantity of food served according to the current economy, our customers complain bitterly.

Fire wood, our source of fuel, is bringing us down. It is very expensive. The fact is, you use, let us say, 100,000 cedis to buy cassava, plantain, fish and other items to cook; after selling the food, you will realism about 80,000 cedis. This means you have a 20,000 cedis loss. What is needed now is big money to cater for the rising cost of our inputs. Nowadays, even money lenders are reluctant to lend out their money. The cash is simply not there. We therefore thrive on credit system. The closure of the University too has done great damage to my business. This is because a great number of our customers are gone. With them around, things were not so bad. Therefore, two things of great concern for me, especially, is the immediate reopening of the University and loans with reasonable interest. If I should have gas for cooking, it would cut down greatly on the cost of fuel.

9.5 An honourable family member: trading as women's way of meeting extended household economic responsibility

Florence is 52 years old and divorced. She is Ga. She is also illiterate.

I came from Otu Blohum-Osu in the Greater Accra Region. I have six children, four girls and two boys. I was married and was divorced in 1981. Frankly speaking, I never went to school. Since my husband left me and the children, things have not been easy at all. It was even worse initially. However, my brother helped me with an initial capital to sell (Obroni Wawu) second hand clothes in Accra. I started the whole trade with 3,000 cedis. Since my ex-husband was no more in Accra, the children go to Sunyani to spend vacations with him.

People were not buying my goods regularly so I switched to the selling of kenkey, this time at Osu-Re. I found the kenkey trade to be very lucrative in the initial stages because my children helped me in the cooking and selling. I had a lot of customers because I prepared my kenkey very well. Problems started when in 1983, there came the shortage of corn. The price of corn went high and even, we normally got a tip off before we were able to locate the exact place to buy maize. The shortage continued to the extent that we no longer had corn to buy.

I therefore switched to the sales and preparation of konkonte. I sold konkonte with palm nut and groundnut soup. The konkonte business was able to sustain us throughout the 1983 famine period. In fact the demand for my konkonte was high because food items like rice, yam plantain and others were non-existent if not extremely expensive. I stopped the konkonte business the following year and went back to selling kenkey. I then had contact with a man from Nsawam who brought me bags of corn regularly.

I must say that, I am the breadwinner of a large family. I care for my brother's children as well as my own; my ex-husband has stopped paying the school fees of our last child who is now in upper six at Accra Academy. My brother's children help me in the kenkey business and I also give them money. Because my kenkey is good tasting, it is liked by many. Now, I have started preparing kenkey in the morning and afternoon in addition to the evening trade. This is because there are many workers around the Osu-Re area. They usually have the breakfast and lunch at my place. I have also started serving soup and okro stew with the kenkey by popular request. On some occasions, people come and place order for large quantities of my kenkey.

One major problem with this kenkey business is that the price of corn determines the size of a ball of kenkey. Sometimes the price goes high and we are forced to reduce the size of a ball in order not to incur losses. However, if we increase the price of the kenkey according to increase in corn price, people don't buy so I rather retain the price and reduce the size. This is because kenkey has a standard price of 100 cedis and 150 cedis, hence I can't sell it at 200 cedis in spite of price increases in corn. Despite this problem, it is not all that bad because, this trade has sustained us and will continue to be my source of income generation.

9.6 Trading, a miracle of survival: Vida's tale of endurance

Vida is 49 years old. She is a Ga and single. She is illiterate.

I was born at Abossey Okai in the Greater Accra Region. My parents told me that, I was just a two year old baby when Nii Kwabena Bonney, who was then the Chief of Osu Alata brought the people of Accra on to the streets to protest against the high cost of goods on the market.[3] I grew up in a very poor family environment. My mother had nine children. There was only one male with eight females. Seven of us children went to elementary school. My second sister and I did not go to school.

Trading has been in the family for many seasons. I must say that I started trading 35 years ago. Even as a girl, I used to carry kenkey and fried fish to sell for my mother. It therefore came as no surprise to me when I found myself selling provisions at the age of 15. My mother looked after us with her kenkey business. When I was 13 years old, I travelled with my father to Ashanti Mampong where he worked for the Government Training School. In Ashanti Mampong, my father introduced me to a Ga woman already living there selling kenkey. I helped this woman to sell her kenkey for a little commission of six pence daily. After three years, my father was transferred by the Government to Agogo. I returned to Accra. When I returned to Accra, I had already saved some amount out of the six pence daily earnings. Using this savings, I started buying a carton of milk which then cost me one shilling two pence. I made some good profit from this. After some years, I stopped the provisions trade and took over my mother's kenkey industry.

I carried on the kenkey industry or trade until I became pregnant with my first child. I also made some money selling fried fish. When I became pregnant, my mother came in to help with the kenkey trade. The role I played was to go to the beach and buy fish for my mother to fry and sell along with the kenkey. This went on till I had my second child. Though I had two young ones to care for, I was rich. I finally left the family trade and went into selling scarfs, panties and cosmetics. The problem with this line of trade is, the pants would easily get dirty causing financial losses to me. Anyway, it was not too bad. I was in this trade even when J.J. Rawlings did his first coup.4 The soldiers brought what they called control price. I lost very big money in that period. To make some money, I went back selling kenkey and fish. I managed to save 20,000 cedis and again went back hawking cosmetics. This involved a lot of walking. This brought to me blood pressure problems. I therefore stopped the cosmetics business.

I stayed home for some months and then branched into spice trading, selling maggi cubes, curry powder, grounded pepper, tin tomatoes, nutmeg and other spices. I have remained in the spice business ever since.

Like any other trader, I have so many problems. If I could have a bigger money, business would be fine. Because of the small capital I have, I can only buy few items at a time for retailing. I usually buy goods at 150,000 cedis and earn just 1,000 cedis profit on it. I would have stopped long ago, except that there is nothing else I can do. I am too old for the kenkey trade.

I don't like borrowing because the money lenders charge too much interest. Perhaps the government can lend us some money with small interest. There is no improvement in my life though I have been trading for such a long time. One thing that bothers me is that we pay 4,000 cedis as license to the toll collectors. They do nothing for us. We pay the 'kayabola's5 boys 200 cedis every morning to sweep and clean my stall. We suffer from too much harassment from the AMA. They come and seize

220

our goods on the pretext of tolls default. By the time you go and pay the penalty, most of your goods will be stolen.

I see a very big difference between the time I used to sell kenkey and fried fish and this our present time. In the past the few pence I earned as profit were able for a rainy day. Now I need about 1,000 a day to feed my granddaughter and I don't make that much daily. Our survival is a miracle. Luckily, I live in our family house so I pay no rent. I use kerosene lantern because I can't afford electricity bills. I envy people who work for the government because they get their salaries even when they are not well and hence are absent from work, the government gives them a big money. As for people like me, when I am sick, nobody cares for me. If I stay home for two days, I will starve. When this government and office people say that trading is good, I laugh because there is nothing in it. The market, to me, is a place you go and spend the day.

9.7 Harassed by authorities, bankrupted by officialdom: Comfort's story

Comfort is 45 years old. She is an Akan (Ashanti). She is divorced and literate.

I was born in the year 1950 at Bonkrong in Nsuta Ashanti. Ours was a large family. My parents gave birth to and brought up seven children. I am the third born. There are three males and four females. My father of blessed memory took education very seriously. I remember as a child how my father used to teach us how to read and write even before we started primary one. My father's faith in education paid off rather handsomely. My two brothers before me are distinguished academicians. The first is a Professor at the University of Ghana, Legon and the other is also a Professor at Cape Coast University. I managed to acquire a certificate in Secretaryship at the Accra Polytechnic. The sister after me is now an accomplished teacher. The rest hold Degrees in various disciplines.

I joined the Barclays Bank in 1968. I worked with the bank for 21 good years as a Branch Secretary. I parted ways with Barclays Bank in 1989. Whenever I think of the circumstances leading to my resignation from the bank, I feel a very deep sense of sadness that pains my soul. I was intimidated. I still feel very bitter so I don't want to talk about it. I will carry the pain to my death. When I was leaving Barclays, the management game me a fairly huge amount of money as my gratuity. I decided to use this money to trade. I therefore bought a land around Mallam Atta Market. I built and furnished a shop/store. I filled the store with goods comprising mainly of tin tomatoes. A few weeks later, Mr E.T. Mensah and his gang from the Accra Metropolitan Assembly came to close my store. They explained that the land on which my store stands was meant for stalls and not stores. By the time I had raised money to go and pay the 350,000 cedis fine imposed on me by the AMA, all the goods in the store had gone bad. I simply went bankrupt. Thus, together with another woman who suffered the same fate, I challenged Mr E.T. Mensah's appointment as a Minister.

To survive, I joined a cousin in the second hand clothes trade. This trade is not profitable at all. I started this second hand business with 300,000 cedis. I am now left with 80,000 cedis. My capital keeps going down. What is killing us is the taxes. The tax we pay is more than our profits. We constantly have to dip into our basic capital to pay taxes. Trade is not paying off because of low capital. For somebody like me, the only way I can raise enough capital is bank borrowing.

Even that is not worthwhile because of the high interest as against my low profit level. What is really annoying is the income tax. They just come and tax us without assessing our volume of trade. The people from the city council come and collect 6,000 cedis from us whenever it suits them. It is not fair. This is killing trade. The UTC stores and other departmental stores are taxed according to their volume of trade recorded on their balance sheets. When I was with the bank, we taxed our customers income according to their profit and loss account. Traders should be taxed based on the assessment of their volume of trade. The Internal Revenue Service is exploiting us by taking more than our profits.

Traders also need special soft loans with a year moratorium. As it is now, I cannot go to the banks for a loan. To sustain my trading, I receive foreign exchange from my son in the USA. I wonder at times how mothers like me would have survived without their sons and daughters abroad. Yet the government is not making it possible for those overseas to register for the 1996 elections. I look forward to the day I will reopen my shop at Mallam Atta. I shall then receive goods on credit and pay my suppliers after selling the goods. I want to leave the second hand clothing business because I am practically working and sweating for the government people to chop.

I have two children, a boy and a girl. The girl is 27. She is a married trained teacher. She pays the rent on my three bedroom flat and my electricity bills. The boy is 25 years old and is in the USA. He frequently sends me some dollars which I invest in my trade. My children are a great blessing to me. I deliberately did not talk about their father because he did not look after the children. By God's grace, I was able to give them some amount of education. They are now responsible adults. All I do is to buy my food, perhaps a few clothes. It is not easy but God is and has always been my provider.

9.8 Prevented from schooling, escaping into marriage: Kaduni's tale of lost educational opportunity

Kaduni is 38 years old. She is a Kassena from the North. She eloped into marriage. She is illiterate and is a bread seller.

I was born at a village called Gia, about two and half miles North-East of Navrongo Central in the Upper East Region. I am 38 years of age, married with four children and the third born of nine children (six boys and three girls) all of the same parents. In terms of the girls only, I am the second born. I lived with both parents, in my father's house in our native community from infancy to late adolescence. My father is a subsistence farmer and my mother, a housewife who used to assist him on the farm.

At the age of three, I was told by my mother that my senior brother who is the first born, left the village for Kumasi to search greener pastures as a result of my father's refusal to send him to school. He returned home later when I was six years of age. He still saw the need for education in the family, bought me school uniform and sent me to Gia Primary school. As soon as my brother left for Kumasi again after having spent four weeks in the house, my parents, especially my father insisted that I stop schooling and help them on the farm as well as in the management of the home in order to reduce the burden on them. My father made it clear to me that I either school and feed myself, clothe myself, live in my own house and be my own father or I stop schooling completely and enjoy the above mentioned opportunities.

Realising the dangers ahead, I left school immediately after having attended class one for only two weeks and that ended my education. This then explains why I have no education background. I am not the only victim but both parents of mine as well as the rest of my brothers and sisters equally had no education background. Having left school at the age of six, I became committed to both farming and household activities such that my parents grew to like me most and hardly did they incur my displeasure. This cordial relationship continued till I was 19 years old when my mother died. Shortly after her death, confusion between my father and I set in. The whole thing started, when my father tried to give me out to his age mate for marriage on the grounds that tradition empowers parents to look for men of their choice to marry their daughters. Not being happy with my father's decision, I fell in love with a man of my own choice. My father became annoyed and vowed not to allow me to get married to this man. Contrary to his wish, I got married to this man, a native of Navrongo-Pungua who came from Accra to spend his annual leave in the house by then.

Notwithstanding my behaviour, my father refused to sanction the marriage and threatened collecting me back. My husband sensing danger of loosing me cut short his stay and made us to leave Navrongo-Pungu for

Accra-Maamobi where the two of us and our four kids are presently living. At the moment there is no any bone of contention between myself and my father, nor between my husband and my father because the harm has already been done and also my husband has done a lot to win the heart of his father-in-law.

On our arrival at Accra, I asked my husband who was a watchman at the Department of Parks and Gardens to give me money to start petty trading which he initially refused to give, on the grounds that when women get money they don't respect their husbands. He stood by his words until we had our first issue in 1983 – after almost five years of marriage before he reconsidered his decision and gave me an amount of 2,000 cedis in a form of special loan without interest to enable me embark upon any business of my choice.

Taking the value of the money into consideration, I decided to go into the retailing of bread for three specific reasons: firstly, it is the trade that needs less capital to start with. Secondly, it is the trade I can conveniently carry out with the little space I have acquired in front of our house from our landlord. And lastly, the family, especially my children can feast on it in case of crisis.

When I first started the business within the first quarter of 1984, there were few bread sellers in Maamobi, specifically along the Alahandu Road, as such I was able to make a lot of profit within the shortest possible time and paid the loan back to my husband – an ex-employee of the above mentioned organisation presently on retirement since 1993. Also part of the profit was used to buy my own clothes and cooking utensils. In effect the business was smoothly running. However, with the recent changes in the family as well as changes in the market trends, I am now facing the following problems in the transaction of my business. My inability to save part of the profit I do get from the business for the possible expansion or diversion of trade. This reason stems from the fact that the little profit I get goes to help feed the family since my husband's pension salary cannot cater for the family. Quite apart, the market is also choked up with bread sellers such that I hardly get enough customers like the olden days. And finally, the problem of lack of storage facilities is worth mentioning as mice occasionally invade the unsold bread in my bedroom.

Having stated the problems I am facing in the transaction of my business, I strongly believe that, if I have adequate capital to construct a locker in my bedroom and also to open my own provision shop along the said road in addition to the retailing of the bread, the aforementioned problems wouldn't have been anything to discuss about.

9.9 Family accommodation: a tale of transferred tenancy

Alice is 32 years old. She is an Agogo. She is unmarried with one child.

She attended Middle School, trained as a seamstress and is a women's clothes seller.

I am 32 years old, born at Agogo in the Ashanti Region, an Akan by birth and a Christian. I am unmarried and I have seven sisters and four brothers all of the same parents. In all we are 12 children and out of this number I am the ninth born and out of the eight girls, I am the last born.

My father is a farmer and my mother, a petty trader. Both parents have no education background. However, they knew the importance of education and sent all of us to at least elementary school. I for one, attended Agogo middle school where I obtained my Middle School Leaving Certificate.

I lived with both parents at Agogo until separation came between my mother and father when I was 16 years of age. My mother left Agogo for Suhum in the Eastern Region where she is currently living on petty trading. At that tender age of 16, I couldn't withstand the discomfort caused by my mother's departure, so I joined her at Suhum in the same year. At Suhum, I took to retailing of sugar cane to help supplement my old lady's coffers.

I transacted this business for almost a year when my mother advised me to join my senior brother who was residing in Accra by then and learn a profession which I can depend on in the future. Based on the advice given by my old lady, I gathered few cedis from my business and made it all the way to Accra-Newtown where my senior brother was living.

On arrival, my brother received me nicely, bought me a sewing machine and sent me to learn sewing at a nearby fashion spot in Newtown where I obtained my profession as a seamstress at the age of 20 years after having gone through two years intensive training.

On completion, my brother left Accra back to Agogo to take care of our father who was left behind with my three junior brothers. On his departure, he handed over his room to me where I am still putting up with my 11 years old daughter. When leaving he told me to use the machine to cater for myself which I saw to be impossible for newly qualified seamstress often find it difficult getting customers. So I was being catered for by a certain man, I was in love with. This man who was supposed to be my future husband, gave me money to the tune of 10,000 cedis to open my own tailoring shop and be sewing. I however, felt that the sewing would not fetch me immediate cash and decided to go into the retailing of women's clothes.

In 1983, my 'would have been' husband flew the country as a result of the 31st December Revolution. This happened at a time when I had picked my child's seed. In effect this man, an exile, is the father of my 11 years old daughter – Gifty.

When my lover left the country for Britain in 1983, he used to write and remit some token sums for the upkeep of the daughter but for almost six years today, no letter and no remittance. So I am now solely responsible for the upbringing of my daughter. What to eat, wear as well as her education now comes from my business – retailing of women's wax print which I have been doing for almost over 12 years today.

When I first started my business all was well, as my responsibilities were not many and also I used to get assistance from my lover. Hence my ability to save and open my own kiosk where I do sit and sell my clothes and occasionally do some little sewing when the need arises.

With the present changes in my life pattern, I am now encountering the following problems in the transaction of my business: lack of adequate finance to purchase different varieties of wax prints that will meet the varying tastes of customers. This problem of lack of finance is further worsened by the fact that no savings is being made because the little profit I accrue from the business goes to my daughter's education as well as feeding. Quite apart the market is also choked up with numerous retailers. And finally the unreliability nature of some customers when it comes to time of payment is also a major problem.

In my opinion, the only solution to the above problems is finance. So that if I am able to get adequate capital to purchase more clothes of different varieties, my market will be expanded. My profit margin will also be increased, my daughter's education becomes less a problem and the problem of customers not being reliable would no longer be any big problem for if one customer fails to pay his/her debt on time another customer may settle his/hers on time. In effect more money leads to the purchase of more wax print which implies more market which means more profit leading to more savings for further investment.

9.10 Inheriting a business: family continuities in trading

Annatu is 27 years old. She is single and is a Fante. She has had no education.

I was born in August 1968 among three sisters and four brothers. My father had two wives among which my mother is the youngest. My father and mother are natives of Mankesim where I was born. Both parents were farmers but presently, they have given farming up due to old age. Since I was born, I have never been to school, because my parents did not recognise its importance. As early as eight years I left my parents to stay with my eldest sister in Accra. While there, I was introduced to trading in the form of hawking. I moved from place to place selling kenkey.

I had to leave my eldest sister for another second sister. This is because I was not being well taken care of while staying with this sister. I was by then 14 years of age and I was engaged in the sales of vegetables, mainly cabbages. To begin with, my sister and I at each day had to wake up, get to the market or farms around to buy our wares. The farms are usually gardens commonly found around moist areas or along drainage in and around Accra Metropolis. At times we buy the entire farm or garden. Initially this business belonged to my sister's husband's Auntie. She bequeathed it to us as soon she married and left for Mecca in Saudi Arabia.

Ever since, this trade has been very helpful and interesting until recently when events are showing signs of change I have lived by the proceeds from this trade ever since I begun. Out of this myself and my sister, apart from taking care of our own selves in Accra here, have been able to rebuild our house in Mankessim where our parents are living. Apart, we constantly remit our parents at our home town. About 60 per cent of their livelihood depends on the two of us.

Although I've no big properties to mention now I can boast my trade because it has sustained me up till now. In the years by I could actually buy a piece of cloth at least once a month, including other needs of mine. Abiba my younger sister is also benefiting from my trade. She is currently learning a vocation in dressmaking at the same time attending a Makarantha school (Islamic school). However my main problem with this trade is the downhill change in trend. A lot more people have resorted to this trade. I guess it is mainly engaged in by those people who are leaving the rural areas into the urban centres. Initially customers from as far as Akosombo come to buy from us. Apart from this place (in front of Kingsway along 37 Achimota High Street passing in front of Roman Ridge and Dzorwulu) and in front of the main Kingsway store in Accra Central, one cannot find cabbages being sold anywhere. But now, even men are selling it; a lot of young girls are hawking it all over. It is a commonplace to see people walking residential areas carrying cabbages. This has affected our profit margin. Again because the trade is common now. It is difficult to control our wares from getting rotten. At times about half of the ware if not sold early gets rotten thereby affecting the business. Again it is difficult to get credit facility for this trade as more people are moving in to buy it on a cash basis. Although I am getting nothing from the trade now I couldn't stop either because of the danger involved in other trade.

9.11 Providing for herself: the teacher's daughter's tale

Cecilia is 23 years old. She is Akan and is single. She has a Middle School background.

I am a native of Asamankese in the Eastern Region of Ghana. My mother is the second of my father's three wives although they have separated now. My mother was a 'chop bar keeper' and my father a teacher. Presently my mother is doing small scale farming. In fact, a kind of gardening around where she lived in Suhum. My father is also a Medical Dispenser. He even injects the sick when necessary, he was a student of one Dr Bannerman.

My trading career begun during my primary school going ages. At the beginning I used to sell sweets to my friends when we were on break. I continued that till I got to middle school. At this period I started cooking rice for sale to pupils. This was where I stopped school for the trade. Before all this I gathered my initial capital from the savings out of what my father used to give me for school. My interest increased when my father could not always provide my needs. I have been in trade for at least over seven years now.

At present I am selling palm wine here (Accra). I had to shift over to this trade because I have left Suhum. More importantly I cannot continue with the cooking of food because I'm staying with a distant relative, who I think could not tolerate the cooking in his house. Also to bring out all the utensils is also a problem. I trek to Nsawam every three or four days to buy my wares. I usually buy between one and three drums. Each drum contains ten gallons of palm wine.

Trading has enabled me take care of myself ever since my parents could not wholly help provide my needs. I must emphasise that, my mother has been a constant beneficiary of my trading activities. Apart, she uses some of the proceeds I remit for the upkeep of my girl child. She will turn three by next year April. Her father does not provide for her apart from me. In fact I have no problem with my present business because it is somewhat less tiresome as compared to the cooking that I used to do at Suhum. Again I quickly sell it out and realise my profit. Although the profit margin is not all that big it is quicker to get. I can't conveniently imagine when I will stop selling this palm wine. Although the quantity sold at each time varies, I still want to remain because it is sustainable.

9.12 Trained for commerce, diverted to trading: Rose's tale of disappointment

Rose is 19 years old. She is Fante and is single.

I hail from Odoben in the Central Region. I completed Agona Swedru Roman Catholic Middle School in 1991. On completion, I furthered my education in Cape Coast where I read a three year course at the Pitman's Institute of Business Studies. I was then being sponsored by my uncle who was then residing in Cape Coast. My real father died when I was about four years old. My uncle also died about one week after I had completed my course at Pitman's. My plans of studying computer was therefore nipped in the bud. Since finding a job became very difficult for me, my mother advised me to trade in the interest of my younger brother because she was also ill. I therefore wrote a letter to my cousin who in London for some help. Considering my mother's illness he gave out £200 on condition that I care for my younger brother and my mother, although he promised to help occasionally.

My mother introduced me to a friend of hers who normally travels to Togo to buy goods at lower process and sells them in Ghana for profit. This woman in turn introduced me to trading a variety of goods ranging from shirts, trousers, shoes, panties, necklaces to canvass. The woman normally takes me to Togo and helps me in the buying of the goods. Due to the economic problems in the country the demand for these goods are very low, so I give the goods out on credit basis. The terms of agreement is to give the buyer about two to three weeks to pay the amount in full.

There are so many problems associated with this business. The problems are: when the day of payment reaches, some of the buyers either postpone the date of payment or they tell me that they don't have money. Others go into hiding to get rid of that embarrassment. Some of the buyers don't pay all the money. They pay to some level and refuse to pay the rest. Since they delay in paying the monies, I don't get the money in bulk or on time to be able to go back to Togo to bring the next consignment. The problem is further compounded by the fact that I use the same money for our family needs. Because of this the money keeps dwindling.

Sometimes, when I am coming from Togo with my goods, the immigration officials at the border take monies and in some cases they seize the goods entirely. I once decided to try Ivory Coast to see whether the goods will be cheaper there, but I ran at a loss and presently I am contemplating on finding a job to be able to survive. Another problem associated with this type of trade is that my success depends not only on the number of friends that I have but also how reliable they are. Many people are always ready to buy my goods on credit when I come from Togo, but the most important thing is the payment. When the people are not reliable I don't give them the goods because profits could be well calculated only when the monies are paid on the stipulated time. Presently, I can only survive in the trading business if I get a huge capital with which I can buy more goods without going to Togo regularly. And even if I get the money to buy a large stock of goods I will be faced with the problem of sales.

9.13 Both trader and schoolgirl: a tale of two worlds

Georgina is 16 years old. She is single and is an Ewe. She has lived away from her parents since she was six years old.

I came from Akatsi in the Volta Region. My parents both come from the Volta Region. I have two sisters and one brother. It was my elder sister who brought me to Accra. I was six years old when I was brought to Accra. Because I was too young, I was made to attend the University Staff

Village Primary School in 1986. I have presently completed the JSS in the same school awaiting results.

At the age of ten, I started working with my sister. We started selling kenkey and fried fish. We buy our corn from Madina in 'American tins' (Olonka). It was recently that we had a lady who constantly supply us with the corn. Through this woman we get the corn a bit cheaper than the Madina price. With the fish, we started by buying from a nearby house. We buy the already fried fish at a reduced price and increase the price a bit for our profit.

I normally help my sister in cooking of the kenkey at dawn. My sister wakes me up around four a.m. After the cooking, I bath and prepare for school. On closing, I come back home to change and take over from my niece who sells the kenkey at the Achimota Square Garden. I sell 'til midnight. I am not much disturbed by this work because I am used to it. In the beginning I encountered a lot of problems. I sometimes feel sleepy in the classroom but mostly I try my possible best not to sleep. I don't get enough time to learn but when it is examination time, my sister gives me the chance to learn. Despite my work at home, I am always among the first five in my class.

Due to low sales at the Achimota Square Gardens we decided to move to Legon Campus. On the campus, my sister decided that we sell 'yokor gari' (gari and beans) with fried plantain behind the Physics Department, kenkey and fried fish at the University Taxi rank and kenkey and fried fish in Commonwealth Hall. We also sell 'wakye' (rice and beans) behind the Physics Department. We initially encountered a lot of problems. There were people selling in these places before we came so our sales was initially low. More so, the people didn't know us. With time they started patronising our food, when they later came to know us. At the moment my sister has travelled, so I do most of the work.

Generally, we make high sales from Monday to Wednesday but from Thursday to Sunday our sales are always low. We also face the problem of low sales during the vacation times, so we normally reduce our stock during vacation to avoid waste. Due to the nature of our business and the behaviour of students, we create cordial relationship in order not to incur their displeasure. My sister advised me to be always tolerant in order to prolong my stay in Commonwealth Hall especially. Occasionally some of the students buy the food on credit and remit us when they receive their loan or sometimes at the end of the month. Presently, we are seriously affected by the continuous closure of the University because our sales keep on going down as more students leave the campus.

9.14 Conclusion: a trade for all seasons

Felicia tells us of her early childhood experiences trading and of her regular arrangements with a transport operator. Travelling for Felicia was all part and parcel of trading; harassment by petty officials a commonplace trading experience. Auntie Babie also tells us of how frequent travelling to Tema was part and parcel of her task load in the trading of fish. Comfort tells us a tale of spousal separation and of how her childhood experience was one of being forced to find an occupation to provide for herself. Similarly Florence tells of spousal separation and the oscillation of her children between her husband's and her own household: her role is unambiguously that of breadwinner and provider for her own children as well those of her brother. Migration is a major component of this pattern. Each trader's story substantiates some aspect of the relationship between gender, domestic obligations, trade and travel in urban Accra.

Several themes recur throughout these biographies. Firstly, it is clear that the economic and financial responsibilities for offspring fall largely upon the shoulders of women. The biographies indicate the unwillingness of fathers to meet the income needs of their children. Interestingly, while this seems to be widely understood as the dominant pattern, offspring still express their emotional hurt at being abandoned or neglected by their fathers. Secondly, the role played by remittances in supporting continued trading by women in a context where social responsibilities eat into their trading capital is evident. The biographies, with their detailed weave of personal and trading history, support the evidence collected from the surveys of traders' travel, the emerging literature on gender issues in Ghana and the detailed anthropological work of a number of separate authors.

Notes

1 Literally translated, 'dadematse' means cutlass chief. However, a Dadematse is the head of a Krobo farming community.
2 'Anifa nifa' refers to 1974 when 'Ghana moved right'. That is when vehicles moved from left to the right side of our roads.
3 The period in question is in reference to the 1948 Riots in Accra and other principal town in the then Gold Coast, to protest against the Colonial government for the high cost of living.
4 The period being referred to is 1979 when Flight Lt J.J. Rawlings and the AFRC staged their *coup d'etat*.
5 'Kayabola' refers to the delinquent juveniles that frequent our major markets performing menial tasks for money.

Dweninimu aben
(jen nee nee MOO AH bay)
The ram's horns – recalls the
proverb, 'The ram, while
slow to anger, is unstoppable
when riled up'.

10 Gender and transport organisation: The case for a more sensitive policy approach

Jeff Turner, Margaret Grieco and Nana Apt

10.1 Traders, travel and the taming of the transport system: a more gender friendly approach

Previous chapters have demonstrated that the interaction between petty trading and the informal public transport sector requires more considered policy attention. Traders frequently experience lengthy waiting times for access to the lower cost forms of public transport. A key element of the delay to journey experienced by traders is accounted for by the considerable variations in the size and condition of vehicles which form the one queue for departure at the lorry stations. There was considerable evidence of negotiation and bargaining within the Accra transport market. Even where a tro-tro is used by a trader, the set fare often only represents one component of the cost. Traders talked of variability in the fares charged for the carriage of their loads by tro-tro even when load size remained the same, similarly, traders indicated that side payments were frequently made to 'bookmen', i.e. brokers, to obtain a seat on the earliest departing vehicle. That paying such a fee in order to get access to public transport where the fares are officially 'fixed' or 'set' is both routine and necessary raises the question of what the real transport costs are and how they are determined. Informal charging practices appear to interact and dovetail with formal charging ones.

Motorised transport organisation could be improved by simple measures such as: i) removing full load restrictions at the lorry parks and permitting pick ups en route; and ii) a reorganisation of taxi charging regimes to permit cost benefits from sharing amongst traders. On a related but different note, a major finding of our research into female traders' experience of the transport system is that better planning for non-motorised transport is required. Wheeled non-motorised transport in a low income economy performs a critical function in the distribution system:

Plate 10   Paving the way: cycle, car and gutter

low cost load carrying capacity is an important element of the commercial functioning of developing economies. Cultural stereotypes imported from the West operate against this non-motorised transport being fully utilised, however, the evidence is that this form of transport is not transitional but will persist and must be planned for if accidents are to be prevented and smooth flows of traffic are to be ensured.

Gender stereotypes work against women's access to the operation of transport technologies. This is readily seen in the area of cycling and the operation of trucks and trolleys. Women continue to carry Africa's load on their heads at cost to their physiologies: segregated non-motorised transport facilities could help to ease this burden. Perceptions are that women are at more risk when operating non-motorised transport than are their male counterparts. Concerns about injury and indeed about the loss of human capital result in their travel being more arduous than that of their brothers. Segregated facilities for non-motorised transport, which are accompanied by effective enforcement so that non-motorised routes are not invaded by other road users or roadside vendors, could benefit Ghana's female petty traders.

We have seen that head load portering by women and girl children is a significant feature of the non-motorised informal public transport system. In opposition to many of the images of Africa which view men as migratory and women as sedentary, these female porters are short term migrants. They use the portering trade as an opportunity to save and to accumulate capital: they maximise their savings by living in very low quality accommodation or by sleeping on the street. These porters are a key element in the traders' transport chain: the design of Accra's central market area and the capital constraints of the petty trading economy guarantee the persistence of female head loading for the foreseeable future. Girl children from rural areas, most particularly the north, will continue to be a component of the kayayoo labour supply. We have suggested that the involvement of children in informal sector employment requires a rethinking on how education is to be delivered. More attention needs to be paid to informal educational arrangements: focusing policy on universal primary education alone is not sufficient where school age girls' earnings are a necessary part of household survival.

Whilst household structure is significantly different in the developing world to that of the developed world, many of the tools used for policy analysis fail to take such differences into account. For example, the definition of what group of family members constitute a household is no easy business in a context where polygamous marriages are pervasive. Similarly, in a context where it is conventional for the partners to an operative marriage to live in separate accommodations, conventional approaches within household analysis are deficient. Yet another feature of the developing country urban household which falls outside of the scope of the conventional Western approaches is the fluctuations in household size which result from the more open boundaries of family membership. Fostering in Ghana precisely generates such fluctuations in household size. In the case of migrant households even greater fluctuations are likely to result from the role these households play as reception institutions for new migrants from their home areas. Both the scale of and the fluctuations in household composition between developing and developed households can be expected to have their impact on role definitions and activity patterns.

Overall, the material collected forces the recognition that households in developing countries have more complex scheduling requirements than those in developed countries with major consequences for infrastructural policies. Travel delays, we have shown, have consequences for girls' education. Deficiencies in infrastructure increase the task burden of the African girl child. These same deficiencies help create an important social role for elderly females in household organisation but, also, contribute towards a heavy task burden falling upon the shoulders of the isolated elderly.

We have attempted to indicate that the transport culture and transport supply are complex phenomena which are likely to vary between different geographical locations. A transport system which affords an appropriate level of diversity, reliability in service provision and an array of low cost modes can do much to ease the burden of the urban poor: a more holistic and culturally sensitive approach to the informal public transport system of developing countries is clearly required. Any attempt to implement technology or policy which fails to pay appropriate attention to such institutional barriers or resources is likely to meet with problems, particularly for women meeting their economic and transport needs. Success lies in understanding the details and harnessing them in transport policies appropriate for the area or region seeking development (Okpala, 1977).

10.2 Home and dry: at Christmas and on rainy days

Through the various chapters of this book, we have seen the travel and transport dimensions of a female trader's life. As a schoolgirl she has to compensate for the unreliabilities and difficulties that a weak infra-structure presents. Her task burden does not lessen as she ages: her responsibilities for others increase. In a society which registers the scale of her effort in its practices of spousal separation, she occasionally affords herself of the benefits of a more expensive transport mode. At Christmas and on rainy days she takes a taxi.

We saw that there are specific gender features of economic involvement in this region which impact greatly upon the informal public transport structure. Women dominate the trading sector: the absence of strong retail distributional systems means that these female traders carry the organisational and social responsibilities for ensuring the local availability of goods. They are major actors in the area of transport organisation: they both adapt their transport behaviour to the poor quality and low reliability of existing informal public transport systems and creatively adapt the local informal public transport system to their business needs. Our purpose was to draw attention to the ways in which different patterns of social organisation give rise to different patterns of transport organisation. From the evidence we have presented, it is clear that the analysis of transport organisation necessitates a recognition of the existence of transport culture. Transport practices, transport priorities and transport arrangements in Ghana reflect the organisation of a culture in which trading is women's business and transport her commercial burden.

Bibliography

Abane, A. (1993), 'Mode choice for the journey to work among formal sector employees in Accra, Ghana', *Journal of Transport Geography*, 1 (4), pp.219–29.

Abrams, P. (1980), 'Social change, social networks and neighbourhood care', *Social Work Service*, 22, pp.12–23.

Abu, K. (1983), 'The separateness of spouses: conjugal resources in an Ashanti town' in Oppong, C. (ed.), *Female and male in West Africa*, George Allen and Unwin: London.

Adenike Oloko, B. (1991), 'Children's work in urban Nigeria: a case study of young Lagos street traders' in Myers, W.E. (ed.), *Protecting working children*, Zed Books in association with UNICEF, pp.11–23.

Agarwal, S., Attah, M., Apt, N., Grieco, M.S., Kwakye, E. A. and Turner, J. (1994), *Bearing the weight: the Kayayoo, Ghana's working girl child*, UNICEF conference on the girl child, India.

Allen, S. and Wolkowitz, C. (1987), *Homeworking: myths and realities*, Macmillan: London.

Ainsworth, M. (1992), *Economic aspects of child fostering in Cote d'Ivoire*, World Bank: Washington DC.

Amponsah, F., Apt, N., Turner, J. and Grieco, M. (1994), *Putting the cart before the car: the use of non-motorised transport by traders in urban Accra*, Report to TRL, UK Social Administration Unit, University of Ghana: Legon, Accra.

Apt van Ham, N.A. (1991), 'Activities, care and support of ageing women in Africa: a Ghanaian case study' in Hoskins, I. (ed.), *Older women as beneficiaries of and contributors to development: International perspectives*, American Association of Retired Persons: Washington DC.

Apt, N.A. (1992), 'Ageing in the community: trends and prospects in Africa', *Community Development Journal*, Vol. 27, No. 2, pp.130–39.

Apt, N.A. (1994), *The situation of elderly women in Ghana*, report to the United Nations: New York.

Apt, N.A. (1995), *Coping with old age in a changing Africa*, Avebury: Aldershot.

Apt, N.A., Blavo, E. and Opoku, S. (1992), *Street children*, Social Administration Unit, University of Ghana: Legon, Accra.

Apt, N.A. and Grieco, M.S. (1994), 'Urbanisation, caring for the elderly and the changing African family: the challenge to social welfare and social policy', *International Social Security Review*, October.

Apt, N.A. and Grieco, M.S. (1994a), *Tracking study of newly trained teachers*, a report commissioned on Ghanaian teacher training provision by ODA: Ghana.

Apt, N.A. and Grieco, M.S. (1994b), *The head teachers' perspective: supplement to newly trained teacher tracking study*, a report prepared for the ODA Teacher Education Project and the Institute for Education Development and Extension, University College of Education Winneba: Ghana.

Apt, N.A. and Grieco, M.S. (1995), *Listening to Street Girls*, commissioned by UNICEF, Ghana.

Apt, N.A., Grieco, M.S., Donkor-Badu, F. and Turner, J. (1994), *Jobs for the boys, loads for the girls: the social organisation of portering in Accra*, report commissioned by the Transport Research Laboratory, UK.

Apt, N.A. and Katila, S. (1994), 'Gender and intergenerational support: the case of Ghanaian women', *Southern African Journal of Gerontology*, Vol. 3, No. 2, October, pp.23–29.

Apt, N.A., Koomson, J., Williams, N. and Grieco, M.S. (1996), 'Family, finance and doorstep trading: the social and economic well-being of Ghana's elderly female traders', *Southern African Journal of Gerontology*.

Ardayfio-Schandorf, E. (1994), 'Household headship and women's earnings in Ghana', in Ardayfio-Schandorf, E. (ed.), *Family and development in Ghana*, Ghana Universities Press: Accra.

Ardener, S. (1964), 'The comparative study of rotating credit associations', *Journal of the Royal Anthropological Institute of Great Britain and Ireland*, 94, (2), pp.202–229.

Asomaning, V., Agarwal, S., Apt, N.A., Grieco, M.S. and Turner, J. (1994), *The missing gender: an explanation of the low enrolment rates of girls in Ghanaian primary schools*, Social Administration Unit, University of Ghana: Accra.

Attah, M. (1993), *Benefits derived by rural women under the UNDP/ILO funded income generating projects at Nsein, Nyamebekyere-Essougya and Funko in the Western region*, Ghana, unpublished dissertation, Diploma in Social Administration, Department of Sociology, University of Ghana, Legon.

Benneh, G., Songsore, J., Amtuzu, A.T., Tutu, K.A and Yangyouru, Y. (1993), *Environmental policies and the urban household in Greater Accra Metropolitan Area*, Stockholm Environmental Institute: Stockholm.

Besley, T., Coate, S. and Loury, G. (1993), 'The economics of rotating credits and savings associations', *American Economic Review*, 83, (4), pp.792–810.

Bevan, P. and Ssewya, A. (1995), *Understanding poverty in Uganda: adding a sociological dimension*, Centre for Study of African Economies: University of Oxford.

Boampong, H. (1981), *Women traders in Accra: problems and prospects*, Department of Sociology, University of Ghana: Legon.

Boateng, E. (1993), 'Ghana' in *Africa south of the Sahara*, Europa: London.

Brannen, J. and Wilson, G. (1987), *Give and take in families: studies in resource distribution*, Allen and Unwin: London.

Bukh, J. (1979), *The village woman in Ghana*, Scandinavian Institute of African Studies: Uppsala.

Burns, L. (1979), *Transportation: temporal and spatial components of accessibility*, Lexington Books: Lexington, Mass.

Carlstein, T., Parkes, D. and Thrift, N. (1978), *Timing space and spacing time*, Vol. 3, Edward Arnold: London.

Chinn, C. (1988), *They worked all their lives: women of the urban poor in England, 1880–1939*, Manchester University Press.

Clark, G. (1989), 'Separation between trading and home for Asante women in Kumasi Central Market, Ghana' in Wilk, R. (ed.), *The household economy: reconsidering the domestic mode of production*, Westview Press: Boulder, Colorado.

Clark, G. (1991), 'Colleagues and customers in unstable market conditions: Kumasi, Ghana', *Ethnology*, Vol. XXX, pp.31–48.

Cleaver, K. and Schreiber, G. (1994), *Reversing the spiral*, World Bank: Washington.

Coffie, E.A., (1992), *Women's work in the informal sector: a case study of women porters in the 31st December market*, undergraduate dissertation, Department of Sociology, University of Ghana: Legon.

Cornwell, J. (1984), *Hard earned lives: accounts of health and illness from East London*, Tavistock: London.

Cutrufelli, M. R. (1983), *Women of Africa*, Pitman Press: Bath, UK.

Dankwa Y., Turner, J., Apt, N., Thompson, G. and Grieco, M. (1994), *Living infrastructure: the children of children in refuse disposal and water provisioning in Ghana*, a report in supplement of household organisation research conducted on behalf of the Overseas Centre, Transport Research Laboratory: Crowthorne, UK.

Derricourt, N. and Miller, C. (1992), 'Empowering older people: an urgent task for community development in an ageing world',

Community Development Journal, Vol. 27, No. 2, pp.117–21.

Di Leonardo, M. (1987), 'Women, families and the work of kinship', *Signs*, Spring, pp.440–53.

Dyck, I. (1990), 'Space, time and renegotiating motherhood: an exploration of the domestic workplace', *Environment and Planning D: Society and Space*, Vol. 8, pp.459–83.

Elson, D. (1991), *Male bias in the development process*, Manchester University Press.

FAWE (1995), *Ghana Chapter Newsletter*.

Finch, J. and Mason, J. (1993), *Negotiating family responsibilities*, Routledge: London.

Forman, F.J. and Sowton, C. (1989), *Taking our time: feminist perspectives on temporality*, Pergamon Press: Oxford.

Fortes, M. (1974), 'Introduction to Legon Family Research Papers No. 1' in Oppong, C. (ed.), *Domestic rights and duties in Ghana*, Institute of African Studies, University of Ghana: Legon.

Foucault, M. (1977), *Discipline and punish*, Peregrine: London.

Fouracre, P.R., Kwakye, E.A., Okyere, J.N. and Silcock, D.T. (1994), 'Public transport in Ghanaian cities – a case of union power', *Transport Reviews*, Vol. 14, No. 1, pp.45–61.

Fouracre, P.R. and Maunder, D.A. (1979), *A review of intermediate public transport in Third World cities*, Proceedings of the PTRC Summer Annual Meeting.

Freire, P. (1970), *Pedagogy of the oppressed*, Penguin: Harmondsworth.

Gabianu, A. Sena (1990), 'The Susu credit system: an ingenious way of financing business outside the formal banking system' in *The long term perspective study of sub-Saharan Africa: Vol. 2, Economic and sectoral policy issues*, The World Bank: Washington DC.

Gardner, G., Jacobs, G.D. and Fouracre, P.R. (1989), *Traffic management in developing countries*, unpublished working paper, Transport Research Laboratory: Crowthorne, UK.

Garlick, P.C. (1971), *African traders and economic development in Ghana*, Oxford: Clarendon Press.

Ghanaian Statistical Service (1992), *Ghana in figures, 1992*, Statistical Service: Accra.

Goody, E.N. (1978), 'Some theoretical and empirical aspects of parenthood in West Africa' in Oppong, C. et al. (eds.), *Marriage, fertility and parenthood in West Africa*, Australian National University Press: Canberra.

Gregory, D. and Urry, J. (1986), *Social relations and spatial structure*, Macmillan: London.

Grieco, M.S. (1995), 'Time pressures and low income families: the implications for "social" transport policy in Europe', *Community Development Journal*.

Grieco, M.S. (1996), *Workers' dilemmas: recruitment, reliability and repeated exchange*, Routledge: London.

Grieco, M.S., Apt, N.A., Dankwa, Y. and Turner, J. (1994a), *At Christmas and on rainy days: the transport costs of market traders in Accra*, report commissioned by the Transport Research Laboratory: Crowthorne, UK.

Grieco, M.S., Apt, N.A. and Turner, J. (1994b), *Home and away: Domestic organisation and low income travel in urban Ghana*, report to Transport Research Laboratory: Crowthorne, UK.

Grieco, M.S., Turner, J. and Kwakye, E.A. (1995), 'A tale of two cultures: ethnicity and cycle use in urban Ghana', *Transport Research Record*, 1441, Washington DC.

Grootaert, C. and Kanbur, R. (1995), 'Child labour: an economic perspective', *International Labour Review*, Vol. 134, No. 2, pp.187–203.

Handa, S. (1994), 'Gender, headship and intrahousehold resource allocation', *World Development*, Vol. 22, No. 10, pp.1535–647.

Hareven, T. (1982), *Family time and industrial time*, Cambridge University Press: Cambridge.

Hillman, M., Adams, J. and Whitelegg, J. (1990), *One false move ...: a study of children's independent mobility*, Policy Studies Institute, London.

Howe, J. and Barwell, I. (1987), *Study of potential for intermediate means of transport*, report for Ministry of Transport and Communications, Ghana on behalf of the World Bank.

Humphries, S. (1981), *Hooligans or rebels?*, Blackwell: Oxford.

Hyde, K.A.L. (1993), 'Sub-Saharan Africa' in King, E.M. and Hill, M.A (eds.), *Women's education in developing countries: Barriers, benefits and policies*, published for the World Bank by the John Hopkins University Press: Baltimore and London.

Joekes, S., (1994), 'Children as a resource: environmental degradation and fertility', *Focus on Gender*, Vol. 2, No. 2, pp.13–18.

Johnson, V., Hill, J. and Ivan-Smith, E. (1995), *Listening to smaller voices: children in an environment of change*, Actionaid: London.

Jones, P.M. (1979), 'New approaches to understanding travel behaviour: the human activity approach' in Hensher, D.A. (ed.), *Behavioural travel modelling*, Croom Helm: London.

Jones, P.M. (1989), 'Household organisation and travel behaviour' in Grieco, M.S., Pickup, L. and Whipp, R, *Gender, transport and employment*, Gower: Aldershot.

Jones, P.M. and Clarke, M.I. (1988), 'The significance and measurement of variability in travel behaviour: a discussion paper', *Transportation*, 15, (1/2), pp.65–87.

Jones, P.M., Dix, M.C., Clarke, M.I. and Heggie, I.G. (1983), *Understanding travel behaviour*, Gower: Aldershot.

Katila, S. (1994), *Fieldwork notes on female market traders in Accra*, Social Administration Unit, University of Ghana: Legon.

Katila, S. (1996), 'From mother to daughter: social networks and entry into the occupation of trading', *Small Business (Piccolo Impressa)*, No. 1.

Katila, S. (1995), 'The Market Queen institution: between democracy and dictatorship', paper presented to the 12th EGOS Colloquium, Istanbul.

Kilson, M. (1974), *African urban kinsmen*, Harvard University Press.

Knox, P.L. (1984), 'Community studies in geography: a review and select bibliography', paper presented to the SSRC Community Studies Workshop, Aston University, 11–13 January.

Little, J. and Peake, L. (eds.) (1988), *Women and cities*, Macmillan: London.

Little, K. (1973), *African women in towns: an aspect of Africa's social revolution*, Cambridge University Press.

Lloyd, C. and Brandon, A. (1993), 'Women's role in maintaining households: family welfare and sexual inequality in Ghana', *Population Studies*, Vol. 47, pp.115–31

Mackenzie, S. (1988), 'Balancing our space and time: the impact of women's organisation on the British city, 1920–1980', in Little, J. and Peake, L. (eds.), *Women and cities*, Macmillan: London.

Mbara, T.C. and Maunder, D.A.C. (1994), *The effect of regular fare increases on stage bus patronage in Harare, Zimbabwe*, Project Report (unpublished) Transport Research Laboratory: Crowthorne, UK.

McDowell, L. (1981), 'Capitalism, patriarchy and the sexual division of space', paper presented to the Conference on the Institutionalisation of Sex Differences, University of Kent.

Moch, L., Fobre, N., Smith, D., Cornell, L. and Tilly, L. (1987), 'Family strategy: a dialogue', *Historical Methods*.

Morris, L. (1990), *The workings of the household*, Polity Press: Cambridge.

Myers, W.E. (ed.) (1991), *Protecting working children*, Zed Books in association with UNICEF.

NCWD (National Council on Women and Development, Ghana) (1995), *The status of women in Ghana (1985–1994)*, Executive summary of the National Report for the Fourth World Conference on Women: Accra, Ghana.

Overseas Development Agency (1994), *Gender issues in Ghana: a review*, prepared by BRIDGE, Institute of Development Studies: Sussex.

Odaga, A. and Heneveld, W. (1995), *Girls and schools in Sub-Saharan Africa: From analyis to action*, World Bank: Washington DC.

Okpala, D.C.I. (1977), 'Received concepts and theories in African studies and urban management strategies: a critique', *Urban Studies*, Vol. 24, No. 2, pp.137–50.

Oppong, C.O. (1994), 'Some roles of women: What do we know?' in Ardayfio-Schandorf, E. (ed.), *Family and development in Ghana*, Ghana Universities Press: Accra.

Organisation of African Unity and the United Children's Fund for OAU International Conference on Assistance to African Children, Dakar, Senegal, 25–27 November 1992, *Africa's children, Africa's future: Human investment priorities for the 1990s.*

Pearson, M. and Grieco, M.S. (1991), 'Spatial mobility begins at home? Re-thinking inter-household organisation' paper presented to the Annual Conference of the Institute of British Geographers, Sheffield University, January, 1991.

Pankaj, T. and Coulthart, A. (1993), 'Non-motorised transport in rural and urban Ghana', *Appropriate Technology*, Vol. 20, No. 1, pp.29–30.

Peil, M. (1970), 'The apprenticeship system in Accra', *Africa*, 40, pp.137–50.

Peil, M. (1995), 'Ghanaian education as seen from an Accra suburb', *International Journal of Educational Development.*

Pellow, D. (1978), 'Work and autonomy: women in Accra', *American Ethnologist*, Vol. 5, No. 5.

Rimmer, P. J. (1986), *From riksha to rapid transit*, Pergammon Press, Sydney.

Roberts, E. (1984), *A woman's place: an oral history of working class women 1890–1940*, Blackwell: Oxford.

Robertson, C. (1975/1976), 'Ga women and change in marketing conditions in the Accra area', *Rural Africana*, Vol. 13, No. 29, pp.157–71.

Robertson, C. (1977), 'The nature and effects of differential access to education in Ga society', *Africa*, 47, pp.208–19.

Robertson, C. (1984), 'Formal or non-formal education? Entrepreneurial women in Ghana', *Comparative Education Review*, 28, pp.639–58.

Ross, E. (1983), 'Survival networks', *History Workshop Journal*, 15, pp.4–28.

Salifu, M. (1993), 'Bicycle safety: Sustaining mobility and environment', *IATSS Research*, Vol. 17, No. 2.

Sawyerr, A.G.C. (1976), *Market traders at Makola Market: a sociological study*, undergraduate dissertation, Department of Sociology, University of Ghana: Legon.

Silcock, D.T. (1981), 'Urban paratransit in the developing world', *Transport Reviews*, 1, (2), pp.151–68.

Sowa, N. (1994), 'Labour in an era of adjustment: the case of Ghana' in Horton, S., Kanbur, R. and Masumdar, D. (eds.), *Labour in an era of adjustment*, Vol. 2, EDI Publications: Washington.

Steel, W. and Aryeetey, E. (1994), 'Informal savings collectors in Ghana: Can they intermediate?', *Finance and Development.*

Thrift, N. (1983), 'On the determination of social action in space and time', *Environment and Planning D Society and Space*, Vol. 1, pp.23–57.

Tolley, R. (1990), *The greening of urban transport: planning for cycling and walking in Western cities*, Belhaven Press: London.

Turner, J. (1994), *Transport patterns and travel behaviour in urban Ghana*, Project Report PR/OSC/047/94, Transport Research Laboratory: Crowthorne, UK.

Turner, J. and Fouracre, P.T. (1995), 'Women and transport in developing countries', *Transport Reviews*.

Twumasi, P.A. (1976), 'The working day of a woman trader: is trading an easy job?', *Journal of Management Studies*, Vol. 2, No. 2, pp.87–91.

UNICEF, Ghana (1993), *Equity in education*.

UNICEF, Ghana (1994), *Childscope field report*: Afram Plains.

United Nations (1991), *The world ageing situation 1991*, United Nations: New York.

United Nations (1995), *Beijing Declaration*.

Warren, D.I. (1981), *Helping networks: how people cope with problems in the urban community*, University of Notre Dame Press: Notre Dame.

Whipp, R. (1987a), 'Calhoun, kinship and community', International *Journal of Sociology and Social Policy*, Vol. 7, No. 1, pp.1–12.

Whipp, R. and Grieco, M.S. (1989), 'Time, task and travel: budgeting for interdependencies' in Grieco, M.S., Pickup, L. and Whipp, R. (eds.), *Gender, transport and employment*, Avebury: Aldershot.

Women and Geography Study Group of the Institute of British Geographers (1984), *Geography and gender: an introduction to feminist geography*, Hutchinson: London.

Woodford-Berger, P. (1981), 'Women in houses: the organisation of residence and work in rural Ghana, *Antropologiska Studier*, 30/31, pp.3–35.

World Bank (1994a), *Averting the old age crisis: Policies to protect the old and promote growth*, World Bank: Washington DC.

World Bank, (1994b), *World Development Report: Infrastructure for Development*, Washington DC.

World Bank (1995), *Ghana: Poverty Past, Present and Future*, Report No. 14504–GH, Washington. DC.

Appendix

High cost/low cost transport options used by urban Ghanaian traders
(Supplementary interviews: 102)

Goods traded	High cost Form	Price	Low cost Form	Price	Gender	Area
T shirts, trousers, sports wear, shirts	(Urvan bus)	C1,500 – C2,000	Urvan bus	C1,000; C520 self and C480 for goods	M	Tema
Plastic cups and plates, saucepans	(Urvan bus)	C1,050	Urvan bus	C920; C520 self and C400 for goods	F	Tema
Panties, bedsheets, towels, sponges, handker-chiefs, socks	(Urvan bus)	C1,400	Urvan bus	C1,150	F	Tema
Electrical parts	(Urvan bus)	C1,500	Urvan bus	C1,000; C520 self and C480 for goods	M	Tema
Paints, nails, door locks, plumbing fixtures	(Taxi)	C10,000	Taxi	C6,260; C260 to Accra and C6,000 back to	M	Tema

Cosmetics, clothes, chains, haircreams	No high cost trips taken	No high cost trips taken	Taxi	Tema C1,200 for the return trip	F	Tema
Bathroom sandals	(Urvan bus)	C1,500	Urvan bus	C1,060; C260 to Accra and C800 for the return trip of person plus goods	F	Tema
Panties, shorts bedsheets, singlets, socks, towels	(Taxi)	C2,000	Taxi	C1,400 for the return trip; C700 for the outward trip and C700 for the return trip	M	Tema
Shoe polish, shoe brush, padlocks, clothes pegs, cassettes, body creams	(Taxi)	C1,500	Taxi	C1,300 for the return trip; C600 in and out for self and C700 for the goods	M	Tema
Clothing materials, chains	(Taxi)	C4,000	Taxi	C3,200 for the return trip; C1,200 in and out for self and C2,000 for the goods	F	Tema
Clothing materials	(Urvan bus)	C2,500	Urvan bus	C1,460; C260 for self to Accra and C1,200 for goods and person on the trip back	M	Tema
Batteries, doorlocks, photo albums, padlocks	(Taxi)	C2,000	Taxi	C1,500; C1,000 for self in and out of Accra and C500 for goods	M	Tema

Breakable plates	(Taxi)	C3,200	Taxi	C2,900; C900 for self in and out of Accra and C2,000 for goods	F	Tema
Body and hair cream, bathing soap, comb, powder	(Urvan bus)	C1,500	Urvan bus	C1,000; C520 for self in and out of Accra and C480 for goods	F	Tema
Secondhand shoes	(Urvan bus)	C1,200	Urvan bus	C1,000; C520 for self in and out of Accra and C480 for goods	M	Tema
Cooking oil, tin tomatoes, rice, sugar	(Taxi)	C400 for self plus one bag of rice, sugar, or box of oil	Taxi	C290 for self and goods to and from Kaneshie	F	Kaneshie
Poultry feed, live birds	(Taxi or Urvan bus)	C390 for goods and self	Taxi or Urvan bus	C190 for return trip to Accra and C50 per bag of feed	M	Kaneshie
Shoe polish, shoe brushes knives	(Taxi or Urvan bus)	C340 for self and goods	Taxi or Urvan bus	C140 for the return trip to Accra and C100 for goods	M	Kaneshie
Alcoholic beverages and soft drinks, in crates and in cartons	(Chartered Urvan bus)	C60,000	Chartered Urvan bus	C40,000 per week for self and goods	M	Kaneshie
Rice, beans, gari	(Urvan bus)	C500	Urvan bus	C240 for self on the return trip to Accra and C100 per bag of goods	F	Kaneshie
Tomatoes	(Taxi)	C500	Taxi	C400 per return trip for self and goods to Accra	F	Kaneshie

251

Beans, oil	(Taxi)	C1,000	Taxi	C500 per return trip for self and goods to Accra	F	Kaneshie
Mosquito coils, tooth-paste	(Urvan bus)	No higher price paid	Urvan bus	C380; C140 in each direction for self and C100 for goods	F	Kaneshie
Panties, singlets, socks	(Urvan bus)	C300	Urvan bus	C140 per return trip for self to Accra, and is not charged for items	M	Kaneshie
Bathroom sandals, chalewotey	(Urvan bus)	C500	Urvan bus	C340; C140 for self in and out to Accra and C200 for goods	M	Kaneshie
Foam cushion covers, table covers	(Urvan bus)	No higher price paid	Urvan bus	C140 for self only. Goods are not paid for	M	Kaneshie
Head caps, socks, sponge, travelling bags	Taxi	C300 for self. Transport-ation of goods not paid	Urvan bus	C140 for self. Transport-ation of goods not paid	M	Kaneshie
Door locks, table lamps, torch light, mosquito spray, lanterns	Taxi	C300 for self. Transport-ation of goods not paid	Urvan bus	C140 for self. Transport-ation of goods not paid	M	Kaneshie
Men's shirts and shorts	No higher price paid	No higher price paid	Urvan bus	C140 for self. Transport-ation of goods not paid	M	Kaneshie
Electrical fixtures	(Taxi)	C300 for self. Transport-ation of goods not paid	Urvan bus	C140 for self. Transport-ation of goods not paid	M	Kaneshie

Second hand clothes	(Taxi)	C800	Taxi	C840; C140 for self in and out of Accra and C700 for goods	M	Kaneshie
Men's shirts and trousers	(Taxi)	C800	Urvan bus	C340; C140 for self in and out of Accra and C200 for goods	M	Kaneshie
Cassettes, batteries	No higher price paid	No higher price paid	Urvan bus	C140 per return trip to Accra. Transportation of goods not paid	M	Kaneshie
Cassettes, batteries, shoe brushes	No higher price paid	No higher price paid	Urvan bus	C140 per return trip to Accra. Transportation of goods not paid	M	Kaneshie
Electrical parts, cosmetics	(Urvan bus)	C2,000	Urvan bus	C240; C140 for self in and out of Accra and C100 for goods	M	Kaneshie
Trousers	(Urvan bus)	C300	Urvan bus	C140 per return trip to Accra, with no payment for the transportation of goods	M	Kaneshie
Paints, brushes, door locks, wall tiles	(Taxi)	C5,000	Taxi	C2,300; C300 for self and C2,000 for goods	M	Kwashi-man
Electrical fittings	No higher price paid	No higher price paid	Urvan bus	C300 for return trip of self, and no charge for goods	M	Kwashi-man

253

Electrical fixtures	No higher price paid	No higher price paid	Taxi	C320 for the return trip to Accra, with no charge for goods	M	Lartebio-korshie
Soaps, biscuits, toilet rolls, cooking oil	(Taxi)	C1,000	Taxi	C880 for the return trip to Accra	M	Lartebio-korshie
Rice, maize, oil, gari in bags	(Mammy trucks)	C18,000	Mammy trucks	C12,140; C140 for self in and out to Accra and C12,000 for goods	F	Teshie
Cooking oil, palm oil, spices, rice	(Taxi)	C3,500	Taxi	C2,700; C300 for self, C2,400 for goods	M	Teshie
Cassava, plantain, green leaves (kondo-mereh), yam	(Taxi)	C2,300	Taxi	C1,800; C300 for self, C1,500 for goods	F	Teshie
Cloths, knives, spoons, matches	(Taxi)	C600	Taxi	C450 for the return trip to Accra	F	Teshie
Not specified	(Urvan and Taxi)	C3,000	Urvan and Taxi	C2,620; C120 to Accra in Urvan and C2,500 from Accra for both self and goods	F	Teshie
Mosquito coil, batteries, exercise books, second hand clothes	Urvan bus	C340 (when she transports more goods)	Urvan bus	C240 for self. Not charged for goods	F	Teshie
Milk, oats, sugar, Milo, toothpaste and other provisions	Taxi	C1,100	Taxi	C600 for the return trip to Accra:C300 in each direction	M	Teshie

Soap, Milo, sugar, toothpaste	(Taxi)	C5,000	Taxi	C3,000 for the return trip to Accra	M	Teshie
Drinks alcohol and minerals, crates	(Chartered Urvan)	C20,000	Chartered Urvan	C16,200 for the return trip to Accra	F	Teshie
Milk, sugar, soap, toilet rolls, oil	(Urvan)	C2,500	Urvan	C920; C120 for self into Accra and C800 for both self and goods back	F	Teshie
Electrical parts	(Urvan bus)	C1,000	Urvan bus	C420; C120 for self into Accra and C300 for both self and goods back	M	Teshie
Oil, Milo, biscuits, baby clothes	(Taxi)	C5,000	Taxi	C3,120; C120 for self into Accra and C3,000 for both self and goods back	F	Achimota
Electrical parts	(Taxi)	C2,000	Taxi	C1,620; C120 for self into Accra and C1,500 for both self and goods back	M	Achimota
Soap, milk, tin foods, plates, cups, spoons	(Taxi)	C3,000	Taxi	C2,120; C120 for self into Accra and C2,000 for both self and goods back	F	Achimota
Cosmetics	No higher amount paid	No higher amount paid	Urvan bus	C340; C120 for self in both directions and C100 for goods	F	Achimota
Bathroom sandals, chalewotey	No higher amount paid	No higher amount paid	Urvan bus	C440; C120 for self in both directions and C200 for goods	F	Achimota

Electrical parts, batteries, doorlocks	(Urvan bus)	C500	Urvan bus	C340; C120 for self in both directions and C100 for goods	M	Achimota
Mangoes	(Taxi)	C2,800	Taxi	C2,000; C800 for self in and C1,200 for goods	F	Achimota
Keyholders, shoe brushes, shoe polish, doorlocks	(Urvan bus)	C1,000	Urvan bus	C480; C120 in either direction for self and C240 for goods	M	Achomota
Cosmetics, Milo, coffee, sugar, gari	(Urvan bus)	C1,500	Urvan bus	C320; C120 for self into Accra and C200 for self and goods on return trip	F	Achimota
Gari, rice, groundnut	No higher amount paid	No higher amount paid	Taxi	C1,920; C120 for self into Accra and C1,800 for self and goods on return	F	Achimota
Stationery, exercise books, text books, pens, pencils	No higher amount paid	No higher amount paid	Urvan bus	C240; C120 for self in each direction and is not charged for goods	F	Achimota
Towels, sponges, biscuits, rice, eggs, sugar and other minerals, trunks	(Taxi)	C3,000	Taxi	C1,320; C120 for self into Accra and C1,200 for self and goods back	M	Achimota

Soap, oil, rice, toothpaste, milk, sugar	(Urvan bus)	C1,200	Urvan bus	C1,000 for return trip to Accra (he pays C57,500 for transport-ation when he buys in bulk)	M	Achimota
Soap, Milo, mosquito spray, Pepsodent cosmetics	(Taxi)	C3,000	Taxi	C2,620; C120 for the outward trip to Accra and C2,500 for goods	F	Achimota
Electrical parts	No higher amount paid	No higher amount paid	Urvan bus	C240; C120 in each direction; no charge for goods	M	Achimota
Oil, rice, coffee, sugar, milk and other provisions	(Taxi)	C3,400	Taxi	C1,830; C130 for self to Accra and C1,700 for goods and self back	F	Abeka Lapaz
Paints, building materials, construction tools	(Taxi)	C5,000	Taxi	C3,130; C130 for self to Accra and C3,000 for goods and self back	F	Abeka Lapaz
Bulbs, soap, biscuits, cigarettes, cloths	(Urvan bus)	C1,000	Urvan bus	C360; C130 for self in both directions and C100 for goods	M	Abeka Lapaz
Milk, sugar, tinfood, cosmetics	No higher amount paid	No higher amount paid	Urvan bus	C260; C130 for self in either direction and does not pay for goods	F	Abeka Lapaz
Electrical parts	No higher amount paid	No higher amount paid	Urvan bus	C400; C150 for self in both directions and C100 for goods	M	Madina

Milk, Milo, provisions	No higher amount paid	No higher amount paid	Urvan bus	C500; C150 for self in both directions and C200 for goods	F	Madina
Cloths, shirts, glasses, school shirts	(Taxi)	C2,500	Taxi	C2,000; C400–500 for a taxi into Accra and C1,500 for self and goods back.	F	Madina
Pepper, tomatoes, spices	(Urvan bus)	C1,000	Urvan bus	C500; C150 or self in each direction and C200 for goods	F	Madina
Oranges	No higher amount paid	No higher amount paid	Urvan bus	C650; C150 for self into Accra and C500 for self and goods back	F	Madina
Soap, milk, tin foods, biscuits	No higher amount paid	No higher amount paid	Urvan bus	C600; C150 for self in both directions and C300 for goods back	F	Madina
Shirts, dresses, glasses, plates	(Taxi)	C6,000	Taxi	C4,400; C400 for self into Accra and C4,000 for goods and self back	F	Madina
Paints and cement	(Hires private transport – cargo trucks)	C60,000	Hires private transport – cargo trucks	C40,000	M	Madina
Rice, beans, maize in bags	(Charters an Urvan bus)	C15,000	Charters an Urvan bus	C13,500	F	Madina

Rice in bags, sugar, oil, biscuits, milk	(Charters an Urvan bus)	C20,000	Charters and Urvan bus	C15,400; C400 for a taxi into Accra and C15,000 to bring goods back	M	Madina
Biscuits, cosmetics, cigarettes, polythene bags, sugar, margarine, matches, soap, blades, cocoa powder, Milo, cooking oil	Taxi (dropping)	C5,260	Taxi	C2,760; C260 for self into Accra and C2,500 for self and goods back	F	Tema
Bathroom sandals, chalewotey	No higher amount paid	No higher amount paid	Urvan bus	C620; C260 for self in each direction and C100 for goods back	F	Tema
Towels and sponges only	(Urvan bus)	C720	Urvan bus	C520; C260 for self in each direction and no charge for goods back	F	Tema
Powdered pepper; tin tomatoes, spices, oil, sugar	Taxi	C1,360; C160 to Accra, C500 for goods and C600 for self back	Urvan bus	C620; C260 for self in each direction and C100 for goods back	F	Tema
Cloths, zips, buttons and pins, lining material, thread	No higher amount paid	No higher amount paid	Urvan bus	C1,020; C260 for self in each direction and C500 for goods back	F	Tema

Bathroom sandals, chalewotey	(Urvan – hired to drop her at specific point)	C4,260; C260 into Accra and C4,000 for person and goods back	Urvan – hired to drop her at specific point	C2,760; C260 for self into Accra and C2,500 for goods and self back	F	Tema
Onions, tomatoes	(Urvan bus)	C2,620; C260 for self in each direction and C2,100 for goods back	Urvan bus	C1,220; C260 for transport-ation of self in each direction and C700 for goods back	F	Tema
Cosmetics	(Urvan bus and taxi	C1,360	Urvan bus to Accra and Taxi back from Accra	C1,060; C260 for transport-ation of self into Accra and C600 for self back and C200 for goods back	F	Tema
Tinned fish; baking powder; spices; salad cream	No higher amount paid	No higher amount paid	Urvan bus	C700; C260 for self in either direction and C180 for goods	F	Tema
Baby dresses, socks, singlets	(Urvan bus)	C820	Urvan bus	C620; C260 for self in either direction and C100 for goods	F	Tema
Beans, kontomereh, yam, gari, palm oil, tomatoes, garden eggs	(Urvan to Accra and taxi back)	C3,000	Urvan to Accra and taxi back	C2150; C150 for self into Accra and C2,000 for self and goods back	F	Madina
Pepper, salt, onion, tomatoes, garden eggs, okra, groundnut paste	(Urvan bus)	C710	Urvan bus	C560; C180 for self in each direction and C200 for goods back	F	Madina

Soap, Milo, milk, sugar	(Urvan bus)	C560; C180 for self in either direction and C200 for goods back	Urvan bus	C460; C180 for self in each direction and C100 for goods back	F	Adenta
Tomatoes, onion, garden eggs, oil, rice, beans	Taxi	C2,100; C300 for self into Accra and C1,800 for self and goods	Urvan	C1,440; C120 for self in each direction and C1,200 for goods back	F	Burma Camp
Cassava, plantain	(Urvan bus)	C12,240; C120 in each direction for self and C12,000 for goods	Urvan bus	C7,740; C120 for self in each direction and C7,500 for goods back	F	Burma Camp
Okro	(Urvan bus)	C740; C120 in each direction for self and C500 for goods	Urvan bus	C340; C120 for self in each direction and C100 for goods back	F	Burma Camp
Cassava, plantain, kontomereh	Urvan to Accra and Taxi back	C1,620; C120 into Accra and C1,500 for person and goods back	Urvan bus	C500; C120 for self in each direction and C260 for goods back	F	Burma Camp
Salt, pepper, tomatoes, fryfish, onion, garden eggs, spices	Urvan bus	C620; C120 for self in each direction by Urvan and C380 for goods back	Urvan bus	C500; C120 for transportation of self in each direction and C260 for goods back	F	Burma Camp
Yams only	Urvan into Accra and Taxi back	C4,120; C120 for self into Accra and C4,000 for goods and self back	Urvan into Accra and Taxi back	C2,120; C120 for self into Accra and C2,000 for goods and self back	F	Burma Camp

Bathroom sandals, charlewotey	(Urvan bus)	C640; C120 for self in each direction and C400 for goods back	Urvan bus	C440; C120 for self in either direction and C200 for goods back	F	Achimota
Biscuits, matches, cigarettes, tin fish	No higher amount paid	No higher amount paid	Urvan bus	C240; C120 in each direction for self with no charge for goods	F	Achimota
Pepsodent, Milo, milk, sugar, biscuits, tin fish, corned beef	Urvan into Accra and Taxi back	C1,120; C120 for self into Accra and C1,000 for goods and self	Urvan bus	C500; C120 for self in each direction and C260 for goods back	F	Achimota

Index

Charging mechanisms for public transport *see* Fares for public transport

Chartering system for hiring public transport vehicles 25, 41, 42, 44

Child care 10, 149, 188, 201–202, 208, 210

Child fostering 11, 133, 142–145, 149, 161, 177, 238

Child labour 3, 11, 12, 63, 121, 131, 138–145, 149
    by girls 145, 153–182, 203, 210
    see also Kayayoos; Maidservants

Children 11
    as an economic resource 7, 131
    support of 10, 11
    see also Child care; Child fostering; Child labour; Intergenerational support

Choice of transport mode 22, 25, 28, 31, 39–55, 91, 102–115, 155
    accessibility factors 103, 107

Christmas
    effect on trading behaviour 28

Collective organisation of transport 48–54
    barriers to 51–53

Confiscation of trucks and goods 101–102, 103, 110, 111, 215

Contracts between traders and transport operators 37, 43

Credit facilities 120–121, 124, 218, 222, 229

Dash (side payments) 31, 32, 43, 111

Daughters *see* Intergenerational support

Decision making 5, 7, 22, 179

Differentiation in the public transport market 13, 23, 30

Divorce 5

Domestic anchor role 12, 133–137, 149, 187, 188, 200–204

Doorstep trading 7, 9–10, 15, 39, 133, 134–135, 177, 187–210

Dropping system for hiring taxis 25, 28, 41

Dyadic relationships 42

Economic responsibilities of women 4, 7, 10, 13, 14, 37, 71, 120, 129–150, 158, 159, 189, 213, 219, 231

Education 3, 14–15, 80, 81, 133, 138–139, 141, 149, 150, 160–161, 175, 221, 237, 238
    of girls 14–15, 153–182

Elderly women 14, 187–210, 238
    support from grandchildren 202

Ethnic structure of Ghana 5, 22, 53–54, 69–70, 99–101, 146–148

Ewe group 5, 53

Extended kinship system 15, 131, 132, 187–210

Family houses *see* Ancestral homes

Family labour 10, 11, 12, 14, 155–160
    see also Child labour

Family structure *see* Household structures

Fanti group 7, 53, 170
    see also Akan group

Fares and charges for transport 13, 21, 22, 23, 25, 28, 30, 32, 33, 37, 41, 45, 53, 105, 106, 107, 235
    see also Choice of transport mode

Female children 3, 12, 14, 63, 121, 139, 144–145, 150, 153–182, 235
    education 153–182
    see also Child labour; Kayayoos

Female headed households 5–7, 9, 11, 42, 129–150
    see also Household structures

Female porters *see* Kayayoos

Financial responsibilities/status of
women traders 4, 7, 10, 13, 14,
37, 71, 120, 129–150, 158, 159,
189, 213, 219, 231
    elderly women 187–210
    of female children 173–178
    see also Trading capital
Formal trading sector 9, 10, 133
Fostering of children 11, 133,
142–145, 149, 161, 177, 238

Ga group 5, 53, 70, 133, 158, 170,
190, 191, 207–208
Ghana Private Road Transport
Union 23
Girls *see* Female children
GPRTU *see* Ghana Private Road
Transport Union
Grandchildren 11, 143, 144, 170,
202, 203–204

Hand pushed/pulled transport 12,
22, 26, 27, 47, 61, 67, 85–126
Hawking 7, 11, 123, 141, 217, 226
Head load carrying 59–81, 89, 163,
235
    see also Kayayoos; Porterage of
    goods
Home working 133–137
    see also Doorstep trading
House girls *see* Maidservants
Household activity patterns 129,
141, 142–145, 149
Household budgets 10–11, 173–178
    see also Financial responsibilities/
    status of women traders;
    Household survival strategies
Household sizes 135–137, 145, 148,
149, 157, 237
Household structures 4–7, 12, 13,
14, 22, 129–150, 210, 237
    see also Ancestral homes;
    Domestic anchor role
Household survival strategies 11,
79, 118–119, 129–150, 162, 178

Human carriage of goods 59–81, 91,
123
    see also Kaya business; Kayanoos;
    Kayayoos; Porterage of goods
Husbands 4, 5, 148, 158, 169,
174–175, 191, 199, 214, 215, 216,
218, 223–224, 225, 231
    neglect of duties 4
    out migration 5
    see also Household structures;
    Spousal separation

Ill health 79, 164, 195, 196, 221
Importing of second hand vehicles
19, 29, 30, 42
Informal public transport 3, 11, 12,
13, 15, 19–33, 39–55, 61, 69, 239
    in Accra 14, 19–33, 43, 46, 132
    see also Hand pushed/pulled
    transport; Porterage of goods;
    Tro-tros
Informal trading sector 7, 9, 10,
21, 81, 133, 214–230, 237
    apprenticeship system 96
    regulation of 110–111
    see also Petty trading
Intergenerational support 9, 144,
156, 187–210
    see also Child labour;
    Grandchildren

Joining system for hiring taxis 25
Journey times (as a factor in choice
of transport mode) 107–18
    see also Waiting times (for
    departure of public transport
    vehicles)

Kaya business 59–81
    see also Kayanoos; Kayayoos
Kayanoos (male porters) 47, 65–66,
89
    see also Truck boys

265